GLOBAL ORGANIZATIONAL THEORY PERSPECTIVES

Jagdish N. Sheth
Brooker Professor of Research
Graduate School of Business
University of Southern California

Golpira S. Eshghi
Associate Professor of Management
Bentley College

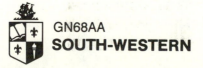
GN68AA
SOUTH-WESTERN

PREFACE

Globalization of the business environment is generating interesting issues and challenges for experts in organization design and management. Even if a company is or wants to remain domestic, it is becoming increasingly necessary for it to inculcate global perspectives among its employees.

Probably the single most important reason for a global perspective in organization design and management is the emergence of global competition in domestic markets. The problem of how to reorganize your resources for cost efficiency and market effectiveness, either to preempt global competitors or to respond to their successful challenge, is the single most important reason for organization change. This is prevalent today in automobiles, consumer electronics, packaged foods, appliances, industrial chemicals, information technologies, and even in highly protected industries such as defense and agriculture. The reorganization issues are more immediate, especially in those industries where global competition has low entry barriers either in terms of liberal trade policy or in terms of foreign acquisition of domestic companies. For example, several European countries including the United Kingdom, France, Germany and the Netherlands have entered the U.S. market through massive acquisitions. On the other hand, a number of Asian countries including Japan, Korea, Taiwan, China and India have entered the U.S. market by export strategy.

Response to this offshore competition is not just defensive but also offensive. The latter has required U.S. companies to enter foreign markets, often reluctantly. This is very evident in the appliance and automobile industries.

Either way, doing business in the global context has forced organizations to redesign themselves for better efficiency and effectiveness.

This volume is designed to supplement standard textbooks in required MBA courses on organization theory and management. It can also be used at the advanced undergraduate level. It is intended to fulfill the accreditation requirements for internationalizing the business curriculum.

The volume is prepared to serve the following needs in organization theory:

- It explores the convergence between comparative management literature and organization theory literature. Both have coexisted for quite some time without sharing their knowledge bases.
- It identifies cross-cultural obstacles an organization is likely to encounter as it transfers its people, money, product and information resources. The only conclusion from the experts seems to be designing an organization structure that is both flexible and adaptive.

- It discusses various types of organization structures (functional, geographic, product, market, etc.) and their appropriateness in different global settings.
- It focuses on issues of control and coordination through different ownership formulas, including joint ventures and strategic alliances.

A number of criteria were used in selecting the papers for this volume:

- They must be managerial in orientation.
- They must be written by authors who are recognized for their contributions to the field.
- The authors must represent a worldwide perspective rather than one limited only to the U.S.

The editors and the Publisher are grateful to the authors and publishers who granted permission to reprint articles included in this volume.

Jagdish N. Sheth
Golpira S. Eshghi

CONTENTS

INTRODUCTION

Organization structure is as important as organization strategy. Often, a new strategy dictated by external environmental forces fails despite top management commitment and bottom management willingness because existing organization structure consisting of procedures, policies, task allocations and reward systems is incompatible or out of alignment with the new strategy. Indeed, existing corporate culture and structure are so deeply rooted that without a crisis of survival, they are hard to change. It is, therefore, easier to select a strategy that fits with the existing structure and culture instead of reorganizing corporate culture or structure to fit the strategy. Fitting a strategy to existing structure implies being "close to your knitting" and continuing to do what the organization knows best how to do. However, there are situations where existing structure and culture may have become obsolete. In that case, fitting the structure to a strategy is inevitable, and often it implies either technology or market diversification.

Alignment of corporate strategy with corporate structure becomes more complex in the global context for two reasons: market diversity and managerial diversity.

As the organization expands its market scope beyond its domestic boundaries, customer, competitive, regulatory and infrastructure differences increase exponentially. Similarly, managerial diversity also increases with global presence. Products, people, procedures and operations increase in their complexity.

In this book, we will focus on organization design and management issues from a global perspective.

Need for a Global Perspective

A number of forces are suggesting that corporations must organize themselves with a global perspective, even if they opt to operate domestically or regionally. Figure 1 summarizes them.

In this section, we will discuss each major environmental force and its impact on organization structure issues.

Global Competition

Two reasons compel an organization to change its structure and culture: survival and competition. In recent years, this has been very true in traditionally regulated industries including airlines, telecommunications and banking as they have become more competitive. It is also true in the global context as many governments allow foreign competition, privatize their public sector businesses, or agree

FIGURE 1

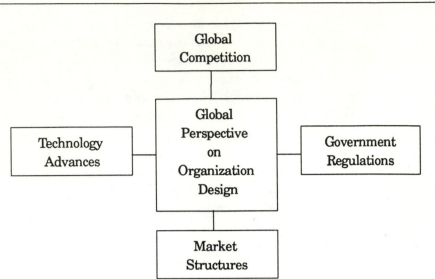

to regional economic integration such as the European Community (EC) beyond 1992.

As organizations experience global competition, they are discovering at least two unique characteristics relevant for organization structure and culture. First, global competition is no longer limited to the Western European nations but is extended to Asian, Eastern European and larger developing countries including India, China, and Brazil. These new global competitors presumably practice different corporate culture and corporate structure theories. For example, Japanese beliefs and practices in consensus management, life-long jobs and strong supplier relationships have suggested that perhaps different ways to organize people and capital resources may not only be desirable but also necessary to compete against them.

Second, competition is becoming increasingly both local and global. On the one hand, a small number of global competitors from Japan, the United States, France and other countries are competing against one another in virtually all markets. On the other hand, in each market, there are also pure domestic competitors. This dual competitive structure is universal across industry sectors including automobiles, pharmaceuticals, telecommunications, chemicals and packaged goods industries, just to name a few. A similar pattern of competition is becoming increasingly prevalent in many services industries including advertising, public accounting, consulting, and even legal services.

How to organize the corporation so that it thinks globally and acts locally has become a major challenge for organization design experts.

Government Regulations

A second major force impacting on global organization and management issues is government rules and regulations. At least three aspects of government regulations seem relevant to organization design.

First, host governments with their national economic agendas are setting policies and procedures for foreign organizations that impact the way they do business both locally and globally. For example, the 1992 economic integration of the European Community (EC) mandates that foreign corporations doing business in the EC must have at least 70 percent locally manufactured components for any assembly operations. This is forcing both the Japanese and the North American multinations to reorganize their businesses in order to access what will presumably be the largest single market in the world. Similarly, many developing nations such as India, Brazil or China insist on domestic production and transfer of technology with only a minority ownership relationship if foreign multinations want access to their emerging markets. Furthermore, these developing nations also insist that manufactured products or components must also be exported or engaged in some form of counter-trade as a way to repatriate their profits and capital. Obviously, such demands are likely to have direct impact on the way an organization will structure itself in the global context.

A second and somewhat related aspect is the international trade policies of different countries. Some nations are dedicated to free market processes as a way of encouraging competition and efficiency. Therefore, they tend to encourage free flow of goods, people, money, and information across national boundaries. Others believe in "guiding" international trade and flows of people, money, products and information in order to protect domestic industries. For example, countries such as Japan, Korea, Taiwan, India and Brazil have been recently criticized for their trade restrictions. Trade policies of nations and economic regions often directly dictate the way a company will organize to do business in different markets.

Finally, most nations, developed as well as developing, (and more recently, Soviet bloc nations) are encouraging foreign participation in their domestic markets. However, economic incentives such as tax havens, employment practices, and environmental regulations vary significantly from country to country, and this requires organizing the business practice uniquely in each market.

Market Structures

Markets in the global context also impact on the organization structure in several ways. First, customers, especially for industrial products and services, are becoming global and they are demanding global presence from their vendors. Recently, we have seen this requirement in the automobile and electronics industries.

Second, market infrastructures including logistics, distribution channels and communication media tend to vary significantly, especially between the advanced and the developing markets. Lack of market infrastructure as well as its diversity often mandates organization change.

Finally, cross-cultural diversity in people's values, business ethics, needs and product or service requirements often suggests that there is no one way to do business globally. A flexible, adaptive organization structure capable of executing a "think globally and act locally" philosophy seems to be increasingly needed.

Technology Advances

At least two technological advances are relevant to global organization and management perspectives. First, advances in computing and communications technologies have enabled corporations to do business on a worldwide basis in real time. Both space and time barriers have crumbled with the development of private dedicated communications networks as well as global access to shared publicly switched networks. This has led to implementation of *global* just-in-time operations in many time-sensitive sectors such as financial services and retailing. Today, we truly have the concept of the global village with the massive development of facsimile, cellular mobile and voice mail services, not to mention electronic mail, video conferencing and electronic data interchange (EDI) capabilities.

Second, there is significant innovation in process technologies. Short cycle times, zero defect, just-in-time and flexible manufacturing and operations are all changing the old concepts of economies of scale and scope. Today, *distributed* manufacturing and business operations located all over the world are a reality in many sectors of economy including electronics and automobiles.

Organization design implications, especially in the global context, are obvious: traditional concepts of hierarchical management control over remotely located operations are giving way to newer concepts of coordination and co-option among decentralized autonomous operational business functional units.

Fundamentally, all the external forces including government regulations, global competition, market structures, and technology advances are suggesting that both *managerial* and *market diversity* are increasing in the global context.

However, not every industry or every company in an industry is likely to be impacted to the same extent or in the same manner from these forces. Therefore, it is unwise to jump on the bandwagon of reorganization simply to imitate competition. In other words, what works for the competition may not work for you.

A Framework for Organization Design

What we need is a conceptual framework with which a corporation can assess the type of organization appropriate for its own unique context. Figure 2 presents that framework.

The fundamental axiom underlying the conceptual framework is that an organization must *distribute* its profit and loss (P&L) responsibilities as close to the source of its market or managerial diversity to balance efficiency and effectiveness.

Single Business Organization (SBO)

When both market and managerial diversity are low, it is best to organize the business as a functional organization on a global basis. All line and staff functions including R&D, manufacturing operations, procurement, sales, service as well as finance, MIS, human resources and legal departments will be organized without any geographical boundaries. For a single business organization (SBO),

FIGURE 2

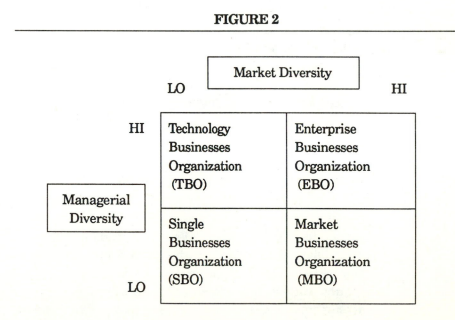

what is needed is global perspective and global allocation of financial, physical and people resources based on their efficiency and effectiveness. Resource allocations may be driven by revenues (markets) or by cost (management functions) depending on corporate culture, top management bias, and efficiency versus effectiveness issues.

The Single Business Organization (SBO) is the simplest and possibly the most efficient form of organization. It is practiced successfully by Japanese subsidiaries. However, over a period of time, with enough market or technology diversification, a functional monolithic organization is forced to make a trade-off between economy of scale and economy of scope.

Market Business Organization (MBO)

If market diversity becomes high, it becomes necessary to reorganize the businesses around its market groups on a global basis. A number of service industries have recently learnt that their customer base is too diverse even though they offer essentially the same expertise or technology. For example, banks have learnt that retail banking is different from investment or corporate banking. The same is true for insurance, consulting, public accounting, medical, legal and other universal services.

Sometimes, market diversity is based not so much on customer differences but on sovereignty differences. For example, social, political, and economic infrastructure differences between advanced nations, communist countries, and developing countries often require market groups by political economies, even though the end users are the same. This is often true in politically sensitive industries such as defense, agriculture, telecommunications, and other economic infrastructure industries.

Technology Business Organization (TBO)

When market diversity is low but managerial diversity is high, it is best to organize businesses around expertise boundaries. We call this Technology Businesses Organization (TBO). Managerial diversity is generated by expertise differences in research, engineering, manufacturing, distribution, sales and services. An organization with *discrete* expertise, which is difficult to transfer from one business to another, will need a TBO design. For example, a company in processed foods is likely to experience managerial diversity if it is also in health care or financial services, even though they may all serve the same customer group. Several years ago, General Foods with discrete technologies such as coffee, carbohydrates, frozen foods, and gelatin tried to reorganize around common markets (breakfast, snack, main meals) and found that it was extremely difficult to converge discrete technologies to focus on a market. They went back to technology expertise groups. We also find that a manufacturing company, when it also enters the service business including value added services, often finds that managerial diversity is so high between manufacturing and services that it needs to organize around its expertise rather than around its markets.

Managerial diversity through expertise discontinuity often arises in R&D, operations and logistics. In fact, the more specialized and dedicated the asset resources (asset specificity) in each of these areas, the greater the discontinuity.

For example, analog and digital technologies tend to be highly discrete in research and development. Therefore, a number of excellent analog based companies have found it extremely difficult to introduce digital technologies without reorganization, even though the same customer buys both technologies. This has been true in test and measurement, telecommunications and electronics. In this context, the company must reorganize around its technology groups.

Similarly, managerial diversity may be localized more in manufacturing operations rather than in R&D. For example, big car manufacturers have been unable to produce small cars without significant reorganization although both R&D and market distribution are similar between big cars and small cars. Indeed, a number of automobile manufacturers have subcontracted from others to manufacture different sizes of automobiles. This is also true in appliances. A company good at making laundry products is unable to transfer its expertise to refrigerators or microwave ovens and vice versa. In this context, it must organize around its product groups.

Finally, physical distribution or logistics may create managerial diversity. This seems to be real between hazardous versus non-hazardous materials, between fresh produce and processed foods, and between finished products and components. The logistics expertise is highly asset-specific and, therefore, requires the business to be organized around its logistics groups. For example, bulk cargo, container cargo and refrigerated cargo groups may become the basis for organization.

In summary, if research and engineering is the primary source of managerial diversity, it is best to organize around technology groupings. If operations is the primary source, it is better to organize around products, and if physical distribution is the primary source of managerial diversity, it is better to organize around logistics.

Enterprise Business Organization (EBO)

When an organization operates or wants to operate in an environment with high market and high managerial diversity, it is both necessary and desirable to design an Enterprise Business Organization (EBO) consisting of a number of fully controlled if not fully owned subsidiaries. Each subsidiary has autonomous manufacturing and marketing operations as well as dedicated staff functions. The Japanese *Zaibastu* are a good example of this organization structure. Recently, both Bell Enterprises Corporation (BEC) in Canada and General Motors in the U.S. have moved toward this model, and one expects IBM, AT&T, General Electric and most of the Fortune 100 companies to become Enterprise Businesses Organizations (EBO) as they diversify their market and technology portfolios. For example, both General Motors and Ford Motor Company have recently expanded into high technology and financial services, while maintaining a strong position in the global automotive business.

The Enterprise Businesses Organization (EBO) requires that profit and loss responsibility be downstreamed to each enterprise business, often with a separate corporate identity and Board of Directors. Therefore, compensation, organization structure, and career pathing are more unique to each enterprise business. The corporate staff of the parent organization tends to be small and is involved in the planning process more as a facilitator and educator and less as a controller and a judge. Each enterprise business is sufficiently autonomous to be bought and sold as a separate business unit with minimal issues of asset separations and settlements.

Connectivity among enterprise businesses and between parent corporation and separate businesses is provided by two processes. The first is an interlocking, internal Board of Directors in which top management of one business enterprise is on the Board of other enterprises and vice versa. This facilitates better coordination and communication. The second process is a corporate image link among all businesses with and through a common corporate identity. Each subsidiary is identified as a company of the parent corporation.

We believe this conceptual framework will be useful in resolving the issues in organization design.

Summary of the Book

This volume on global organization theory perspectives is organized around four substantive areas. The first area discusses integrating comparative management knowledge with organization theory knowledge. Both disciplines have coexisted for quite some time without sharing knowledge with each other. However, globalization of business enterprises makes it inevitable that they learn from each other. The second area focuses on cross-cultural issues. Fundamentally, it deals with the issues of cultural barriers to transfer of resources (technology, people, money, information) across national boundaries. The fundamental message from all the readings is that an adaptive organization with flexible structure is the only way to organize to manage cross-cultural issues.

The third area relates to structural issues. It is similar in description to what we have described in this Introduction. Again, the emphasis is on such key structural output issues as interdependence, control, coordination and co-option. The last area focuses on ownership, strategic alliances and joint ventures as processes with which to gain control and coordination in the multinational context.

I _____ THE IMPORTANCE OF GLOBAL PERSPECTIVES _____

1. COMPARATIVE MANAGEMENT AND ORGANIZATION THEORY: A MARRIAGE NEEDED

ANANT R. NEGANDHI

Anant R. Negandhi (Ph.D.— Michigan State University) is Professor of Organization Theory and Behavior and International Business, Graduate School of Business Administration, Kent State University, Kent, Ohio.

An avenue for integration between two seemingly related areas, namely, cross-cultural comparative management, and organization theory, is provided as a result of an examination of recent developments and changes in the organization theory discipline. It is argued that such integration will enrich research studies undertaken by scholars of different orientations.

Integration between the cross-cultural comparative management and organization theory areas is needed. Scholars working in these two areas appear to be pursuing their research inquiries more independently than is conceptually and methodologically desirable.

Although some cross-cultural organization studies were conducted prior to the 1950s, the large-scale projects on industrialization of developing countries at four major universities, namely, M.I.T., Chicago, California, and Princeton, during the 1950s provided a major impetus to the comparative management area. Scholars from various social disciplines—psychology, sociology, social and cultural anthropology, economics, political science, etc.— contributed toward these efforts. The differing backgrounds of these scholars are reflected in their conceptualizations and methodologies as well as in their specific findings (1, 3, 10, 23, 36, 40, 46). In spite of these differences in orientation, however, there appears to be some convergence of the overall findings of cross-cultural management studies, which can be stated as follows:

1. There is no one way of doing things. The principle of equifinality applies to the functioning of social organizations (42); managers may achieve given objectives through various methods (3, 21, 23, 41).
2. There is no universal applicability of either authoritarian or participating-democratic management styles. In general, the United States can

Reprinted from *Academy of Management Review*, Vol. 18, No. 2, 1975, pp. 334-344 by permission of the publisher.

best be characterized as following democratic-participative style, while Germany, France, and most of the developing countries are authoritarian in their management style. The authoritarian style is not necessarily dysfunctional in developing countries. This perhaps may be the "right type" of leadership (3, 4, 5, 10, 21, 23, 34, 36, 38, 46, 47, 48).

3. More objective measures are brought to bear in making managerial decisions with respect to compensation, objectives, goal setting, etc., in the developed countries; subjective judgment (emotions, religious beliefs) often enters the decision making processes in the developing countries (3, 4, 5, 10, 21, 23, 41, 46, 53).

4. There are similarities and differences among the managers around the world. Similarities are explained in terms of industrialization or the industrial subculture. Differences are explained in terms of cultural variables. The cultural factors are considered the most important influencing variables (3, 6, 21, 23, 25, 45, 46, 50).

Conceptual and Methodological Orientations of Comparative Management Scholars

There are important conceptual and methodological differences among the cross-cultural management researchers. The conceptual and methodological approaches utilized by the comparative management theorists can be divided roughly into the following groups: (a) economic development orientation; (b) environmental approach; and (c) the behavioral approach.

Economic Development Orientation

This concern can be traced to the initial large-scale projects undertaken at the four universities noted above in the 1950s (23). The basic premise was simple: Managerial input plays an important role in achieving rapid industrial and economic development in underdeveloped countries. The approach was essentially a macro or aggregate approach and, accordingly, it was concentrated on the examination of basic trends of managerial development rather than analysis of specific management practices at the firm or micro level.

This level of concern in cross-cultural management studies leads to a link, theoretically and empirically, with economic development theorists. The area or discipline of economic development itself, if not vague, is too general to be suitable for testing the well-conceptualized hypotheses necessary for building any discipline. As a result, the cross-cultural management field did not progress far beyond identifying and noting the importance of managerial input in economic development.

Environmental Approach

Utilizing economic development as a main premise, the environmental approach in cross-cultural management studies attempted to highlight the impact of external environmental factors, e.g., socioeconomic, political, legal, and cultural, on management practices and effectiveness. It is essentially a macro approach. The work of Farmer and Richman (18, 52) exemplifies this concern. The underlying hypothesis here is that managerial practices and effectiveness are the functions of external environmental variables and, accordingly, interfirm differences in both practices and effectiveness can be explained on the basis of differences in environmental conditions facing firms in different locations and/or countries.

The classification of environmental variables provided by Farmer and Richman (18) and others (52) has been useful in drawing attention to the significant external variables affecting the workings of complex organizations. The overemphasis on environmental factors, however, has led to the belief that individual enterprises are basically passive agents of external environments. This may not be so. A manager is not necessarily a passive agent. Both an organization and a decision maker (manager) interact with the environmental stimuli and attempt to mold them in order to achieve desired goals and objectives (46, 52). As Boddewyn has aptly remarked, "A real danger exists . . . of letting environment crowd the comparative analysis. Comparisons are somewhat precariously balanced between management itself and its environment" (6, p. 12). One therefore needs to take care "not to throw out the management baby with the environment bath or smother it in a blanket of social context" (6, p. 12).

Conceptually and operationally, the environment approach has not progressed beyond providing arbitrary classifications for separating environmental factors into certain groups: economic, social, cultural, etc. In other words, various environmental factors have not been operationalized, nor have testable hypotheses emerged from this approach.

The Behavioral Approach

The behavioral approach in cross-cultural management studies attempts to explain behavioral patterns between individuals and groups in organizational settings. Here, basically, authors have concentrated on three different aspects:

1. Understanding the "National Character Profiles" and deducing from this knowledge certain aspects of organizational behavior patterns (10, 39).
2. Attitudes and perceptions of managers concerning some key management concepts and activities (3, 4, 5, 21, 40, 51, 54).
3. Prevalent beliefs, value systems, and need hierarchies in a given society (10).

The basic assumption here is that attitudes, beliefs, value systems, and need hierarchies are functions of a given culture. Therefore, by establishing relationships between these concepts and managerial practices and effectiveness, one can deduce the impact of cultural variables on management practices and effectiveness.

From the massive data generated during the last decade or so, one can easily be convinced that the attitudes, beliefs, values, and need hierarchies, are different in different societies. They are even different among different subgroups (ethnic and/or occupational) within a given society. However, the claim regarding the linkage between *culture* and *attitudes*, *attitudes* and *behavior*, and *behavior* and *effectiveness* raises a variety of conceptual and methodological problems.

First, most of these concepts are ill-defined, and their operational measures are poorly conceived. For example, as Ajiferuke and Boddewyn have stated, "Culture is one of those terms that defy a single all-purpose definition, and there are almost as many meanings of culture as people using the term" (1, p. 154). It appears that culture, although used as an independent variable in most cross-cultural management studies, has a most obscure identity and often is used as a residual variable. Second, if one is interested in understanding and explaining interfirm differences in managerial practices and effectiveness, as is presumed in the comparative management area, there is increasing evidence to support the contention that management practices, behavior, and effectiveness are as much, if not more so, functions of such contextual variables as size, technology, location, and market conditions as they are of sociocultural variables (8, 26, 27).

In summary, an understanding of the impact of sociocultural variables on management practices and effectiveness should include attention to the relevant developments and findings in the organization theory discipline.

Recent Changes in the Organization Theory Area _____

The last two decades have brought many fundamental changes in the area of organization theory. These changes have resulted in a proliferation of different approaches (29) and in shifts in basic orientations for the study of complex organizations (42). Although the Weberian model of bureaucracy still dominates the literature on complex organizations, the shift from a descriptive to an analytical level is not only noticeable, but it has become necessary for scholars aspiring to publish in reputable journals.

Starting from a mere characterization of the bureaucratic phenomenon, research efforts to study complex organizations have advanced to the point of seeking an explanation for the causes of specific structural arrangements and tracing the consequences of particular structures on behavior patterns and the effectiveness of an organization. The emphasis now is to establish empirically the reasons why different degrees of variation exist in the hierarchical structure of individual organizations and to examine the impact of different structural patterns on behavior and effectiveness.

In addition to the shift from a descriptive to an analytical level, the perspective for studying complex organizations has changed. Organizational studies undertaken during the last decade were concentrated primarily on examining the impact of such internal variables as size, technology, workflow, leadership style, managerial strategies, and location on organizational structures, behavior patterns, and effectiveness. This so-called closed systems approach can easily be discerned in the studies by Indik (27), Caplow (8), Woodward (60, 61), Harvey (24), Perrow (47, 48), Hickson and his colleagues (26) (size and technology), and the Ohio State University and University of Michigan studies on leadership (32, 53).

Briefly, scholars utilizing the closed-systems approach conceive the units of their specific studies as independent of external environmental influences. As Emery and Trist have stated, "Thinking in terms of a closed system . . . allows most of its problems to be analyzed without reference to its external environment" (14). In contrast, an open-systems approach, by its very name, requires consideration of the influence of the external environment of an organization on the internal properties of the organization (11, 13, 14, 37, 42, 43, 44, 55, 56, 57, 58).

In order to understand the open-systems perspective, one needs to examine the overall systems and general systems concepts and the usefulness of these concepts in studying complex organizations. A system has been defined as "a regularly interacting or interdependent group of items forming a unified whole" which "is in or tends to be in equilibrium" (59). Alternately, it is defined as "a set of objects together with relationships between the objects and between their attributes" (59). The interdependence and interlinking of various parts of subsystems within a given system seem to be the main differentiating attributes of a system. These attributes thus force one to think in terms of *multiple causation*, rather than in terms of single causes.

The general systems approach, conceived at a still higher level of abstraction, visualizes the study of all living organisms within this singular framework in order to test hypotheses at cross-levels of living systems, which include the cell, organ, organism, group, organization, society, and the supernational system (37). The key attributes of general systems are: subsystems or different components in a given system, holism, open systems, input-transformation-output phenomenon, system boundaries, negative entropy, steady state, dynamic equilibrium, feedback mechanism, cybernetics, hierarchy, internal elaboration, multiple goal seeking, and equifinality (28).

It is indeed challenging to utilize such abstract attributes in understanding the functioning of complex organizations. However, the present state of knowledge, as well as the understanding of these concepts, is so minimal that the utilization of them has created considerable confusion among scholars of different disciplines (28).

Until such time as these general systems concepts are fully developed and operationalized, the so-called midrange approach, contingency theory, seems to be providing a realistic means of utilizing some of the salient attributes of the systems concept for the study of complex organizations (28). As Kast and Rosenzweig have stated:

> The general tenor of the contingency view is somewhere between simplistic, specific principles and complex, vague notions. It is a midrange concept which recognizes the complexity involved in managing modern organizations but uses patterns of relationships and / or configurations of subsystems in order to facilitate improved practice. The art of management depends on a reasonable success rate for actions in a probabilistic environment. Our hope is that systems concepts and contingency views, while continually being refined by scientists / researchers / theorists, will also be made more applicable (28).

By utilizing this perspective, scholars such as Lawrence and Lorsch (30), Burns and Stalker (7), and Woodward (60, 61) have made considerable contributions to our understanding of the structuring and functioning of complex organizations. It is this very perspective in organization theory which, in this author's opinion, can provide a bridge for anchoring the cross-cultural management area within the overall organization theory discipline. To facilitate such an integration, however, the contingency theory perspective needs broadening and enlarging.

Present Limitations of Contingency Theory

Judging from the various current organizational studies undertaken with the contingency perspective, it appears that researchers have conceived the contingency approach very restrictively. For example, the studies by Burns and Stalker (7), Lawrence and Lorsch (30), and Woodward (60, 61), which have been identified and referred to in literature as representing the contingency approach, have merely utilized technological and market factors which affect the organization structure and effectiveness. In addition to these factors, organizational functioning is dependent upon many other variables, such as size, task agents or publics, the power and bargaining positions of other social organizations, and sociocultural variables. For example, the studies of Dill (11), Thompson (55, 56), and Thorelli (57) indicate clearly how organization structure and effectiveness are affected by the nature of task environment agents. Similarly, those working with health and welfare organizations, such as Lefton and Rosengren (31), Hage (20), and Hall (22), to mention a few, have shown the impact of interorganizational relationships on the structure and effectiveness of a given organization. Finally, as Crozier has pointed out, "Organizational systems are cultural answers to the problems encountered by human beings in achieving their collective ends. . . . The structure of an organization system can be viewed not only as an institutional answer to handle these power relationships but also as the rules of the games members have to play. Within the limit of the game, the players' strategies are rational; but the game itself is a man-made construct which is heavily dependent on the cultural capacities and attitudes of the people concerned" (9, pp. 49-50).

The Integrating Model

An enlarged perspective on contingency theory, with the inclusion of the so-called contextual (closed systems) variables, environmental factors, and sociocultural variables, can provide a comprehensive understanding of the factors affecting the structuring and functioning of complex organizations. The integrating model shown in Figure 1 can provide a means of including these so-called closed-systems and open-systems variables. As shown in the diagram, one can conceptualize these variables by visualizing three successive environment organization boundaries: (a) *organizational environment*; (b) *task environment*; and (c) *societal environment*.

The *organization environment* can be conceived as the environment existing within the "closed system" that marks the boundaries of the organization. This layer of the environment is largely under the purview of the managers or decision makers. Size, technology, organizational climate, and human and capital resources of the firm are some of the important variables identified within this environmental layer. Indik (27), Woodward (60, 61), Hickson et al. (26), Perrow (47, 48), Litwin and Stringer (33) and others throw considerable light on the impact of this organizational environment on organizational patterns and effectiveness.

The *task environment* has been identified by Dill as "that part of the total environment of management, which is potentially relevant to goal setting and goal attainment" (11). Similarly, Thorelli has defined it as "that part of the total setting with which the organization is transacting and in which it is competing" (57). The research studies by Dill (11), Thompson (55, 56), and Lawrence and Lorsch (30), as well

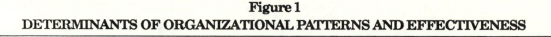

Figure 1
DETERMINANTS OF ORGANIZATIONAL PATTERNS AND EFFECTIVENESS

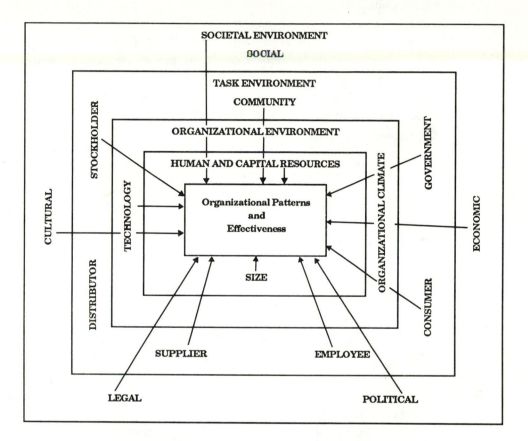

as the author's studies in cross-national settings (43), clearly show the impact of this environmental layer on organizational patterns and effectiveness.

Lastly, one can conceive the third layer of environment, *societal environment*, as the macro-environment (economic, political, social, cultural, legal) in a given nation. It is within this third layer of environment that cross-cultural comparative management theorists can make useful contributions by examining the impact of sociocultural variables on organizational structuring and functioning. However, it is clear from looking at the diagram that these scholars, as well as those working with the organizational environment layer variables (size, technology, etc.) and the task environment layer, need to be concerned about controlling "other" variables not specifically investigated by them. In other words, an individual research design should specify which of the variables are included and which are excluded in the particular study and should show how those that were excluded are being controlled in order to avoid the contamination problem.

The systems framework as outlined here and utilized by contingency theorists also demands that the "patterns of relationships" rather than the causal linkages be stressed (28). This then requires that multivariate models be used. For example, those interested in examining the impact for size on the organization structure should ask additional questions pertaining to the effects on their specific independent variable, size, generated by other variables within the organization environment layer; and, more ambitiously, determine the effects of the task environment and sociocultural factors on size. Similarly, those who consider themselves to be open-system and cross-cultural theorists should be cognizant of the impact of variables in other environmental layers. By so doing, individual scholars will be compelled to take into consideration the problem of contaminating variables and will become aware of the dangers of overgeneralization of their specific findings. It is hoped that in this manner individual studies will become more "additive" in building and expanding the area of knowledge dealing with the functioning of social organizations.

In the light of these last two comments, a disclaimer must now be added to the integrating model presented above. The environmental layers and the specific variables are by no means all-inclusive. This classification schema is offered as a beginning step, and further thoughts on building a comprehensive integrating model are, indeed, needed.

Notes _____

1. Ajiferuke, M., and J. Boddewyn. "Culture and Other Explanatory Variables in Comparative Management Studies," *Academy of Management Journal*, Vol. 13 (1970), 153-163.

2. Auclair, G. "Managerial Role Conflict: A Cross-Cultural Comparison" (Paper presented at the 76th Annual Convention, American Psychological Association, San Francisco, September, 1968).

3. Barrett, G. V., and B. M. Bass. "Comparative Surveys of Managerial Attitudes and Behavior," in J. Boddewyn (Ed.), *Comparative Management: Teaching, Research, and Training* (New York: Graduate School of Business Administration, 1970), pp. 179-207.

4. Barrett, G. V., and E. C. Ryterband. "Cross-Cultural Comparisons of Corporate Objectives on Exercise Objectives" (Paper presented at the 66th Annual Convention, American Psychological Association, San Francisco, September, 1968).

5. Barrett, G. V., and E. C. Ryterband. "Life Goals of United States and European Managers, " *Proceedings, XVI International Congress of Applied Psychology* (Amsterdam: Swets and Zeitlinger, 1969), pp. 413-418.

6. Boddewyn, Jean. "Comparative Concepts in Management Administration and Organization," *Memmo* (New York: Graduate School of Business Administration, 1966), 12.

7. Burns, T., and G. M. Stalker. *The Management of Innovation* (London: Tavistock, 1961).

8. Caplow, Theodore. "Organizational Size," *Administrative Science Quarterly*, Vol. 1 (1957), 484-505.

9. Crozier, M. " The Cultural Determinants of Organizational Behavior," in Anant R. Negandhi (Ed.), *Environmental Settings in Organizational Functioning* (Kent, Ohio: Comparative Administration Research Institute, Kent State University, 1973), pp. 49-58.

10. Davis, Stanley M. *Comparative Management: Cultural and Organizational Perspectives* (Englewood Cliffs: Prentice-Hall, 1971).

11. Dill, William R. "Environment as an Influence on Managerial Autonomy," *Administrative Science Quarterly*, Vol. 2, (1958), 409-443.

12. Eisenstadt, S. H. "Bureaucracy, Bureaucratinization, and Debureaucratinization," in A. Etzioni (Ed.), *Complex Organization: A Sociological Reader* (New York: Holt, Rinehart, and Winston, 1964), p. 276.

13. Emery, F. E., and E. L. Trist. " The Causal Texture of Organizational Environments," *Human Relations,* Vol. 18 (1965), 21-32.

14. Emery, F. E, and E. L. Trist. "Socio-Technical Systems," *Systems Thinking* (Harmondsworth, England: Penguin Books, 1969), 281.

15. England, G. W. "Personal Value System Analysis as an Aid to Understanding Organizational Behavior: A Comparative Study in Japan, Korea and the United States" (Paper presented at the Exchange Seminar on Comparative Organizations , Amsterdam, 1970).

16. Etzioni, Amitai. *Modern Organizations* (Englewood Cliffs, N.J.: Prentice-Hall, 1964).

17. Evan, William M. " The Organizational Set: Toward a Theory of Interorganizational Relations," in James Thompson (Ed.), *Approaches to Organizational Design* (Pittsburgh, Pa.: University of Pittsburgh, 1966).

18. Farmer, R. N., and Barry M. Richman. *Comparative Management and Economic Progress* (Homewood, Ill.: Irwin, 1965).

19. Glasser, B., and A. Strauss. *Awareness of Dying* (Chicago: Aldine, 1965).

20. Hage, Gerald. "A Strategy for Creating Interdependent Delivery Systems to Meet Complex Needs," in Anant R. Negandhi (Ed.), *Organization*

Theory and Interorganizational Analysis (Kent, Ohio: Comparative Administration Research Institute, Kent State University, 1973), pp. 17-43.

21. Haire, M., D. E. Ghiselli, and L. W. Porter, *Managerial Thinking: An International Study* (New York: Wiley, 1966).

22. Hall, Richard H., and John P. Clark, "Problems in the Study of Interorganizational Relationships," in Anant R. Negandhi (Ed.), *Organization Theory and Interorganizational Analysis* (Kent, Ohio: Comparative Administration Research Institute, Kent State University, 1973), pp.45-66.

23. Harbinson F., and C. Myers. *Management in the Industrial World* (New York: McGraw-Hill, 1959).

24. Harvey, Edward. "Technology and the Structure of Organizations," *American Sociological Review*, Vol. 33 (1968), 247-259.

25. Hesseling, P., and E. E. Konnen. "Culture and Subculture in a Decision-Making Exercise," *Human Relations,* Vol. 20 (1969), 31-51.

26. Hickson, D., D. S. Pugh, and D. C. Pheysey, "Operations Technology and Organization Structure: An Empirical Reappraisal," *Administrative Science Quarterly,* Vol. 14, No. 3 (1969), 378-397.

27. Indik, Bernard P. "Some Effects of Organization Size on Member Attitudes and Behavior," *Human Relations*, Vol. 16 (1963), 369-384.

28. Kast, Fremont E., and James E. Rosenzweig, "General Systems Theory: Applications for Organization and Management," *Academy of Management Journal,* Vol. 15, No. 4 (1972), 463.

29. Koontz, H., and C. O'Donnell. *Principles of Management* (New York: McGraw-Hill, 1968).

30. Lawrence, Paul R., and Jay W. Lorsch. *Organization and Environment* (Homewood, Ill.: Irwin, 1969).

31. Lefton, M., and W. R. Rosengren. "Organizations and Clients: Lateral and Longitudinal Dimensions," *American Sociological Review,* Vol. 31 (1966), 802-810.

32. Likert, Rensis. *The Human Organization: Its Management and Value* (New York: McGraw-Hill, 1967).

33. Litwin, G. H., and R. A. Stringer, Jr. *Motivation and Organizational Climate* (Boston: Harvard Business School, 1968).

34. McCann, Eugene. "An Aspect of Management Philosophy in the United States and Latin America," *Academy of Management Journal*, Vol. 7, No. 2 (1964), 149-152.

35. McMillan, Charles J., et al. "The Structure of Work Organizations Across Societies," *Academy of Management Journal*, Vol. 16, No. 4 (1973), 555-568.

36. Meade, R. D. "An Experimental Study of Leadership in India," *Journal of Social Psychology*, Vol. 72 (1967), 35-43.

37. Miller, J. G. "Toward a General Theory for the Behavioral Sciences," *American Psychologist*, Vol. 10 (1955), 513-551.

38. Mouton, J., and R. Blake. "Issues in Transnational Organization and Development," in B. M. Bass, R. C. Cooper, and J. A. Haas (Eds.), *Managing for Accomplishment* (Lexington, Mass.: Heath Lexington, 1970), pp. 208-224.

39. Narain, Dhirendra. *Annals*, March 1967, 124-132.

40. Nath, R. "A Methodological Review of Cross-Cultural Management Research," in J. Boddewyn (Ed.), *Comparative Management and Marketing* (Glenview, Ill.: Scott, Foresman, 1969), pp. 195-222.

41. Negandhi, Anant R. *Management and Economic Development: The Case of Taiwan* (The Hague: Martinus Nijhoff, 1973).

42. Negandhi, Anant R. (Ed.), *Modern Organizational Theory* (Kent, Ohio: Kent State University Press, 1973), pp. 102-131.

43. Negandhi, Anant R. *Organization Theory in an Open System Perspective* (New York: The Dunellen Co., Inc., 1974).

44. Negandhi, Anant R., and B. C. Reimann. "Correlates of Decentralization: Closed- and Open-Systems Perspectives," *Academy of Management Journal*, Vol. 16, No. 4 (1973), 570-582.

45. Oberg, W. "Cross-Cultural Perspectives on Management Principles," *Academy of Management Journal*, Vol. 6 (1963), 129-143.

46. Parsons, Talcott, et al. *Theories of Society* (New York: Free Press, 1961), 38-41.

47. Perrow, Charles: "A Framework for the Comparative Analysis of Organization," *American Sociological Review*, Vol. 32 (1967), 192-208.

48. Perrow, Charles. "Some Reflections on Technology and Organizational Analysis," in A. R. Negandhi (Ed.), *Comparative Administration and Management: Conceptual Schemes and Research Findings* (Kent, Ohio: Bureau of Economic and Business Research, Kent State University, 1969), pp. 33-44.

49. Prasad, S. B., and A. R. Negandhi. *Managerialism for Economic Development* (The Hague: Martinus Nijhoff, 1968).

50. Roberts, K. H. "On Looking at an Elephant: An Evaluation of Cross-Cultural Research Related to Organizations," *Psychological Bulletin*, November 1970.

51. Ryterband, E. C., and G. V. Barrett. "Managers' Values and Their Relationship to the Management of Tasks: A Cross-Cultural Comparison," in B. M. Bass, R. C. Cooper, and J. A. Haas (Eds.), *Managing for Accomplishment* (Lexington, Mass.: Heath Lexington, 1970).

52. Schollhammer, Hans. "Comparative Management Theory Jungle," *Academy of Management Journal,* Vol. 12 (1969), 81-97.

53. Stogdill, Ralph M. *Managers, Employees, Organizations* (Columbus, Ohio: The Ohio State University Bureau of Business Research, 1965).

54. Thiagarajan, K. M. *A Cross-Cultural Study of the Relationships Between Personal Values and Managerial Behavior*, Technical Report 23, NONR NOOO14-67A (Rochester, N.Y.: University of Rochester, Management Research Center, 1968).

55. Thompson, James D. *Organizations in Action* (New York: McGraw-Hill, 1967).

56. Thompson, J. D., and W. J. McEwen. "Organizational Goals and Environment: Goal-Setting as an Interaction Process," *American Sociological Review*, Vol. 13, No. 1 (1958), 23-31.

57. Thorelli, Hans B. "Organizational Theory: An Ecological View," *Proceedings of the Academy of Management*, 1967, pp. 66-84.

58. Von Bertalanffy, L. " The Theory of Open Systems in Physics and Biology," *Science,* Vol. 3 (1950), 23-29.

59. *Webster's Seventh New Collegiate Dictionary* (Springfield, Mass.: Merriam, 1967), p. 895.

60. Woodward, Joan. *Industrial Organization: Theory and Practice* (London: Oxford University Press, 1965).

61. Woodward, Joan. " Technology, Managerial Control, and Organizational Behavior," in A. R. Negandhi, et al. (Eds.), *Organizational Behavior Models* (Kent, Ohio: Bureau of Economic and Business Research, Kent State University, 1970).

2. CONVERGENCE/DIVERGENCE: A TEMPORAL REVIEW OF THE JAPANESE ENTERPRISE AND ITS MANAGEMENT

DEXTER DUNPHY

D. C. Dunphy is Professor of Management, Australian Graduate School of Management, University of New South Wales. Correspondence regarding this article may be sent to him at: Australian Graduate School of Management, University of New South Wales, P.O. Box 1, Kensington, N.S.W. 2033, Australia.

The convergence/divergence debate, which has been a central theme in the English language literature on the Japanese enterprise and its management, is summarized. Evidence for and against convergence between Japanese and Western organizations is reviewed during specific historical periods, and the adequacy of competing models that explain differences between managerial practices in Japanese and Western enterprises is examined.

Japan was isolated from Western influences throughout most of its history. Since modernization during the Meiji period (1868-1911), the forms taken by Japanese economic organizations as Japan industrialized have fascinated both Western and Japanese observers. Even the earliest Western commentators saw the Japanese enterprise as different. As early as 1915, Veblen outlined some of these differences and set the tone for the ensuing debate about organizational life in Japan. He argued that as countries modernize, their organizational structures and value systems inevitably converge. Since Veblen, the central debate in Western literature on the Japanese enterprise has continued to revolve around this convergence theory.

That Japanese enterprises developed distinctive characteristics has been generally accepted. However, how different Japanese enterprises were, in what ways they were different, and whether these differences were disappearing, have been debated continuously. To the proponents of convergence theory, these differences were simply vanishing vestigial remnants of an increasingly irrelevant feudal culture. However, to others they were enduring elements of a massive cultural continuity or innovative contributions to the evolving strategies of a nation attempting to seize world economic leadership.

Reprinted from *Academy of Management Review*, Vol. 12, No. 3, 1987, pp. 445-459 by permission of the publisher.

This review of the convergence/divergence debate is based on an annotated bibliography covering approximately 500 books and articles of significance culled in a comprehensive search of the English language literature on Japanese organizations (Dunphy & Stening, 1984). The debate is summarized historically, which is a very different approach from methods of analysis such as meta-analysis, which summarize cumulative research studies as if time were irrelevant. Such approaches are inappropriate for examining convergence, where change over time is the necessary focus of attention.

Before 1970—The Rise of Convergence Theory

On the whole, writers before 1970 favored convergence theory; they saw the distinctive features of Japanese enterprises as obstacles to economic progress. Harbison, the most thorough advocate, rashly predicted that "unless basic rather than trivial or technical changes in the broad philosophy of organization building are forthcoming, Japan is destined to fall behind in the ranks of modern industrialized nations" (1959, p. 254). Clearly, some Japanese management practices disturbed Western researchers. Yoshino wrote: "Even a very cursory examination reveals that not only does Japan's managerial system differ from its counterparts in other highly industrialized nations, but in many of its aspects, it runs counter to what are considered sound principles of management in the Western world, particularly in the United States" (1968, p. ix).

However, Western commentators did not always accept convergence theory in its simplest form. Ballon (1969b), for instance, discussed the remuneration system but concluded the Japanese were unlikely to abandon it despite pressures for change. Karsh and Cole (1968) also saw factors undermining the traditional "nenko" (seniority-related) wage system but noted that their data could support both convergence and divergence theories. Early studies showed that some Japanese practices were retained while others were abandoned. This could be interpreted as either a transitional period in a wholesale move to Westernization or as selective adaptation in particular areas of company operations, without modification of prevailing cultural values.

This latter position was adopted by the cultural determinists. Abegglen (1958) initiated the culturalist counterattack on convergence theory; he argued that the Japanese system of organization was a natural outgrowth of traditional social relationships and values. Although the Japanese enterprise was different, it was not necessarily imperfect or inferior; the adoption of Western techniques did not mean the end of the Japanese ethos. He concluded "although the technology of modern industry was introduced into Japan, the factory organization at the same time developed consistent with the historical customs and attitudes of the Japanese and with the social system as it existed prior to the introduction of modern industry" (Abegglen, 1973, p. 16). Clearly Abegglen was attacking the technological determinism underlying convergence theory. Later, after studying employment patterns of 25 large companies in 1956 and 1966, he noted the persistence of low workforce mobility and other aspects of the permanent system in Japan. He concluded that this showed the durability of Japan's approach to industrial organization (Abegglen, 1973).

During this period, some Japanese writers were more critical than Westerners of the unique characteristics of Japanese firms. For example, Takezawa (1966) referred to automatic promotion and slow decision-making processes as pathologies, and Odaka (1963) criticized Japanese practices as preindustrial. Imai (1969) wrote of the divided loyalties of "shukko" (lent) employees, of the absolutist power of company presidents, of the inefficiency and collective irresponsibility of the "ringi" (collective) system of decision making. He argued for wholesale adoption of a Western merit-based, nonpermanent employment system. Writing in 1968, Yoshino indicated that arguments like this led to considerable rethinking among Japanese managers. He wrote: "Evidence has been presented that there is a growing incompatibility between the traditional managerial attitudes and patterns and the evolving environment. In the past few years progressive Japanese management is intensifying its efforts to modify its practices and ideologies to meet the challenges of a changing environment" (p. 274). All this seemed to indicate the immediacy of a massive convergence to Western practice. (See, for example, Yamada, 1969.)

Vogel, in 1979, commented:

> During the 1950's and 1960's under government guidance many smaller firms were consolidated in order to modernize, and new American technology and management were introduced. For a time companies were even considering copying the American pattern whereby workers could be dismissed and laid off more easily and hired in mid-career. . . . By the late 1960's when Japanese businesses started outperforming companies in the West, Japanese management intellectuals were satisfied that their seniority system was preferable to the dominant Western pattern, and they began to articulate a new philosophy of management (p. 134).

Rather than culture or technology determining management policies and practice, Japanese managers chose a distinctively Japanese approach because it yielded *results*. Several writers now argued that Western companies operating in Japan needed to modify their management practices and personnel policies toward those of the Japanese (Ballon, 1967, 1968, 1969a; Glazer, 1968; Hirono, 1969; Yoshino, 1968), but for adaptation to take place, Western managers needed to identify what made the Japanese enterprise different from the Western enterprise.

Early surveys of workers' values in Japan emphasized the familial aspects of the Japanese workplace (Ballon, 1969c; Bennett & Ishino, 1963; Prasad, 1968), the ideal of harmony (Ballon, 1969a; Brown, 1966; De Mente, 1968), the importance of reciprocal obligation (Chandler, 1966; Whitehill, 1964a, 1964b; Whitehill & Takezawa, 1961), and the importance of group motivation (Brown, 1966; Takamiya, 1969). Rohlen's study (1970) of a company training program gave valuable insight into how cultural continuity in values was maintained by management.

One major weakness of theories of cultural determination was the failure of researchers to develop a) a model of how general social values affect the values of managers and workers, and b) a model of change. If general social values such as feudalism and familism are all-powerful, why would the status quo shift? A search for a theory of change began. Abegglen (1957) provided evidence that better educated Japanese employees were more autonomous and less tradition-oriented than less educated employees. This had obvious implications for organizational change in a system which recruited managers on the basis of educational attainment. Takamiya (1969) argued that a particular strength of Japanese managers included their ability to recognize changing environmental factors and their courage in abandoning old conventions in such circumstances.

The study of Japanese managerial values and style illustrates this flexibility. Many descriptions of Japanese culture stress the centrality of strong paternalistic values. In the late 1960s, traditional Japanese managers were often characterized as patriarchal or despotic (Levine, 1958), and absolutist (Imai, 1969). Yoshino (1968) traced the evolution of Japanese entrepreneurial ideology from the Meiji era, showing the early influence of Samurai ideology and the fusion of this tradition with U.S. management philosophy after World War II. Strong nationalistic attitudes were maintained but traditional Japanese paternalism was modified by an infusion of U.S. human relations theories (Tanaka, 1969). A major crosscultural study of managerial values demonstrated the extent of the value change (Haire, Ghiselli, & Porter, 1966). Japanese managers favored participative approaches more than the managers of any other nation. They also ranked second (to U.S. managers) in belief in the capacity of people to exercise leadership and initiative.

Attention was also devoted to documenting unique features of the Japanese economic and political environment and its effects on business operations (e.g., Adams & Kobayashi, 1969; Miller, 1963; Yoshino, 1968). This more sociological approach suggested social-structural rather than cultural reasons for the rather different goals of Japanese managers (for instance, a greater attention to growth than profit, as Suzuki, 1969, noted).

1970-1973—Growing Doubts About Convergence with the West _____

This was a period of new theoretical developments. Dore (1973) advanced his late developer hypothesis and used it to *reverse* the traditional thrust of convergence theory. Japan, he argued, was creating new structures because of its late industrial development and it was to these structures that Britain would converge, rather than vice versa. In a historical analysis of employer-employee relations in Japan, Evans (1970) argued that culture and history were determining factors in the unique solutions developed, making convergence irrelevant. Cole (1973) vigorously attacked both convergence and historicism as explanations of economic development and advanced a functional alternatives approach as a better explanation of permanent employment in Japan.

A significant theoretical debate was being held during this period, focusing on the permanent employment system. Marsh and Mannari (1971, 1972) and Cole (1971, 1972, 1973) provided statistical analyses which clarified the extent of interfirm mobility. There was significantly less interfirm mobility in Japan than in the U.S., but the term "permanent employment" is misleading, if taken to imply that most Japanese workers stay with the one firm for life. Marsh and Mannari (1971) also strongly attacked the notion, advanced by proponents of the cultural thesis, that the traditional value of loyalty led to a higher proportion of Japanese versus American workers remaining with the one firm. In their view, Japanese workers were motivated by the same rewards as Western workers, but Japanese firms rewarded different behavior. These writers were attacking the cultural determinists by arguing for the pull of incentives rather than the push of culture.

The impact of Japanese values on business practice was given a more sophisticated theoretical base at this time, particularly by Nakane (1972, 1973). Doi (1973) made a more detailed analysis of the impact dependence has on interpersonal behavior in organizational settings. De Bettignies (1971) also traced aspects of organization behavior and management to child rearing practices and family structure. Yet, just as these generalized descriptions of core values were emerging, England and Koike (1970) published empirical work illustrating the diversity of values among the Japanese managers they studied, and Parkanskii

(1973) examined the adoption of American management methods by Japanese companies. Once again this raised the issue of the relevance of societal values to managerial practice.

Kelley and Reeser (1973) used an interesting methodology to explore this issue. They studied branch managers at Hawaiian banks to test if the managerial values of American managers of Japanese ancestry were different from those of Caucasian ancestry. On the whole, the managerial values were similar, but managers of Japanese ancestry had distinctive attitudes regarding long-term employment, company commitment, respect for formal authority, teamwork, and paternalism. Whether these attitudes translated into practice was not studied; nevertheless, this was substantive support for the impact of cultural values on managerial attitudes.

Tsurumi (1973) initiated an examination of the overseas operation of Japanese multinationals, which became a more significant area of inquiry as Japanese overseas operations assumed increasing significance. Up until this time, convergence had been discussed largely in relation to Japanese firms operating in Japan. Now the convergence debate was widening to examine whether Japanese firms abroad preserved their distinctively Japanese organizational practices or adapted to local practices.

1974-1977—Strategic Choice Versus Determinism _____

During the period 1974-1977, case studies of Japanese organizations in Japan expanded. Rohlen's *For Harmony and Strength* (1974) detailed how company members were socialized into company culture, becoming committed members of a clan-like organization. This vital theoretical link showed that managers selected cultural values and consciously inculcated them into new organizational employees. It appeared that cultural determinism was more a mindful management strategy for building organization commitment than an impersonal cultural force. Most of the remaining case studies published during this period reflected an emerging interest in the relationship of business strategy to structure, an interest reflected in the title of the First Fuji Conference: "Strategy and Structure of Big Business" (Nakagawa, 1975) and in an important article by Drucker: "Economic Realities and Enterprise Strategy" (1975). This period followed the oil shock (1970-1974) which affected Japanese economic strategies dramatically. Strategy and structure were explored in studies centering mainly on the development of Zaibatsu (large financial, commercial, and industrial combined) or Zaibatsu-like groupings (Azumi & McMillan, 1975; Hill, 1977a, 1977b; Lyons, 1976; Nakagawa, 1975; Rutledge, 1974; Tindall, 1974; Tsuchiya, 1975;

Yanagihara, 1974; Yasouka, 1975). This research linked variations in Japanese business practices to both the position these enterprises held in the economy and to the strategic goals of the businesses. Kono's (1976) comparison of Japanese and U.S. approaches to long-range planning showed that variations in national practice were rational adaptations to different economic environments. Managers of large Japanese organizations adopted Western strategic techniques, but they used these techniques to evolve organizational strategies which reflected Japanese, rather than Western, business priorities.

Hazama (1977) traced the development of Japanese personnel practices from the Meiji period, showing how their adoption also followed from strategic choices. However, Marsh and Mannari (1976) argued, from their analysis of three manufacturing firms, that the more "Japanese" a social organizational variable is, the less it has to do with performance. Therefore, one is left with this question: If Japanese personnel practices follow from strategic choices made in a distinctive economic environment, why were these practices irrelevant to performance? Although Marsh and Mannari used questionnaire responses and not direct measures of performance, their study exposed the fallacy of *assuming* that Japanese-style personnel practices necessarily contributed to Japanese economic success. Other studies showed that these personnel practices do not necessarily create more satisfied employees, although it is often assumed that they do (Azumi & McMillan, 1976; Odaka, 1975).

The increasing success of Japanese overseas operations raised the issue whether distinctive Japanese business practices were exportable. Exportability represented a critical test for cultural determinism because if Japanese practices were a response to Japan's unique cultural tradition and environment, these should not be easily exportable to different cultures. What happened, however, was that the whole convergence debate was recycled regarding Japanese offshore operations. Yamazaki, Kobayashi, and Doi (1977) argued that the difference was only transitional for Japanese-type multinational enterprises, and that these would converge toward Western-type multinationals. Yoshihara (1977) formed a similar conclusion, but used a culturalist basis. He argued that Japanese-style management did not transfer easily because it was designed for a culturally homogeneous workforce. Yoshino (1975) also questioned whether the international divisions of Japanese companies could develop a system more relevant to other cultures. By contrast, Murano and Tomb (1974) argued that it was these peculiarly Japanese management practices that would enhance the acceptability of Japanese enterprises in host countries and would ensure the success of their operations.

Actual analyses of the operations of Japanese firms abroad were sparse at this time. Johnson, Ouchi, and Kraar started to fill this vacuum. Johnson and Ouchi argued that Japanese methods were transferable to the U.S.; they claimed that 20 such companies in the U.S. were "out-performing American companies in the same industries" (1974, p. 61). Later, Johnson (1977) stated that only one-half of the Japanese companies were more successful than their U.S. counterparts, but the employees of Japanese companies operating in the U.S. had higher job satisfaction. Kraar's (1975) studies of Japanese operations in the U.S. also showed that employees were enthusiastic about such personnel practices as job security, shared decision making, in-house training, and profit sharing.

Most early empirical studies of the exportability of Japanese management practices were made in the U.S., and this could have influenced the conclusions. There may have been a consistent bias in selecting Japanese managers who were sent to the U.S. subsidiaries of Japanese companies. Similarly, there also may have been reactions unique to the intersection of two specific cultures. Traditionally, the strongly unionized workforces of Britain and Australia, for example, have resisted the introduction of profit sharing.

Empirical studies of Japanese operations in countries other than the U.S. were rare at this time, but informed observers wrote impressionistic articles. Harari and Zeira (1974) and Tsurumi (1976) argued that Japanese personnel policies created problems in employee morale aboard. Key jobs were reserved for Japanese employees, and they were given special rewards. Also, Japanese managers were unfamiliar with local workforce expectations and imposed an inappropriate management style. Sim's (1977) comparative study of U.S., British, and Japanese firms also indicated that the greater centralization of Japanese firms decreased performance in key areas, but Yoshihara (1976) rejected such criticisms for Japanese subsidiaries in Thailand.

A major contribution was made by England's comparative studies of the values of Japanese managers and employees (England, 1975, 1978; Whitely & England, 1977), which showed that Japanese managers had the most homogeneous value system of any group studied. Japanese managers were pragmatic; they valued competence and achievement at the personal level and size and growth at the enterprise level. Later, Whitely and England (1977) produced evidence about the culture versus stage of industrialization debate, indicating that both these factors influenced managerial values. The methodology employed neatly demonstrated the complementarity of what had been regarded as competing explanations.

Ronen and Kraut (1977) used three data sets on employees' attitudes and found that most countries clustered with others on the basis of a similar cultural history. Countries such as Japan, with culturally distinct attitudes, had unique languages and cultures. The powerful impact of this unique culture on employees' values was illustrated again by Harari and Zeira (1974), who showed that Japanese employees have similar values regardless of whether they are working for Japanese or non-Japanese firms, or whether they are working in Japan or overseas. Weinshall and Tawara (1977/78) studied two divisions of a foreign-owned shipping company in Japan, one with Japanese managers and the other with non-Japanese managers. The authors observed completely different styles of management in the two divisions, indicating that values do affect practice. The above studies suggest that Japan may represent an extreme case of cultural determinism—its culture is more powerfully determining because of a long history of cultural isolation. Therefore, Japanese firms continued to maintain some consistently different goals, strategies, and personnel practices, and Japanese managers and workers continued to exhibit some consistent and distinctive values and behaviors in the workplace. There was little evidence for convergence.

1978-1980—Comparative Studies of Personnel Practices _____

More systematic comparative research was carried out during the period 1978-1980. The prime focus was Japanese overseas operations, particularly those in the U.S. Cook (1978) studied Japanese and U.S. management styles in the banking industry in California. She found that neither management policy nor managerial personnel practices were significantly different between Japanese-controlled and U.S.-controlled banks. Pascale (1978) and Maguire and Pascale (1978) compared U.S. subsidiaries of Japanese companies with their U.S. counterparts and concluded that Japanese companies did not outperform American ones. They identified few differences in management practices; the main exceptions were communications initiated by Japanese managers and more consultative decision making.

This is consistent with Bass and Burger's (1979) finding that Japanese managers, more than managers of any other nationality, prefer two-way to one-way communication and are better at it. Pascale and Maguire (1980) again found more similarities than differences between Japanese and U.S. companies and argued that this may reflect convergence. Takamiya (1979) reported similar results for European and U.S. subsidiaries of Japanese enterprises. Lincoln, Olson, and Hanada (1978) surveyed 54 Japanese business organizations in California, finding no strong evidence for distinctively Japanese practices, except for reduced job specialization. However, Kagono et al. (1980) surveyed the operations of

Japanese firms in the U.S. and identified some clear differences in management practices. These studies indicated that Japanese firms operating in the U.S. showed fewer distinctive characteristics than Japanese firms operating in Japan, but evidence for the Japanese maintaining both distinctive values and practices in Japan remained strong. For example, Whitehill and Takezawa (1978) concluded that Japanese managers and employees surveyed in Japan had different and more homogeneous values when compared to managers and workers in the U.S. Ishida (1980) found substantial differences between the behavior of Japanese workers in Japan and European workers in Europe. Dore (1979) explained the particular nature of these Japanese "home" values in terms of the late industrial development of Japan which resulted in there being no tradition of free wage labor. For the most part, Japanese firms in Japan remained distinctively Japanese but they adapted their practices abroad, maintaining fewer, if any, peculiarly Japanese practices. Clearly culture does affect operations to a substantial degree, but local culture dominates the culture of the parent company. This, together with Whitely and England's study (1977) reviewed above, suggests three major determinants of a company's culture—national stage of industrialization, national culture of the parent company, and local culture.

Ouchi and Jaeger (1978) analyzed two culturally-based modal organizations: Type A (North American and Western European) and Type J (Japanese and Chinese). They argued for the emergence of a new hybrid form, Type Z, which they saw as particularly suited to the modern world. This was a revision of convergence theory. Rather than Japanese management practices increasingly approximating those of the U.S., or vice versa, they both were evolving toward a new form that represented a combination of both. However, often it is unclear whether these authors are making descriptive or prescriptive statements, and their methodology has since come under attack.

Reflecting a renewed general interest in power by social scientists, there was a strong upsurge of interest in the nature of power and control in the Japanese system. Earlier research (Azumi & McMillan, 1975; Sim, 1977) had established that Japanese organizations were more centralized than Western organizations and that different functions were decentralized in these organizations. Suzuki (1980), in his study of diversification of firms in Japan, confirmed that there was stronger centralized control over subsidiaries in Japan. However, Lincoln et al. (1978) did not find these larger structural differences in Japanese firms operating in California. Once again, the evidence favored local adaptability rather than general convergence.

Fruin (1980) studied the development of the Kikkoman Shoyu Company, Limited, a well-known family firm in Japan. He concluded that the Japanese system of job security and fringe benefits did not derive from family paternalism. The system is not characteristic of family-owned companies. Paternalism developed as a managerial reaction against union activism rather than from traditional management values and practices. Therefore, the ways in which the Japanese structure authority and power are more the result of managerial choice than adherence to tradition. Values and traditions were used as rationalizations after the event.

Clutterbuck (1978), Fruin (1978), and Magota (1979) questioned the universality of raises and promotion based on seniority, demonstrating considerable variation in practice than popular stereotypes indicated. However, the most comprehensive study of human resource development practices to date was by Levine and Kawada (1980). This historical study covered several key industries and examined how and why Japanese enterprises set up internal systems for key workers, thus building up a highly versatile, loyal core of permanent employees in a particular firm. The authors stressed that this internal labor market system had substantial benefits for the elite firms that developed it, confirming Fruin's argument that these are rational choices by managers interested in financial returns, not the repetition of traditional solutions.

1981-1983—The Emergence of Voluntarism _____

Although convergence continued to be a major focus of debate in the literature of this period, there was no increased convergence in attitudes about the subject. Ballon (1983) continued to declare the uniqueness and originality of the Japanese system, and Kubota (1982) argued that this developed directly from Japan's social structure. In his view, unless the social structure of Japan changed significantly, there would be no convergence. Takezawa and Whitehill (1981) replicated their 1968 study and found no decrease of the differences in work attitudes between Japanese and U.S. employees, yet Marsh and Mannari (1981) continued to argue for convergence to the West on the basis of what they perceived as a weakening of the seniority system and of employees' commitment. Similarly, Ouchi (1981a, 1981b, 1982) and Pascale and Athos (1981) continued to argue for the convergence of both Japanese and Western organizations into a mixed model. By arguing for the overwhelming importance of staff, skills, style, and superordinate goals, Pascale and Athos (1981) ignored earlier work indicating that Japanese organizations have systematic strategic and structural differences. Theoretical and methodological critiques of Ouchi's work were made by Sullivan (1983), and Schein (1981) criticized Ouchi, Pascale, and Athos, particularly for not answering the question of the cross-cultural transferability of management practices.

Marsland and Beer (1983) argued that although Japanese human resource policies and practices are consistent with Japanese values and culture, these policies and practices are neither an inevitable nor natural outcome of the values and culture. Novel philosophies and practices may be introduced by managers if they are made compatible with the culture. This seems consistent with Fruin's (1980) idea that traditional values could be used as rationalizations for novel practices.

Some Japanese personnel practices, such as consultative decision making, are maintained more persistently in Japanese firms operating abroad. This may be because they are more central to the Japanese managerial belief system. Support for this view can be derived from two studies by Lincoln, Olson, and Hanada (1978, 1981), which show that Japanese managers and workers strongly prefer firms with maximum vertical and minimal horizontal differentiation. Alternatively (or additionally), some Japanese personnel practices could persist abroad because they are more compatible with local culture than are other Japanese personnel practices. Ishida (1981a, 1981b) presented evidence that elements that benefit employees, such as employment security and participation in management, are transferred more easily to other cultural settings, but elements requiring significant efforts at adaptation, such as collectivism and long-term commitment to the same employer, cannot be transferred easily. Other studies supported this conclusion (Iida, 1983; White & Trevor, 1983, and a 1981 Jetro survey cited in Sethi, Namiki, & Swanson, 1984). Schonberger (1982a, 1982b) provided evidence that Japanese manufacturing techniques such as just-in-time production also transfer readily to the U.S. There could be a theoretical advantage in defining culture compatibility more clearly and in devising ways of testing it empirically.

Authors questioned whether the high performance of Japanese organizations at home or abroad should be attributed to personnel practices. Instead, they argued that production management techniques explained the high performance (Hayes, 1981; Wheelwright, 1981), but did not provide supporting empirical data. It may be that for the Japanese, attention to building socio-technical systems rather than simply technical systems led to high productivity. Another useful theoretical contribution was made by Howard and Teramoto (1981). These authors argued that the most important differences between Japanese and Western management were not cultural but metacultural. In their view, the Japanese were superior in understanding the functions of social practices because of their more elaborate vocabulary for social processes. Maruyama's (1982) discussion of cultural mindscapes is also pitched at this metacultural level. This kind of analysis could increase the depth of understanding of cultural influences beyond that provided by surveys of attitude, but methodologically it is primarily intuitive and qualitative; systematic content analysis could strengthen such an approach.

Conclusions _____

The key emerging issues of the convergence debate are: How do Western and Japanese organizations differ? Are these differences disappearing over time (convergence hypothesis) or being maintained (divergence hypothesis)? and What theoretical viewpoint(s) best explains these trends?

When operating in Japan, most large Japanese firms exhibit differences from Western firms: They have different relationships with key stakeholders (particularly government bodies and financial institutions) and they have different goals (e.g., longer term corporate growth, more centralized power structures). However, the most distinctive differences relate to (a) personnel practices and decision-making processes, and (b) manufacturing philosophies and practices.

Despite continued assertions of convergence, hard evidence does not support convergence toward the Western model for Japanese firms operating in Japan. This may have been an option in the late 1960s and early 1970s, but the Japanese decided to retain and develop their own system which was showing impressive results. The Japanese have continued to borrow technology, techniques, and managerial practices from the West and have integrated such borrowing into their overall mode of operation. Two major exceptions to this anticonvergence conclusion are the modification of their paternalistic management style toward a more egalitarian or Western style and the adoption of corporate planning strategies.

On the other hand, non- Japanese firms in Japan and abroad could be converging toward a Japanese model, as suggested by Dore's (1973) late developer hypothesis. Some Western firms have revised manufacturing and personnel practices toward a Japanese model (e.g., Ouchi, 1981a, 1981b), but most Western managers operating outside Japan have followed successful Western models, particularly since the publication of Peters and Waterman's (1982) *In Search of Excellence*. Japan's greatest future influence may be in East Asia, where countries such as South Korea, Taiwan, and Singapore are using Japan as an economic development model. Literature on cultural clusters suggests that if culture is an important variable, Japanese methods should transfer more readily to other Asian countries of similar cultures (Hicks & Redding, undated, 1982).

The third possibility is that Japanese and Western firms may be converging to a new common form, as suggested by Ouchi (1981a, 1981b). However, evidence (e.g., Takezawa & Whitehill, 1981; Schein, 1981; Sullivan, 1983) does not support this possibility, at least for firms in Japan. Although Veblen (1915) and others argued for convergence on the basis of technological determinism, this has not occurred as predicted, and evidence shows that similar general technology can be operated by differing social systems. At the factory floor level for instance, Japanese managers prefer multiskilled personnel to the specialization of labor that prevails in the U.S. In organization-wide personnel policies, they prefer permanent employment. Therefore, the persistence of distinctive practices may relate more to cultural than technological factors. Although Abegglen (1958) and others argued for cultural determinism, this does not account for significant changes in Japanese practices such as the modification of management style. A more sophisticated view of the role of social values can be articulated. First, the relative cultural homogeneity of the Japanese people makes culture a more powerful and uniform force in Japan than in more pluralist societies. Second, Japanese managerial and political elites have played a critical role in choosing, from available local and foreign cultural options, those practices which suited their own ends. They used traditional values to legitimize such practices, powerful socialization processes to inculcate associated behaviors, and material and moral incentives to reinforce these behaviors.

Important in the pattern of such choices are emerging economic strategies of national and enterprise groups, strategies influenced by the limited physical resources of a small island state whose people are its main resource. The characteristic personnel policies of Japanese elite enterprises fit the Japanese cultural tradition, but some have been innovations rather than traditional practices. These are practices, however, that serve the interests of dominant elites. This may be more a matter of ensuring control of the workforce than directly raising productivity. If so, one may assume that Japanese enterprise practices in Japan will continue to diverge from those in the West while they both ensure control and do not decrease productivity in the longer term.

Japanese overseas operations vary in the extent to which they maintain Japanese personnel practices, but there is a marked shift to adapt to local culture. When operating abroad, Japanese managers prefer familiar personnel practices, but modify their behavior over time as they become aware that only some practices are compatible with local values. Vestigial remnants of Japanese company culture are those which are culturally compatible and which also ensure flexibility of operations (e.g., broader job definition), employee commitment (e.g., participative practices), or control by the parent company (Japanese in key senior positions).

Another theoretical standpoint attempts to explain the distinctive features of the Japanese firm in functionalist terms. In this view, these distinctive features are adaptive to the larger society. There is historical evidence that key political actors in Japan gave priority to the modernization of industry and commerce and made conscious decisions which shaped the basic features of the Japanese corporate environment (Vogel, 1979). The integration between large Japanese corporations and government bodies such as MITI (Ministry of International Trade and Industry) stems from early government sponsorship and control of many industries. Typically, functionalism implies a hidden hand theory of social fit, but in the Japanese case there has been a continuing debate about the goals, role, and activities of large corporations. Therefore, a high degree of fit is not surprising, particularly when harmony is a central Japanese value. However, when operating overseas, some Japanese companies have failed to appreciate that key stakeholder relationships (e.g., government) are different and in the U.S., for example, have ended up with major lawsuits against them (Sethi et al., 1984).

Conspicuously absent from most of the literature is a voluntaristic theory which explains the unique characteristics of Japanese enterprises in terms of conscious problem solving by key elites in Japan, yet studies reviewed here (e.g., Kono, 1976; Rohlen, 1974) provide considerable evidence for this. The uniqueness of Japanese management practices in Japan appears to be a mindful response by Japanese managers to their particular economic and cultural environment. Their evolving approach to organization development has been a flexible, innovative process of choice; it is understood that cultural values are only one important factor in achieving goals. A divergent enterprise system has been maintained in Japan by Japanese managers because it has shown results over the long term. For the same reason, Japanese managers operating abroad have learned to manage differently than they do at home. This is evidence for a voluntaristic theory of enterprise building in which cultural traditions and larger social structures are subsumed by the collective, interactive strategic decision making of members of the business elite.

References _____

Abegglen, J. C. (1957) Subordination and autonomy attitudes of Japanese workers. *American Journal of Sociology*, 63, 181-189.

Abegglen, J. C. (1958) *The Japanese factory: Aspects of its social organization.* Glencoe, IL: Free Press.

Abegglen, J. C. (1973) *Management and worker: The Japanese solution.* Tokyo: Kodansha International.

Adams, T. F. M. & Kobayashi, N. (1969) *The world of Japanese business*. Tokyo: Kodansha International.

Azumi, K., & McMillan, C. J. (1975) Culture and organization structure: A comparison of Japanese and British organizations. *International Studies of Management and Organization*, 5(1). 35-47.

Azumi, K., & McMillan, C. J. (1976) Worker sentiment in the Japanese factory: Its organizational determinants. In L. Austin (Ed.), *Japan: The paradox of progress* (pp. 215-229). New Haven, CT: Yale University Press.

Ballon, R. J. (Ed.) (1967) *Joint ventures and Japan*. Tokyo: Sophia-Tuttle.

Ballon, R. J. (Ed.) (1968) *Doing business in Japan*. Tokyo: Sophia-Tuttle.

Ballon, R. J. (1969a) The Japanese dimensions of industrial enterprises. In R. J. Ballon (Ed.), *The Japanese employee* (pp.3-40). Tokyo: Sophia University.

Ballon, R. J. (1969b) Lifelong remuneration system. In R. J. Ballon (Ed.), *The Japanese employee* (pp. 123-165). Tokyo: Sophia University.

Ballon, R. J. (1969c) Participative employment. In R. J. Ballon (Ed.), *The Japanese employee* (pp. 63-76). Tokyo: Sophia University.

Ballon, R. J. (1983) Non-Western work organizations. *Asia Pacific Journal of Management*, 1, 1-14.

Bass, B. M., & Burger, P. C. (1979) *Assessment of managers: An international comparison*. New York: Free Press.

Bennett, J. W., & Ishino, I. (1963) *Paternalism in the Japanese economy: Anthropological studies of Oyabun-Kobun patterns*. Minneapolis: University of Minnesota Press.

Brown, W. (1966) Japanese management: The cultural background. *Monumenta Nipponica*, 21(1-2), 47-60.

Chandler, M. K. (1966) Management rights: Made in Japan. *Columbia Journal of World Business,* 1(1), 131-140.

Clutterbuck, D. (1978) Calculator company puts its managers to the test. *International Management*, 33(4), 35-36.

Cole, R. E. (1971) *Japanese blue collar: The changing tradition*. Berkeley: University of California Press.

Cole, R. E. (1972) Permanent employment in Japan: Facts and fantasies. *Industrial and Labor Relations Review*, 26, 615-630.

Cole, R. E. (1973) Functional alternatives and economic development: An empirical example of permanent employment in Japan. *American Sociological Review*, 38, 424-438.

Cook, N. E. (1978) Human resource management style: A comparative study of Japanese and American banks in California. *Dissertation Abstracts International*, 39, 355A, University Microfilms No. 7811343.

De Bettignies, H. C. (1971) Japanese organizational behavior: A psychocultural approach. In D. Graves (Ed.), *Managerial research: A cross-cultural perspective* (pp. 15-93). San Francisco: Jossey-Bass.

De Mente, B. (1968) The Japanese executive and his management philosophy. *Worldwide P & I Planning*, 2(1), 42-50.

Doi, T. (1973) *The anatomy of dependence*. Tokyo: Kodansha International.

Dore, R. P. (1973) *British factory, Japanese factory: The origins of national diversity in industrial relations*. Berkeley: University of California Press.

Dore, R. P. (1979) More about late development. *Journal of Japanese Studies*, 5, 137-151.

Drucker, P. F. (1975) Economic realities and enterprise strategy. In E. F. Vogel (Ed.), *Modern Japanese organization and decision making* (pp. 228-248). Berkeley: University of California Press.

Dunphy, D. C., & Stening, B. W. (1984) *Japanese organization behaviour and management: An annotated bibliography*. Hong Kong: Asian Research Service.

England, G. W., & Koike, R. (1970) Personal value systems of Japanese managers. *Journal of Cross-Cultural Psychology*, 1, 21-40.

England, G. W. (1975) *The manager and his values: An international perspective from the United States, Japan, Korea, India and Australia*. Cambridge, MA: Ballinger.

England, G. W. (1978) Managers and their value systems: A five-country comparative study. *Columbia Journal of World Business,* 13(2), 35-44.

Evans, R. (1970) Evolution of the Japanese system of employer-employee relations, 1868-1945, *Business History Review*, 44(1), 110-125.

Fruin, W. M. (1978) The Japanese company controversy. *Journal of Japanese Studies*, 4, 267-300.

Fruin, W. M. (1980) The family as a firm and the firm as a family in Japan: The case of Kikkoman Shoyu Company Limited. *Journal of Family History*, 5, 432-449.

Glazer, H. (1968) *The international businessman in Japan: The Japanese image*. Tokyo: Sophia University.

Haire, M., Ghiselli, E. E., & Porter, L. W. (1966) *Managerial thinking: An international study*. New York: Wiley.

Harari, E., & Zeira, Y. (1974) Morale problems in non-American multinational corporations in the United States. *Management International Review*, 14(6), 43-57.

Harbison, F. (1959) Management in Japan. In F. Harbison & C. A. Myers (Eds.), *Management in the industrial world: An international analysis* (pp. 249-264). New York: McGraw-Hill.

Hayes, R. H. (1981) Why Japanese factories work. *Harvard Business Review,* 59(4), 56-66.

Hazama, H. (1977) Formation of the management system in Meiji Japan: Personnel management in large corporations. *Developing Economies,* 15, 402-419.

Hesseling, P., & Konnen, E. (1969) Culture and subculture in a decision-making exercise. *Human Relations,* 22, 31-51.

Hicks, G. L., & Redding, S. G. (undated) *Uncovering the sources of East Asian economic growth.* Unpublished manuscript.

Hicks, G. L., & Redding, S. G. (1982) *Industrial East Asia and the post-Confucian hypothesis.* Unpublished manuscript.

Hill, R. (1977a, April) Japanese company boss who gives no orders. *International Management,* 32, 27-29.

Hill, R. (1977b, April) Japanese fibres firm restructures to restore profits. *International Management,* 32, 41-43.

Hirono, R. (1969) Personnel management in foreign corporations. In R. J. Ballon (Ed.,), *The Japanese employee* (pp. 251-271). Tokyo: Sophia University.

Howard, N., & Teramoto, Y. (1981) The really important difference between Japanese and Western management. *Management International Review,* 21(3), 19-30.

Iida, T. (1983) Transferability of Japanese management systems and practices into Australian companies. *Human Resource Management Australia,* 21(3) 23-27.

Imai, M. (1960) Shukko, Jomukai, Ringi—The ingredients of executive selection in Japan. *Personnel,* 46(4), 20-30.

Ishida, H. (1980) Japanese workers and the quality of working life. *Sumitomo Quarterly,* 4(6), 15-18.

Ishida, H. (1981a) Human resources management in overseas Japanese firms. *Japanese Economic Studies,* 10(1), 53-81.

Ishida, H. (1981b) Japanese-style human resource management: Can it be exported? *Sumitomo Quarterly,* 5(6), 15-18.

Johnson, R. T. (1977) Success and failure of Japanese subsidiaries in America. *Columbia Journal of World Business,* 12(1), 30-37.

Johnson, R. T., and Ouchi, W. G. (1974) Made in America (under Japanese management). *Harvard Business Review,* 52(5), 61-69.

Kagono, T., et al. (1980) Mechanistic vs. organic management systems: A comparative study of adaptive patterns of U.S. and Japanese firms. *Kobe Annual Reports*, 115-139.

Karsh, B., & Cole, R. E. (1968) Industrialization and the convergence hypothesis: Some aspects of contemporary Japan. *Journal of Social Issues*, 24(4), 45-64.

Kelley, L., & Reeser, C. (1973) The persistence of culture as a determinant of differentiated attitudes on the part of American managers of Japanese ancestry. *Academy of Management Journal*, 16, 67-76.

Kobayashi, S. (1971) *Creative management*. New York: American Management Association.

Kono, T. (1976) Long range planning— Japan-USA: A comparative study. *Long Range Planning*, 9(5), 61-71.

Kraar, L. (1975) The Japanese are coming—with their own style of management. *Fortune*, 91(3), 116-121.

Kubota, A. (1982) Japanese employment system and Japanese social structure. *Asia Pacific Community*, 15(6), 96-120.

Levine, S. B. (1958) *Industrial relations in postwar Japan*. Urbana: University of Illinois.

Levine, S. B., & Kawada, S. B. (1980) *Human resources in Japanese industrial development*. Princeton, NJ: Princeton University Press.

Lincoln, J. R., Olson, J., & Hanada, M. (1978) Cultural effects on organizational structures: The case of Japanese firms in the United States. *American Sociological Review*, 43, 829-847.

Lincoln, J. R., Olson, J., & Hanada, M. (1981) Cultural orientations and individual reactions to organizations: A study of employees of Japanese-owned firms. *Administrative Science Quarterly*, 26, 93-115.

Lyons, N. (1976) *The Sony vision*. New York: Crown.

Magota, R. (1979) The end of the seniority-related (Nenko) wage system. *Japanese Economic Studies*, 7(3), 71-125.

Maguire, M. A., & Pascale, R. T. (1978) Communication, decision-making and implementation among managers in Japanese and American managed companies in the United States. *Sociology and Social Research*, 63, 1-23.

Marsh, R. M., & Mannari, H. (1971) Lifetime commitment in Japan: Roles, norms and values. *American Journal of Sociology*, 76, 795-812.

Marsh, R. M., & Mannari, H. (1972) A new look at 'lifetime commitment' in Japanese industry. *Economic Development and Cultural Change*, 20, 611-630.

Marsh, R. M., & Mannari, H. (1976) *Modernization and the Japanese factory*. Princeton, NJ: Princeton University Press.

Marsh, R. M., & Mannari, H. (1981) Divergence and convergence in industrial organizations: The Japanese case. In G. Dlugos & D. Weiermair (Eds.), *Management under differing value systems: Political, social and economical perspective in a changing world* (pp. 447-460). Berlin: Walter de Gruyter.

Marsland, S., & Beer, M. (1983) The evolution of Japanese management: Lessons for U.S. managers. *Organizational Dynamics*, 11(3), 49-67.

Maruyama, M. (1982) Mindscapes, workers, and management: Japan and the U.S.A. in S. M. Lee & G. Schwendiman (Eds.), *Japanese management: Cultural and environmental considerations* (pp. 53-71). New York: Praeger.

Miller, S. S. (1963) Management by Omikoshi: Traditional features of modern business in Japan. *Management International*, 3(1), 59-69.

Murano, T., & Tomb, J. O. (1974, Winter) Japan's future multinationals: Imitators or innovators? *The McKinsey Quarterly*, 39-48.

Nakagawa, K. (1975) Business strategy and industrial structure in pre-World-War-II Japan. *Strategy and Structure of Big Business: Proceedings of the First Fuji Conference*, 3-38.

Nakane, C. (1972) *Human relations in Japan.* Summary translation of Tateshakai no ningen kankei (Personal relations in a vertical society). Japan: Ministry of Foreign Affairs.

Nakane, C. (1973) *Japanese society.* Middlesex: Penguin Books.

Odaka, K. (1963) Traditionalism, democracy in Japanese industry. *Industrial Relations*, 3, 95-103.

Odaka, K. (1975) *Toward industrial democracy: Management and workers in modern Japan.* Cambridge, MA: Harvard University Press.

Ouchi, W. G. (1981a) Organizational paradigms: A commentary on Japanese management and theory Z organizations. *Organizational Dynamics*, 9(4), 36-43.

Ouchi, W. G. (1981b) *Theory Z: How American business can meet the Japanese challenge.* Reading, MA: Addison-Wesley.

Ouchi, W. G. (1982) Theory Z: An elaboration of methodology and findings. *Journal of Contemporary Business*, 11(2), 27-41.

Ouchi, W. G., & Jaeger, A. M. (1978) Type Z organization: Stability in the midst of mobility. *Academy of Management Review*, 3, 305-314.

Parkanskii, A. (1973) Export of American methods of management to Japan. *Japanese Economic Studies*, 2(2), 65-76.

Pascale, R. T. (1978) Communication and decision-making across cultures—Japanese and American comparisons. *Administrative Science Quarterly*, 23, 91-110.

Pascale, R. T., & Maguire, M. A. (1980) Comparison of selected work factors in Japan and the United States. *Human Relations*, 33, 433-455.

Pascale, R. T., & Athos, A. G. (1981) *The art of Japanese management: Applications for American executives*. New York: Simon & Schuster.

Peters, T. J., & Waterman, R. H. (1982) *In search of excellence: Lessons from America's best-run companies*. New York: Harper & Row.

Prasad, S. B. (1968) A new system of authority in Japanese management. *Journal of Asian and African Studies*, 3, 216-225.

Rohlen, T. P. (1970) Sponsorship of cultural continuity in Japan: A company training program. *Journal of Asian and African Studies*, 5, 184-192.

Rohlen, T. P. (1974) *For harmony and strength: Japanese white-collar organization in anthropological perspective*. Berkeley: University of California Press.

Ronen, S., & Kraut, A. I. (1977) Similarities among countries based on employee work values and attitudes. *Columbia Journal of World Business*, 12(2), 89-96.

Rutledge, P. (1974) Bringing Mitsui together again. *International Management*, 29(2), 28-31.

Schein, E. H. (1981) Does Japanese management style have a message for American managers? *Sloan Management Review*, 23(1), 55-68.

Schonberger, R. J. (1982a) The transfer of Japanese manufacturing management approaches to U.S. industry. *Academy of Management Review*, 7, 479-487.

Schonberger, R. J. (1982b) *Japanese manufacturing techniques: Nine hidden lessons in simplicity*. New York: Free Press.

Sethi, S. P., Namiki, N., & Swanson, C. L. (1984) *The false promise of the Japanese miracle*. Boston: Pitman.

Sim, A. B. (1977) Decentralized management of subsidiaries and their performance—Comparative study of American, British and Japanese subsidiaries in Malaysia. *Management International Review*, 17(2), 45-51.

Sullivan, J. (1983) A critique of theory Z. *Academy of Management Review*, 8, 132-142.

Suzuki, H. (1969) Innovation and integration in Japanese management: The fusion of Oriental and Occidental civilizations. *The Role of Management: Innovation, Integration, Internationalization: Proceedings of the 15th CIOS International Management Congress*, 31-37.

Suzuki, Y. (1980) The strategy and structure of top 100 Japanese industrial enterprises 1950-1970. *Strategic Management Journal*, 1, 265-291.

Takamiya, M. (1979) *Japanese multinationals in Europe: Internal operations and their public policy implications*. Berlin: International Institute of Management.

Takamiya, S. (1969) Characteristics of Japanese management and its recent tendencies: Effectiveness of Japanese management. *The Role of Management:*

Innovation, Integration, Internationalization: Proceedings of the 15th CIOS International Management Congress, 394-405.

Takezawa, S. (1966) Socio-cultural aspects of management in Japan: Historical development and new challenges. *International Labour Review*, 94, 148-174.

Takezawa, S., & Whitehill, A. M. (1981) *Workways: Japan and America*. Tokyo: Japan Institute of Labor.

Tanaka, S. (1969) The relationship between management behaviour and social structure. *The Role of Management: Innovation, Integration, Internationalization: Proceedings of the 15th CIOS International Management Congress*, 147-159.

Tindall, R. E. (1974) Mitsubishi group: World's largest multinational enterprise? *Michigan State University Business Topics*, 22(2), 27-34.

Tsuchiya, M. (1975) Management organization of vertically integrated non-Zaibatsu business. *Strategy and Structure of Big Business: Proceedings of the First Fuji Conference*, 65-78.

Tsurumi, Y. (1973) Japanese multinational firms. *Journal of World Trade Law*, 7(1), 74-90.

Tsurumi, Y. (1976) *The Japanese are coming: A multinational interaction of firms and policies*. Cambridge, MA: Ballinger.

Veblen, T. (1954) The opportunity of Japan. In L. Ardzrooni (Ed.), Essays in our changing order (pp. 248-266). New York: Viking Press. (Reprinted from *Journal of Race Development*, 6, July, 1915).

Vogel, E. F. (1979) *Japan as number one: Lessons for America*. Cambridge, MA: Harvard University Press.

Weinshall, T. D., & Tawara, J. (1977/78) The managerial structure of a nationally mixed organization in Japan: A sociometric case study. *Organization and Administrative Sciences*, 8, 209-217.

Wheelright, S. C. (1981) Japan—Where operations really are strategic. *Harvard Business Review*, 59(4), 67-74.

White, M., & Trevor, M. (1983) *Under Japanese management*. London: Heinemann.

Whitehill, A. M. (1964a) Cultural values and employee attitudes: United States and Japan. *Journal of Applied Psychology*, 48, 69-72.

Whitehill, A. M. (1964b) Cultural variations in group attraction. *Sociology and Social Research*, 48, 469-477.

Whitehill, A. M., & Takezawa, S. (1961) *Cultural values in management-worker relations*. Chapel Hill, NC: University of North Carolina.

Whitehill, A. M., & Takezawa, S. (1978) Workplace harmony: Another Japanese 'miracle'? *Columbia Journal of World Business*, 13(3), 25-39.

Whitely, W., & England, G. W. (1977) Managerial values as a reflection of culture and the process of industrialization. *Academy of Management Journal*, 20, 439-453.

Yamada, T. (1969) Japanese management practices—change is on the way as traditional habits are challenged. *Conference Board Record*, 6(11), 22-23.

Yamazaki, K., Kobayashi, N., & Doi, T. (1977) Toward Japanese-type multinational corporations. *Japanese Economic Studies*, 5(4), 41-70.

Yanagihara, N. (1974) The strategy and structure of Japanese industrial corporations. *KSU Economic and Business Review*, 24-45.

Yasouka, S. (1975) The tradition of family business in the strategic decision process and management structure of Zaibatsu business: Mitsui, Sumitomo, and Mitsubishi. *Strategy and Structure of Big Business: Proceedings of the First Fuji Conference*, 81-101.

Yoshihara, H. (1976) Personnel management of Japanese companies in Thailand. *Kobe Economic and Business Review*, 23rd Annual Report, 11-62.

Yoshihara, H. (1977) The Japanese multinational. *Long Range Planning*, 10(2), 41-45.

Yoshino, M. Y. (1968) Japan's managerial system: *Tradition and innovation.* Cambridge, MA: MIT Press.

Yoshino, M. Y. (1975) Emerging Japanese multinational enterprises. In E. F. Vogel (Ed.), *Modern Japanese organization and decision-making* (pp. 146-166). Berkeley: University of California Press.

II _____ CULTURE AND ORGANIZATIONS _____

Cross-Cultural Management: Transformations and Adaptations
Rose Knotts

New Challenges for Japanese Multinationals: Is Organization Adaptation Their Achilles Heel?
Christopher A. Bartlett and Hideki Yoshihara

Cultural Constraints on Transfer of Technology Across Nations: Implications for Research in International and Comparative Management
Ben L. Kedia and Rabi S. Bhagat

3. CROSS-CULTURAL MANAGEMENT: TRANSFORMATIONS AND ADAPTATIONS

ROSE KNOTTS

Rose Knotts is an associate professor of management at the University of North Texas. She was editor of the Academy of Management Newsletter for three years. This article is her first appearance in Business Horizons.

The cross-cultural communication forced by today's business environment can be the source of irritation and lost business. The problems, and the solutions, are described here.

1. Smiling fish is a:
   a. term used by Middle Easterners to describe American tourists.
   b. French chef working in a Japanese kitchen.
   c. dish served in China in which the fish is still alive.
2. In England, to table an issue or motion means to:
   a. put it aside until later.
   b. send it to arbitration.
   c. bring it up and discuss it.
3. Allah is the Supreme Being of which religious group?
   a. Shintos
   b. Buddhists
   c. Moslems

If you answered C to all three questions, you probably have a reasonable grasp of cross-cultural orientations.

The growing population of international students and employees in the U.S., the disproportionate trade deficits among countries, the popularity of international acquisitions and joint ventures, and increasing international interactions among companies today force leaders in U.S. organizations to learn to interact and communicate more efficiently with a greater variety of cultures. The problems and results of mismanagement and miscommunication are evident daily. The problems are not likely to dissipate merely with increased interactions among other cultures, and the results of perfunctory relations and communications are not likely to improve. The responsibility for acknowledging this increasing problem and the obligation for eliminating its sources rest firmly with the organization's leaders. Unfortunately, many organizations are not aware of cur-

Reprinted from *Business Horizons*, January–February 1989, pp. 29–33 by permission of the publisher.

rent trends or the changes occurring around them in the international business environment.

An understanding of some of the aspects of intercultural interactions represents an important step toward being able to adapt to and confront these complex situations. This article discusses some of the aspects and ramifications of interacting with other cultures.

Cross-Cultural Interaction Limitations_____

A primary source of misunderstanding among cultures is the differences in values and priorities. Some of the most common lie in the way dissimilar cultures perceive time, thought patterns, personal space, material possessions, family roles and relationships, language, religion, personal achievement, competitiveness and individuality, social behavior, and other interrelated environmental and subjective issues. Another important source of miscommunication and misunderstanding is in the perceptions of the leaders, managers, and communicators about the persons with whom they are dealing. For example, if people presume their values and habits are superior and more sophisticated than those of other cultures, this attitude will be reflected in the way they communicate. Some of the factors that affect intercultural relationships are outlined below.

Time

Americans place an exceptionally high priority on time, perceiving it as a commodity that holds value. Conserving time to them is an efficient process, a significant asset. Many cultures, conversely, place more worth on relationships and a decelerated, more relaxed lifestyle. If an American tries to coerce others to conform to his tempo, members of other cultures may find it offensive and avoid doing business with him. They may think he or she is someone who is "more interested in business than people" or who thinks "being punctual for an occasion or appointment is a fundamental goal of life." Before some business people will conduct business or interact with others, an amicable relationship must first be established.

Thought Patterns

Americans declare that their past is behind them; however, some cultures believe that a person's past is in front of him, since he can view what has happened. Americans assert that their future is in front of them; others believe that the future is behind them, because they cannot see into the future. Additionally, many Americans would like to foresee the future so they could take advantage of impending opportunities or events. Other cultures believe it fortunate that one cannot see the future because that way he or she is not exposed to negative information that would likely cause worry or pain.

In the *Going International* film series, George Renwick describes the Arab's speech and thought behavior as moving in loops, whereas the American's speech and thought behavior is direct or linear. Those unaware of these patterns could confound the process and cause negative consequences by forward, abrupt, or aggressive communication. Other thought and perceptual traditions influence behavior and communication patterns and could lead to unexpected outcomes if leaders do not take the time and effort to understand them.

Personal Space

Cultures maintain unwritten rules on the distance one member remains from another in face-to-face interactions, in lines, and in public places. Although the distance is affected by the relationships of the people involved, one member of a culture may be offended if someone from another culture, in which personal distance rules are different, violates the space rule by "invading" his space. Americans are typically made uncomfortable by the closer conversation distance of Arabs and Africans; Arabs and Africans may feel rejection by the lengthy personal distance of Americans.

> "Those cultures that place little or no great significance on possessions may feel that it is vulgar, greedy, and disrespectful to flaunt wealth, and cannot relate to the values held by those who do."

Many Americans dislike it when another touches them on the arm or shoulder, but it is more a personal preference than a cultural rule. In some cultures, however, it is inappropriate to touch another person with the hand (especially the left hand), particularly if the party is of the opposite sex. Managers should learn the personal space and touching rules of the society in which they are working so they do not offend host nationals or make them uncomfortable.

Material Possessions

U.S. advertisements reinforce "more is better" or "bigger is better" values. Business publications print annual lists of the largest corporations, the highest-compensated executives, the wealthiest persons *ad nauseum*. Consequently, the attention devoted to these accomplishments prompts Americans to equate success with material wealth. Those cultures that place little or no great significance on possessions may feel that it is vulgar, greedy, and disrespectful to flaunt wealth, and cannot relate to the values held by those who do. Managers need to know the value of material possessions not only in facilitating the communication process, but also when trying to motivate those of other cultures.

Family Roles and Relationships

In many societies, family roles and relationships are very traditional, personal, and predictable. The husband is the provider, the wife supervises the household, and males in the household are more valued than females. Each member of the family has a designated role and the responsibility for maintaining *status quo* for those roles. Peer pressures preserve the roles, and work situations and business interactions are less influential than familial responsibilities. One American businessman became very disconcerted to learn upon his arrival in Egypt that the man with whom he had an appointment was in another city to attend the funeral of his brother. Although the death had occurred a couple of weeks earlier, the Egyptian businessman had neglected to telephone the American and inform him of the expected absence. Rather than show his displeasure at the inconvenience placed upon him, the American capitalized upon the opportunity and pretended the purpose of his trip was to express his personal condolences. An expression of impatience or anger would have probably severed all future relations; the expression of sympathy was most suitable to the occasion. This philosophy is illustrated by a Latin American parable: "Man does not live to work—man works to live." To maintain open communication and good relations, family roles and relations must be honored.

Language

All cultures use verbal and nonverbal communication systems or languages, and each culture's vocabulary reflects its primary values and composition. Eskimos use many words and expressions for snow and its components, Arabs have numerous words for camels, and Americans have multiple words and meanings for computers and accessories. Although words themselves have no meaning (meaning comes from people), managers should observe and respect the role and composition of languages and other subtle cultural cues.

In his book, *Big Business Blunders*, David Ricks details numerous problems that have developed as a result of words or behaviors in one culture or language having opposite or obscene meanings in another.[1] Even within a language, accents, usages, or differences in the way things are said can create disharmony. Terpstra and David indicate that "while an American would say that he put some gas in his truck, drove to his girlfriend's apartment, took the elevator to her floor, and rang the doorbell, an Englishman would say that he put some petrol in his lorry, drove to his girlfriend's flat, took the lift to her floor, and then knocked her up."[2] Ricks also noted some of the problems that developed as a result of a difference in the meaning of words between British and American English.

Religion

Religion is the dominant force in the daily lives of some peoples, such as Arabs. Arab life revolves around prayer times, holidays, and daily events, and many occurrences are justified in the name of religion. Phrases such as "it was Allah's will" are used as rationalizations for a major disaster or disruption of business. Successful foreign businesses operating in cultures where religion governs business and social practices are those who respect and deal with their hosts' customs, such as prayer requirements and dietary restrictions.

Businesses should also be aware that if changes affect religious and cultural patterns, resistance from religious and government leaders can result. One can sense the problems that may occur by examining the Iranian revolution of the early eighties, when many Iranian leaders felt threatened by cultural changes that were developing. Additionally, a disregard or lack of respect for cultural traditions can result in loss of communication or business, or in consequences even more serious.

Personal Achievement

Achievement is another value espoused by the traditional American business person. The success and prestige of our business leaders are measured by the magnitude of their organization, the amount of their compensation, and their location in the hierarchy. The larger the organization and compensation and the higher the stature, traditionally the greater the adoration. In other cultures, especially where family time is meaningful, the quality of relationships and time spent with family are the symbols of success and prestige. When Americans (perhaps subconsciously) communicate this acquisitive attitude to a culture that does not share their achievement motivation, communication channels can be damaged or severed.

Competitiveness and Individuality

Competitiveness and individuality are other values supported by most American business persons. Within reason, competitiveness is considered to be a natural, desired trait. Consequently, individual ambition within an organization is encouraged and rewarded. In some international business cultures, aggressive behaviors that demonstrate individuality and competitiveness are discouraged. Instead, team spirit and consensus are valued traits. Problems, misunderstandings, or miscommunications occur when these opposing values enter into communications and behaviors. For example, in the haste to pursue business, aggressiveness can demonstrate a lack of concern that alienates many international associates. Since many cultures value modesty, team spirit, collectivity, and patience, the competitiveness and individualistic demeanor conveyed in American interpersonal verbal communications, advertisements, physical gestures, status symbols, and so forth represents unacceptable behavior.

Social Behavior

Punctuality is expected in most U.S. business situations, but tardiness is acceptable in numerous social situations. For a number of reasons, however, punctuality is not a revered characteristic in many of the world's societies. The typical American psyche lacks patience with those cultures that do not value punctuality. Consequently, those who supervise persons from cultures that do not revere punctuality may appear pompous or unreasonable.

Noisy eating habits and belching are almost never acceptable in U.S. culture; they are expected as evidence of satisfaction in others. Some Chinese cultures feel it is polite to take a portion of each food served. One American businessman learned of this custom only after taking some Chinese businessmen to a cafeteria. Each Chinese wound up with three trays of food and the American exceeded his daily expense account.

Many behaviors seen by Americans as innocuous are considered inappropriate in other cultures. Such behaviors as showing of the soles of one's feet, touching with or delivering objects with one's left hand, or speaking first may create cross-cultural conflicts.

Ethnocentric Attitudes

Persons who believe their cultural values, habits, or religion are superior to all others possess *ethnocentric* attitudes. Unfortunately, ethnocentric attitudes usually surface in the form of patronization, superiority, disrespect, or inflexibility.

One form of ethnocentricity is seen in stereotyping. If a communicator imagines that a person from another culture will react in a particular way, he will usually convey this attitude in his speech, expectations, or behavior. A man attending an international-relations banquet was seated across from another man who possessed Asian physical characteristics. Wishing to advance international relations, he asked the Asian, "Likee foodee?" The man politely nodded his head. During the program, the Asian was introduced as an award-winning professor of economics at a prestigious university and was asked to make a few projections about world trade imbalances. After a brief discussion in perfect English, the Asian professor sat down, glanced across at his astonished neighbor and asked, "Likee talkee?" To avoid similar embarrassing situations, managers should not make assumptions from physical appearances, attributes, or other superficial characteristics.

To prevent stereotypes from negatively affecting his or her actions, the manager should be prudent. Some precautions are discussed below.

Flexibility and Sincerity

Flexibility is possibly the most important of the precautions necessary to minimize mistakes and misunderstandings in intercultural relationships. While it is logical that all stereotypes are not necessarily negative, assumptions about others should be limited or guarded so the circumstances, situation, or actions of others are interpreted correctly. A flexible manager will cautiously analyze the responses and reactions of subordinates in an attempt to correctly interpret what their cultural reactions indicate.

Sincerity is another characteristic that contributes to the understanding of intercultural interactions. If a manager adopts a sincere attitude by patiently accepting a subordinate from another culture, that empathy will normally be received in a trusting, positive manner.

Intercultural Socialization

Intercultural socialization involves becoming aware of the other culture's habits, actions, and reasons behind behaviors. Americans presume they are the safest, most sanitary culture in the world, but a large majority of the automobiles in the U.S. would not pass inspection in West Germany. The Japanese (and other cultures) think Americans are unhygienic for locating the toilet and bathing facility in the same area. Many cultures think the American habit of sitting on a toilet seat very unsanitary.

There is usually a logical reason for cultural habits and rules, but the reason is not necessarily universal. Managers from all cultures should be willing to accept other cultures' habits and actions and consider that they might be logical or proper. Other cultures' rules and behaviors may seem strange, but they are usually established on historical or religious traditions. Many cultures shake hands upon meeting or greeting others, while bowing is customary in others. Leaving food or drink after dining is considered polite in some cultures, but impolite in others. To prevent social blunders with influential leaders or primary decision makers, managers should follow the rules of etiquette of their cultures.

Establishment of Relationships

Although Americans conduct business with persons they do not know, this practice is not customary in other cultures. One Mexican businessman said on a recent news report, "Why should I do business with a person I do not know?" For the Mexican businessman an amicable relationship was mandatory before transacting business.

To establish relationships, American managers must devote time to becoming acquainted with prospective business partners. Certainly a prerequisite to this process is to learn about their culture and traditions and then dedicate time to becoming familiar with the clients. A word of caution, however: in the process of getting to know another, one needs to learn what subjects are permissible, what subjects to avoid, and what questions to expect. Asking about a man's wife in some cultures is equivalent to asking an American man about his sex life. Additionally, you should not be offended if an Asian inquires about the size of your salary or the price of your home or car. Those are not impolite questions in his culture.

The American adage that the world is getting smaller symbolizes the idea that we are becoming more mobile and interacting with more cultures. To successfully meet this challenge, it is imperative that managers adapt to different situations. Flexibility and adaptability are important at the upper levels of management as well as in the lower levels. The book *Megatrends*[3] noted that business had developed from a national economy to a world economy; this trend does not affect the upper levels of management any more than lower levels. Accompanying the increase of social and economic interaction, the entire organization must become more interculturally adept. Those proactive establishments that implement progressive measures for confronting and adapting to the changes occurring in the work environment will be better prepared and more adept at facilitating and operating in the intercultural era that is upon us.

Notes

1. David A. Ricks, *Big Business Blunders: Mistakes in Multinational Marketing* (Homewood, Ill.: Dow Jones-Irwin, 1979).
2. Vern Terpstra and David Kenneth, *The Cultural Environment of International Business* (Cincinnati: South-Western Publishers, 1985).
3. John Naisbett, *Megatrends* (New York: Warner Books, 1982).

4. NEW CHALLENGES FOR JAPANESE MULTINATIONALS: IS ORGANIZATION ADAPTATION THEIR ACHILLES HEEL?

CHRISTOPHER A. BARTLETT

Christopher A. Bartlett is an associate professor of Business Administration at Harvard University's Graduate School of Business Administration. He received an economics degree from the University of Queensland, Australia (1964), and both the masters and doctorate degrees in business administration from Harvard University (1971 and 1979). He has held various staff and line management positions including marketing manager with Alcoa, a management consultant at McKinsey and Company's London office, and general manager of Baxter Laboratories' subsidiary company in France. His major interests focus on strategic management, and organization process and design, particularly as these issues relate to the management of multinational organizations. He has published in many leading journals including California Management Review, Harvard Business Review, Journal of Business Strategy, *and* Sloan Management Review.

HIDEKI YOSHIHARA

Professor Hideki Yoshihara is on the faculty of Kobe University's Research Institute for Economics and Business Administration.

As the number, size, and complexity of Japanese multinational companies' (MNCs) overseas operations increase, many of them have begun to realize that they face some fundamental and difficult organizational challenges. Drawing on research undertaken with several large and successful Japanese MNCs, the authors define the nature and source of some of these organizational challenges, and describe some approaches that can be taken to resolving them. The article starts with a brief assessment of the traditional organizational capabilities and existing managerial approaches of Japanese companies, comparing them to the emerging challenges in the international environment. Then, after identifying some constraints and barriers to an effective response to the new demands, the authors propose a series of actions to overcome the problems.

Bartlett, Christopher A., and Yoshihara, Hideki. New Challenges for Japanese Multinationals: Is Organization Adaptation Their Achilles Heel?" *Human Resource Management* 27, no. 1 (Spring 1988): 19-43. Copyright © 1988 John Wiley & Sons, Inc. Reprinted by permission of John Wiley & Sons, Inc.

We would like to acknowledge the helpful comments of Sumantra Ghoshal, Kichiro Hayashi, Nitin Nohria, M. Y. Yoshino and an anonymous reviewer.

The doubling of the stock of Japanese foreign direct investment between 1980 and 1986 provides clear evidence that Japanese multinational companies (MNCs) are at a critical juncture in their development. Spurred on by mounting political pressures, fast developing competitive forces and a plunging dollar, many of the best known of these companies are in the process of radically and rapidly altering their global posture.

Over the past decade, most have made some important transitions: from export-based strategies to ones based more on substantial foreign investment; from a concentration on less-developed and newly industrialized countries towards a major presence in the industrialized developed nations; and from a centralized management philosophy to one emphasizing more localization and delegation. Suddenly, their international organizations have been transformed from a tight Japanese core with a scattering of assembly plants in developing countries, to a much larger worldwide network of complex, integrated, self-sufficient national companies.

Yet, even in companies that were at the vanguard of the Japanese export invasion of overseas markets, there often seems to be a remarkable lack of understanding about the international operating environment and little sophistication in the management of the newly evolving worldwide organization. In many ways, their current problems are similar to those of their American counterparts when they were building their international organizations in the immediate post-war decades. But in addition to the limitations of an ethnocentric perspective, the Japanese manager must also overcome the huge obstacle presented by an organizational system that is strongly rooted in Japanese culture, and in many ways is ill-suited to the newly imposed internationalization task.[1]

In the process of undertaking a broader study comparing the organizational structures, processes and capabilities of European, American and Japanese MNCs, we were asked by some Japanese managers to describe the nature of the challenge they faced, to draw some general conclusions and make broad recommendations for action. Drawing on data obtained from our sample of Japanese companies — some of the countries' largest and most successful MNCs —we have tried to define the nature and sources of some of their common problems, and outline some approaches to resolving them.

Although the analysis and recommendations directly concern Japanese companies, the findings also have relevance for managers of American and European companies. In recent years, much has been written about the Japanese organizational forms and management processes as the source of their outstanding success.[2] Our study of some of their leading MNCs, however, indicates that their organization may represent a major impediment to the global restructuring of their operations. This is important for Western managers to understand since it is creating a strategic window of opportunity for them in the battle for global market share. In some sense, the battle has shifted to one of organizational capability, and these companies first able to overcome the challenges of managing a globally integrated organization while retaining their market sensitivity and innovative flexibility will have a major advantage.[3]

The paper starts with a brief assessment of the traditional approaches and existing capabilities of Japanese companies, and evaluates them against the emerging challenges in the international environment. After identifying some constraints and barriers to effective response to these new demands, we propose some actions to overcome the problems, drawing on the experiences of some of the companies we studied.

Japanese MNCs: Traditional Approaches _____

All multinational companies (MNCs) are partial captives of their historical development and their national origin, but until recent years most Japanese companies have been pretty comfortable prisoners. The pattern and timing of their international development and the influence of their national culture have been important contributors to their outstanding success in the international environment in the postwar era.

For many reasons — for example, the country's geographic and political isolation and the late arrival of the industrial revolution — Japanese companies expanded internationally somewhat later than their European and American counterparts. Although many had engaged in some earlier efforts to capture incremented export sales to neighboring Asian markets, it was only when the postwar domestic boom slowed that most Japanese companies began to regard overseas expansion as an important element in their strategy.[4]

When internationalization finally gained momentum within these companies, some unique Japan-bound institutional and cultural factors encouraged most of them to expand primarily through export rather than through foreign investment as the Europeans and Americans had done in an earlier era. First, the drive for international expansion was motivated in large part by companies' need to ensure the continued advancement of employees, in their domestic organization. In a system of lifetime employment, growth was the engine that fueled organizational vitality and self-renewal, and export orders became an important element of that growth. Second, the Japanese management system was so culture-dependent that it tended to impede the development of international investments. Even beyond the obvious language barriers, the basic decision processes were built on an assumption that participants with shared values could engage in intensive face-to-face discussions and negotiations — conditions difficult to achieve where managers were continents apart.[5] Finally, through historical good fortune, trading companies were well-established Japanese institutions that had far more overseas knowledge and contacts than almost any manufacturer. Their existence facilitated the development of exports, and reduced the need for companies to establish strong foreign operations of their own.[6]

While these various internal factors were shaping the decision of most Japanese companies to build their international operations primarily through export, external forces were reinforcing this approach. Most basically, Japan's Ministry of Finance (MOF) had to approve all overseas investment, and at least until the late 1960s, were strongly biased towards upstream natural resource projects and downstream trade-related operations rather than off shore manufacturing investments.[7]

But such policies were not too damaging to most companies since an export strategy based on assets, expertise and strategic control concentrated in Japan fit perfectly with the international environment of the time. GATT negotiations had brought tariffs to their lowest levels in half a century. Revolutions in air travel, telecommunications, and shipping caused transport and communications barriers to crumble in the 1960s and 1970s. At the same time, new product and process technologies, the rising cost of R&D, and shortening product life cycles were all reinforcing the need for global scale economies.[8]

As a result, in consumer electronics, automobiles, office equipment, electronic components, industrial machinery and many other industries, Japanese companies with strategies based on standardized products, global scale operations and central control were able to take market share from European and American MNCs. Having expanded abroad in an earlier era of high tariffs and logistical barriers, these more mature international companies had built their operations on a foundation of independent national companies offering products developed and manufactured for their local market. To respond to the new environmental conditions, these well-established Western MNCs had to scramble to redesign their products, rationalize their manufacturing facilities, and establish control over their various national operations. Unburdened by such diverse, and independent worldwide organizations, most Japanese companies found their centralized Japanese organization configurations to be the source of great strategic advantage.

International Trends: Emerging Challenges _____

The various globalizing forces that emerged in the immediate postwar decades and dominated the competitive environment of the 1960s and 1970s, continued to exert their influence into the 1980s. In recent years, however, these forces have been joined, and to some extent counterbalanced by some other trends that have emerged, at least in part in reaction to the powerful impact of the globalizing forces of the previous era. These new trends present a challenge to the strategy and management processes of those companies that followed centrally-driven global strategies.

In contrast to the earlier influences that favored larger global scale manufacturing operations, such as those developed in Japanese companies like Toyota, Komatsu and Canon, the recent trend towards flexible manufacturing processes employing robotics, computer-aided design and manufacturing, and other emerging technologies has had the effect of reducing minimum efficient scale in many industry segments. In the words of Mr. C. J. van der Klugt, President and Chairman of the Board of Management of Dutch electronics giant, Philips, "The debate about global products will be short-lived when flexible automation becomes the dominant production technology."[9]

Perhaps as important as their impact on manufacturing scale has been the way in which these new technologies have allowed a broadening of the range of product variations that can be produced efficiently. As Mr. van der Klugt points out, "Basic models . . . will easily be able to be translated into more individualized models." This reinforces a market trend that is also emerging in the 1980s. Perhaps reacting to an overdose of homogenized and standardized global products, consumers have begun to demand products more tailored to their specific needs. A Matsushita manager explained that in response to this shift away from standardized items, his company was being forced to produce more models in smaller runs. In tape recorders, for example, the company had doubled the number of offered models since 1976, but sales per model had declined 60% in the same period. "Increasingly, we are having to grasp the consumers not en masse, but as target groups — even down to the individual," he said.

The trend towards more locally differentiated products is reinforced by the growing importance of software in a large number of industries—from telecommunications to computers to consumer electronics. This trend is requiring companies to adapt standard hardware-oriented products into hardware plus software systems and services that need to be much more sensitive and responsive to local market differences.

Coupled with a continually accelerating product life cycle, the need for more flexible and differentiated products and systems gives an important competitive edge to companies that are closest to their markets. Those with sensitive, flexible, and responsive product development and manufacturing capabilities close to the consumer, often have an advantage over those relying on globally standardized products from distant and inflexible global scale plants. It is through following such an approach for example that the upstart British company, Amstrad, has been able to build a major market position against established global competitors, right at the time when the low cost Japanese companies were trying to establish positions in the U.K. as their beachhead for a broader European attack.

But the most important countertrend of the late 1970s and 1980s has been the reactions of many national governments to the dramatic success of the global companies, and particularly to the Japanese. In the 1960s, large MNCs may have held "sovereignty at bay," to quote Vernon's classic phrase, but by the late 1970s national interests were certainly striking back.[10] Faced with the rapid penetration of their markets by foreign-sourced products shipped by efficient global companies, many countries began to bend, sidestep and even ignore trade agreements in their attempt to stem the import flood. The trend spread from developing to industrialized countries, and even the United States, long the champion of free trade, began negotiating orderly marketing agreements and voluntary trade restraints with Japan.

Well into the 1980s, the political stakes kept rising. Those companies that responded to mounting protectionist pressures by increasing the number of local assembly plants found themselves facing still tougher host government demands. Through increasingly sophisticated industrial policies, governments began to intervene more in companies' foreign investment strategies. So-called "screwdriver plants," set up to assemble knock-down kits, have become an unacceptable way to circumvent the trade barriers. Local content laws, technology transfer requirements, and a host of other national legislation is designed to force global companies to move an increasing part of their value-added operations into the host country, and establish themselves as truly local national entities.[11]

The combined impact of these emerging forces has been dramatic. Under pressure to adapt their export-based, centrally controlled operations, Japanese companies have made major commitments to expanding their overseas operations. The rapid rise in the value of the yen in recent years (going from a dollar exchange rate of 239 yen in the fourth quarter of 1985 to 159 a year later) has only made the need to change their dependence on a Japan-centered sourcing strategy more urgent.

As their overseas operations became larger, more diverse, and increasingly complex, many Japanese companies began feeling the need to modify old organizational structures and management processes to allow them to manage the new reality. The managers we talked to recognized that the key success factor in this massive reorientation of their international strategy was their ability to surmount the substantial barriers that lay in the way of the required organizational adaptation.

Barriers to Response _____

Like the European and American companies that met the same challenges in an earlier era, the Japanese companies that are becoming true multinational companies in the 1980s are facing barriers to the adaptation of their strategy and structure. In the sample of companies we studied, we were conscious of three major impediments that seemed common to all of them—the constraints of the Japanese organization processes, the limitations of the traditional strategic assumptions, and the barriers due to management mentality.

Japanese Organization System

We described earlier why the discussion-intensive, group-oriented characteristics of the Japanese management system fit well with the requirements of a centralized export-based strategy. The classic process of *nemawashi* (consensus building) and *ringi* (shared decision making) required close physical proximity and shared cultural values.[12] As an increasingly important part of the company's asset base and task responsibilities were shifted offshore, however, strains began to appear. Unlike the more systems-oriented approach in American-based companies, this people-dependent and communication-intensive management process is not easily stretched over barriers of distance, time, language and culture.

In the companies we studied, there were two key ingredients that allowed their management processes to operate internationally—a group of Japanese managers who knew the company, its strategies and processes, and were willing to go abroad as the linkages in the worldwide organizational process; and a travel budget and logistical arrangement that allowed these widely dispersed managers to engage in the intensive discussions and negotiations that were at the center of the management system of each of these companies.[13]

Kao, the leading Japanese branded package goods company, provides a good illustration of this dependence on the use of individuals to link the organization. Despite the modest size of its overseas operations—small soap and detergent companies in seven southeast Asian countries and a couple of larger industrial operations in Spain and Mexico—this company has a cadre of sixty expatriate Japanese managers and technicians running overseas operations with only 2,000 employees. This is more than double the number of American expatriates its U.S. based competitor Procter and Gamble has in an international business with total sales over twenty times larger. More significantly, all of the top management positions in Kao's overseas companies and most of the level below that are Japanese nationals; in P&G only five of the forty-four subsidiary general managers are American. A similar contrast can be made between Matsushita and 3M. The former has over 800 expatriates in an international business with 40,000 employees; the American company has less than 100 expatriates to manage its 38,000 foreign employees.

As the size and complexity of foreign operations has grown, the need for expatriate managers has increased. But, for many companies, demand is outstripping supply. Takeda, the chemical and pharmaceuticals company which had deliberately created and nurtured a large pool of employees for overseas postings, now finds many of them are uninterested in future international assignments. The contributing causes are numerous. Overseas allowances to compensate for differences in foreign salary levels have shrunk, numerous examples of managers losing career opportunities due to being out of touch with headquarters have surfaced, and the strains on families have become clear, particularly when wives stay at home to ensure children receive a good Japanese education. The problem has become so widespread that the expression "escaping from overseas banishment" has achieved currency in the business jargon common among Japanese managers today.

The operation of the Japanese management system internationally has also become strained by pure logistics. The need for detailed information sharing and intensive face-to-face consultations and negotiations has led Japanese companies to spend huge amounts on travel and communications. In 1984, for example, NEC Japan personnel made over 10,000 overseas trips. Companies are becoming increasingly aware of the substantial financial and human cost that such intensive travel is placing on their organizations. Indeed, many feel that managers are already stretched beyond reasonable limits, but without any other means of coordinating their worldwide operations, they are obliged to expand this system of "jet age nemawashi" as one manager called it.

But there is another side to the limitation of the Japanese management system in the international environment. To participate in the system one needs a thorough understanding of the complex culturally based decision processes, an established internal network of contacts, and an ability to communicate intensively in Japanese. The very nature of the system makes it virtually impenetrable to non- Japanese except at the periphery, and even then, in the most superficial way.[14] In almost all Japanese MNCs the core of the decision making process remains purely Japanese. Because of this, many foreigners recognize that not only is their career advancement limited to the national organization, but even there, they must operate in an environment in which their influence and power is often constrained. The lower starting salaries and slower promotion process prescribed by the Japanese system also serve as major barriers to entry for most individuals considering joining foreign affiliates of Japanese companies. In the words of one disillusioned American manager in the U.S. subsidiary of a large Japanese company, "It is ironic that the very factors that have made this company's management of its production workers abroad so successful (participation in decision making, job security and advancement opportunities, and an egalitarian attitude) all seem to be missing from their treatment of management. I am becoming very doubtful that I can look forward to a satisfying career here."

As a consequence, several of the Japanese companies we studied had experienced difficulty recruiting and keeping the most talented individuals for their foreign operations. This, in turn, reinforced the Japanese managers' inclination to keep parent company expatriates at the center of all key decisions, and a vicious cycle was established.

Institutionalized Strategic Roles

The classic Japanese company's pattern of international expansion from Asian countries to other developing nations, and finally to industrialized markets, influenced the perception of the appropriate strategic role and organizational responsibilities that could be assigned to overseas units. By concentrating first in developing markets, companies found it relatively easy to meet local demands with the more basic and mature products that had succeeded in the Japanese market. Sony's international business was built on the base established by its ubiquitous transistor radio; Komatsu found ready acceptance for its all purpose bulldozer; Kao could sell its basic soap and detergent lines. Although all of these companies tried to be sensitive to local market needs and to modify their products where necessary, there was little need to challenge the established product technologies and marketing approaches, and local sales companies became the delivery pipelines for products and strategies developed at the center.

Similarly, when manufacturing began to move offshore, the first plants were simple assembly operations built in response to the demands of host governments in the developing countries that had provided the first export markets. Matsushita's approach was typical: it set up plants with equipment it either built or specified, trained local workers in manufacturing techniques it developed, and supplied the operations with components and subassemblers it manufactured in

Japan. The limited supply of skilled managers in many of these companies meant that expatriates took most key positions, and the company found it easy to direct, support, and control such operations from the center.

This proved to be such a successful means of managing that some of the strong strategic assumptions that emerged in this phase of development became institutionalized.[15] Among the most powerful was the conviction that the center's role was to direct, support, and control the activities of foreign operations. Under this assumption and practice, overseas companies became dependent units whose role was to implement corporate directions.

As these companies expanded into more developed countries, the situation changed dramatically. There was an ample supply of sophisticated managers and technical people, the markets were at least as advanced as Japan's and sometimes more so, and the feasibility of supporting, directing and controlling a larger number of more diverse, more sophisticated national operations became questionable. Yet, in many companies, the institutionalized assumptions and practices were hard to break. Many of the companies we studied still tried to sense and respond to market, technological and competitive environment of the developed country from the center, just as they had done so successfully for less-developed markets. But the new situation was infinitely more complex, more diverse, and more dynamic than before, and the center's capacity and capability to perform the task were soon overloaded.

NEC is one company that has successfully emerged from these constraining assumptions as later examples illustrate, but only after it learned from the problems they caused in the early years of its U.S. telecommunications operations. While the company's central product development group was concentrating on an electronic switch based on an analog system, a strong preference was emerging in the U.S. for digital technology. Although NEC management in New York tried to communicate their perception of the developing "digital fever," it was only after the enormously successful market penetration by its Canadian competitor, Northern Telecom, that the central group finally began work on a digital switch.

Even after developing hardware that was more responsive to the more advanced U.S. market, the fact that NEC had concentrated its major software capability in Tokyo to serve worldwide market needs continued to constrain its viability. The telecommunications systems and market needs in North America were so different that there were almost continuous requests on headquarters for major software changes. But the Tokyo group resisted such demands and even when they did agree, it took a long time to communicate, interpret and negotiate every change between the U.S. and Japan. As a result, NEC's early reputation in regarded dependency as being synonymous with exploitation.[18] One manager in a South American subsidiary complained that new products and new programs came down from Japan so fast that they had no time to think or question them. Besides, they had no significant spare resources to make changes, and little opportunity to influence central strategy: "We feel a bit like the peasant woman whose husband ensures her loyalty and fidelity by keeping her barefoot and pregnant," he said.

Despite these numerous operational, motivational and even political problems and pressures, the persistence of this headquarters-dominated strategic posture is still a widespread phenomenon in Japanese MNCs. It is embodied in their culturally bounded centralized decision processes; it is reinforced by the accumulation and concentration of assets, resources and skills in the home country; and it is defended by the many vested organizational interests whose power base rested on their ability to support and control overseas operations.

Constrained Management Mentality

The third barrier we saw impeding the adaptation of some Japanese companies to the new international forces was one that had also represented an important problem for their European and American counterparts. It related to a management mentality that resisted the need to change Japanese products, strategies or organization approaches to accommodate the diverse and changing international demands. Even in some of the most globally oriented companies in Japan, we were surprised to find managers whose attitudes reflected a view of the emerging international changes not as sources of new opportunity or even as normal environmental developments to which the company had to adjust. Rather they seemed to be viewed as destructive forces to be resisted, since they were forcing the company to compromise its existing efficient operations and its effective organizational processes.[19] Such narrow views and ethnocentric biases have developed as a result of a long history of management isolation from international business. They were reinforced by the insulating effects of the strong cultural aspect of their management systems, and for some, became justified by the initial success of their companies using such an approach in international markets.

As a result, the localization programs introduced by many large Japanese companies were often undertaken under sufferance, primarily in response to government pressure for greater local content or increased local employment. Rarely at the middle management level did we see a recognition that such changes could actually offer major strategic benefits for their companies. In Toray, the large Japanese textile company, the international managing director fought a long hard battle to convince management to build a new polypropolene film plant

the North American market was as a company with excellent hardware but
adapted software.

However, the problems associated with the strategic dependence of su
sidiaries on the center were not limited to the decreased efficiency of centralize
direction and control, and the limited capacity of headquarters to support mor
complex and demanding overseas activities. We also saw evidence of motivational problems as managers in overseas companies became increasingly frustrated
by their constrained roles and limited responsibilities. Yet, as indicated in our
earlier argument, the Japanese organizational systems locked them out of headquarters management processes and prevented them from working to change the
assumptions, even when the capabilities of the foreign operation seemed to indicate that a different role and relationship would be appropriate.[16]

For example, when Matsushita acquired Motorola's TV operations in the U.S.,
the operation had a strong R&D capability. Within the first year after acquisition
this group had developed a synthesizer tuner that was adopted by the parent
company for worldwide models. However, the U.S. group became frustrated
when ten Japanese engineers arrived to provide direction and coordination with
Matsushita's main development departments in Japan. They soon recognized
they were out of the mainstream of development, and felt they had lost much of
their freedom. Within a short period of time half the group had left, including
most of the best engineers, and the flow of innovations from Motorola stopped.
The group took on a local design and production engineering role. The assumption that only central groups could provide innovation and leadership became a
self-fulfilling prophesy.

Even in many developing countries, subsidiary company managers felt they
had matured to a stage where they could assume substantially more responsibility, and the headquarters' assumption of their strategic dependency became
increasingly frustrating. Some managers in Matsushita's Asian operations told
us they resented the fact that the Japanese domestic plants would retain the
production of the newest products and guard the latest technologies. By col-
laborating with three other local companies, Matsushita's Taiwan joint venture
even went as far as to develop independently its own picture-in-a-picture TV, not
only to ensure it had the technology, but also to prove that it had the capability to
do so.

The constrained strategic role of overseas subsidiaries has also had unfortunate political repercussions for many Japanese MNCs. Widespread perceptions
of corporate imperialism led to anti- Japanese riots in southeast Asia in the early
1970s.[17] The lingering presence of such perceptions presents a continuing risk
for Japanese companies operating in developing countries where some have

in the U.S. He is now engaged in an even more difficult struggle with corporate technical staff who insist that the new plant must be operated strictly on Japanese lines. Yet increasingly their European and American competitors were recognizing that by dispersing their assets and resources they could capitalize on some important yet underutilized potential assets. Perhaps the most important was an exposure to a wider range of stimuli (consumer needs, technological changes, competitive actions) that could trigger innovative responses. Equally important was the improved access such operations provided to a worldwide pool of management talent and technological skills—some of the scarcest of all management resources.[20] In many Japanese companies, parochial management attitudes impede the full exploitation of such potential benefits.

For example, as Kao expanded aggressively in East Asian markets during the 1970s, top management emphasized the importance at contributing to the national economies in which it operated. But while the company made every effort to employ locals, build local plants, and even transfer its mature technology, the strong tradition of competing through technologically superior products and highly efficient operations led most managers to regard these companies as little more than foreign appendages that gave the company local market access. Thus while the localization of assets, responsibilities and resources continued to build capabilities in the overseas operations, such newly developed capability went underutilized. In contrast, Unilever's management had long regarded its overseas companies in even the least developed countries as important sources both of new ideas and management personnel. Its Turkish subsidiary developed a vegetable oil equivalent of the middle-eastern clarified butter product, ghee; its Indian company adapted advanced detergent technology to local stream washing practices by developing a process to make detergent bars to replace the dominant bar soap product. In such an entrepreneurial subsidiary environment, local management was developed into a valuable corporate resource, who were transferred throughout the company and promoted to the most senior corporate positions.

In recent years, however, many of these narrower traditional management views began to broaden and the ethnocentric biases began to break down. Unfortunately, they have been replaced, at least in some quarters, by a more disturbing trend in management attitudes — a growing management chauvinism, or even in some cases, arrogance. Fed by the phenomenal success of many Japanese companies abroad, some managers we interviewed questioned the need to change either the existing management processes or the strategic posture of their companies' international operations. Younger managers in particular seemed convinced that the Japanese way of managing was superior and should not be compromised. Many whose management experience was concentrated in the last decade appeared to have taken to heart the popular slogan "Japan as number one," and developed an attitude that a winning team should not change its approach.[21]

Whether due to limited international exposure or a chauvinistic inflexibility, such mentalities in the managers of Japanese multinationals represent important barriers to their companies' adaptation. As we will discuss in the next section, they are barriers that are difficult to break down.

Prescriptions and Recommendations _____

As the foreign direct investment statistics so dramatically indicate, the transformation of Japanese multinational enterprise is already in full swing. As foreign subsidiaries become larger, more sophisticated and more strategically important, the question facing most companies is not whether to, but how to, manage the emerging reconfiguration of assets and redistribution of responsibilities. High on the list of priorities for most managers in Japanese MNCs are questions relating to the three important barriers to internationalization we identified. Drawing heavily on the lessons and experiences of the companies we observed, but also adding our own normative suggestions where we observed gaps in current practice, we have drawn up a brief list of recommendations and prescriptions for Japanese managers as they attempt to meet these challenges.

Open the Organizational System

The first and most basic barrier we identified was one that is culturally built into the Japanese management system. We do not suggest that companies abandon their consensus-building values and their group-oriented processes. We do, however, suggest that these processes be made a little less impenetrable by "outsiders." Such changes will not be made quickly or easily, but unless companies begin to make some effort, they will remain culture-bound captives of their ethnocentric biases.

There are two important thrusts to this approach: one is to educate the non-Japanese and provide them with knowledge, contacts and opportunity to enter the company's management processes; the second is to create the conditions within the company to allow foreign managers to become legitimate participants in the ongoing processes.[22]

The task of educating foreign managers in ways that will help them gain access to their Japanese company's systems should begin at the point of their employment—in the company's overseas operations. The most basic step is to provide employees with some form of formal education on the norms, practices and values of the company. Matsushita represents a good example of a company that has taken steps to ensure that all new employees worldwide are exposed to an education program to inform them of the company's philosophies, beliefs and practices. All foreign employees are exposed to training built around a series of video tapes that have been prepared in Japanese, English, Spanish and Chinese. Topics include the company's overall philosophy, manufacturing practices, personnel management, and marketing approaches.

If the acculturation process stops there, however, there is a risk that many employees may be left with some knowledge of a new system that is greatly different from anything they have had experience with before, and a vague feeling that they will never be able to penetrate it. More than theoretical knowledge, the non-Japanese needs the tools to help enter the systems and the experience of operating in it. Ideally, he or she should become proficient in Japanese, but the reality is that the language is difficult and few develop the proficiency to participate in the complex and subtle discussions that lead to decisions in the Japanese system.

But while none of the companies we studied was successful in developing any kind of Japanese language fluency in their overseas operations, they found that just offering regular language and culture classes had two important side benefits. First, it gave non-Japanese managers a basic communication skill that led to a greater sense of social ease with their Japanese colleagues.[23] Perhaps more importantly, by offering such programs to their management they sent a signal of their willingness to break down barriers and include them in the mainstream of the decision processes.

The language barrier is only the first that must be overcome, however, and the next important step in opening the management system to non-Japanese is to ensure that the tight internal social systems do not routinely exclude them from the daily business processes. In most Japanese companies, there are formal and informal mechanisms that have tended to institutionalize the exclusion of non-Japanese from the decision process. "Contact positions" staffed by Japanese whose main task is to communicate back to headquarters can short circuit linkages between local managers and the parent company; after-hours meetings of expatriate Japanese managers to discuss the day's activities can become the real decision-making forum; and the practice of having expatriate Japanese make most visits to headquarters alone or perhaps with foreigners tagging along in token roles can reinforce the image of local managers being on the periphery. To different degrees, in every company we studied, the non-Japanese were very aware of—and highly frustrated by—such exclusion from the management mainstream. Many had become cynical and viewed those discussions and decisions in which they were involved as charades, designed to reach conclusions already agreed by their Japanese colleagues over late night drinks or received in a telex from Tokyo. Unfortunately, there were many occasions in which such assumptions were correct.

Because of the larger number of expatriates typically used by Japanese companies, the temptation to develop a two-tiered management system and parallel communication channels will always be great. However, working around local management, rather than with them is not only extremely demotivating, it is also highly inefficient. As the local nationals become more familiar with the system's processes and norms, and as they develop more contacts and relationships, it is important to leverage their knowledge and expertise by bringing them into discussions and negotiations on key issues early, and by ensuring that their involvement is real and not token. Companies serious about doing so can help ensure it occurs by making their expatriate managers understand that their success in doing so is regarded as important as their achievement in the marketplace.

But foreigners will never be integrated into Japanese systems until they have contacts and credibility in the parent company headquarters. Building such relationships takes time and persistence as managers at Sony have discovered. Twelve years after it first established regular quarterly meetings between top managers in its Japanese and American companies, the company feels it is only now beginning to achieve good communications. For this reason, it is important that key foreign managers are brought to Japan frequently not just for brief visits, but also for extended stays of several months, and when possible, for even longer term assignments. They must be given the opportunity not only to meet but also to work with their Japanese counterparts. Although they may never build up the network of personal relationships that a Japanese manager would have, they can at least penetrate the ranks and overcome the perceptions of being an "outsider."[24]

Ajinomoto, the Japanese giant, is one company that has tried to achieve this objective as part of its training program. The company brings most foreign technicians and some managers to Japan for a three- to six-month training program in which they not only work and train with their Japanese counterparts, they live and eat together in the same company facilities. The foreigners are given sufficient language training to develop a 300 word vocabulary— enough to communicate with and get to know their colleagues. NEC has gone even further. Through the efforts of its international personnel division, it has established a program by which non- Japanese managers from its overseas operations are rotated through two year parent company assignments. At the end of their time in Japan, these individuals not only have a good understanding of the company's strategies and technologies, they also appreciate much better the values, norms and practices of their Japanese parent company, and they have begun to develop the contacts and channels to communicate more effectively to headquarters.

Mr. Tabuchi, president of Nomura Securities, also recognized this need. He said: "Without true internationalization a company cannot be prosperous in the future. It may be very advantageous to have blue-eyed executives at the corporate head office. By changing the form of our processes and thinking, we can change the content."

But there is no point in preparing foreign managers for participation in the corporate system if the headquarters group remains unreceptive. In NEC's experience, the most effective way of opening their organizational system has been to internationalize a larger proportion of its management group to make them more conscious of the importance of foreign operations and more open to their ideas. By giving a broad group of key managers the experience of living and working abroad, the company has greatly improved understanding of the differences in national environments and their sensitivity to the difficulties of operating at long distances from the corporate headquarters. Furthermore, by giving parent company expatriates the opportunity to develop relationships with foreign managers while simultaneously improving their language abilities, NEC's top management believes it has been able to significantly increase the openness and enhance the quality of the overall management process.

Develop the Foreign Operation Role

The second barrier to an effective response to the new demands for national responsiveness lies in the historical attitude of Japanese companies toward their foreign operations as dependent children, and several companies are now trying to break out of the constraints of a parent-subsidiary relationship based on dependency by the subsidiary company and direction, support and control by the parent.

The overall objective can be thought of as developing the world-wide national organizations into an interconnected network of competence centers, capable not only of implementing the company's strategy but also of making important contributions to it.[25] While this means removing the constraints that often limit the role of local operations, it does not imply reducing the important role that the central groups play in determining the company's strategic direction by scanning the global environment, analyzing trends, and developing responses. It only suggests that there will be a diminishing ability to sense and respond to the growing diversity of demands and the increasing rate of change from headquarters. By creating multiple groups with the responsibility and resources to develop innovative responses to emerging national opportunities and threats, the company not only increases the total capacity and scope of its innovative capability, it also creates an internally competitive environment that tends to sharpen managers' entrepreneurial edge.

The challenge is a substantial one. It involves redefining the basic role and responsibilities of the company's foreign operations, and restructuring their relationship with the parent company. This is not a task that can be quickly achieved. Its successful implementation depends on the sequential development of the national organization in three stages —resources should be transferred, local knowledge, skills and expertise must be developed, and finally responsibilities can be expanded.[26]

The first task of transferring resources may be a painful decision for the company, but it is not difficult to implement. In responding to protectionist pressures or to host governments' legislation for higher local content or increased technology transfer, many companies have managed to build plants, expand capacity or establish development laboratories in their overseas subsidiaries. The mistake has been that many have stopped there, expecting that this injection of capital will make the foreign operation more productive or innovative. The problem is that while the physical assets may be expanded, the local entity is still operating with its limited internal skills and capabilities, and is being managed under the old dependency/control management relationship.

In 1985, ten years after its establishment, Matsushita's plant in Cardiff, Wales was still highly dependent on the parent company for direction and support. In an unusual step for a Japanese chief executive, company president Mr. Toshihiko Yamashita used an interview with the *Financial Times* to express his unhappiness with the situation, suggesting that the plant needed to be more creative and innovative and rely less on headquarters. " They have to become self-sufficient and stand on their own two feet," he said.

To become more self-sufficient, however, top management must be willing to develop the skills and knowledge base within national companies so they can break their dependence on the parent. The first need is to build a management group with the potential to act in the new role planned for the national company. Their profile may be quite different from the good solid operating managers who succeeded in the past by implementing well.

Some companies have tried to bring in the required creativity and leadership by recruiting experienced managers into senior positions. But having gained all of their extensive experience managing in another way, these individuals are sometimes less flexible in making the adjustments necessary to fit into a different management system. Indeed, many will accept the position only on the condition they have operating freedom and autonomy. Such an arrangement represents too traumatic a break from their past for most Japanese organizations, and can end in failure.

One of the earliest and most publicized examples of this problem occurred when Sony recruited Harvey Schein, a manager with extensive senior management experience in large U.S. companies to head up its North American company. While providing the necessary leadership, drive and independence, he also created in the U.S. company an organization system and management process that isolated it and inhibited its relationship with Japan. After five years he resigned. However, after gradually building better communications and understanding through regular quarterly meetings, the isolation and antagonism had been broken down so effectively that the parent company even adopted the internal budgeting and planning systems developed in its American unit.

Learning from the traumatic experiences of those who tried rapid change of their local personnel and systems, more companies are attempting to upgrade the quality of their national operations gradually, by recruiting high-potential managers at the entry level, often from good business schools and by building relationships slowly as Sony has done. Even here the challenge is to overcome the reputation of Japanese companies as offering limited responsibility, slow advancement, and poor salaries. But those willing to spend the substantial time and effort developing a positive image on selected campuses find the effort rewarding.

The next task in developing an independent local capability is to ensure the new recruits are allowed to grow to their full potential in the national company. This requires the commitment of headquarters to train and develop these managers and technical experts and provide them with the fullest understanding of existing company knowledge and expertise in their field. But the development process involves more than knowledge transfer. It requires giving these individuals the managerial freedom and organizational support to build their expertise, test their ideas, and develop their sense of independence.

An example will illustrate the effective implementation of these steps. NEC's decision to develop an advanced software capability in its U.S. telecommunications company was made in response to two problems: the difficulty of responding to U.S. market needs with only a central software capability, and the chronic shortage of software engineers in Tokyo. The company hoped not only to become more responsive to the market, but also to capitalize on its access to American engineering talent. Recruiting of software engineers began in the early 1980s, and initially they were given responsibility only for "patching" problems in software at customer sites. When this embryonic group requested funding for two personal computers for a development project, they were given the resources. Soon they had created an innovative means for patching software from a central terminal rather than having to make individual site visits (an innovation subsequently adopted by the parent company). To ensure local managers would be properly trained, the company sent to the U.S. as engineering vice president, the manager responsible for the software development for the company's latest switch. He recruited an expanded group of engineers and asked headquarters to transfer still more responsibility. When he felt they were sufficiently familiar with the company systems, he created a separate design engineering department, and obtained authorization to expand from 20 to 50 engineers in the first year. Almost immediately, the group was able to undertake major independent software development for the U.S. market.

Within a few years the U.S. group had evolved from its dependency role as deliverer of centrally developed products to become a substantially free-standing unit, able to sense market needs and opportunities and develop innovative responses. Furthermore, by tapping into valuable local technical resources, it had built itself into an important corporate resource, able to make valuable contributions such as the software patching system which could be adopted by the broader corporate system.

Thus, having developed strong innovative capabilities in its various national operations, management can evolve the role of that company from dependent subsidiary, to self-sufficient national company, to contributing corporate resource. The role of headquarters shifts from controlling and supporting the activities of dependent operations to coordinating worldwide centers of competence, monitoring their innovations and new proposals, and integrating their various capabilities into an interdependent global network of operations.

Broaden Managers' Perspectives

Our first two recommendations represent fairly radical proposals to change the company's organization processes and strategic orientation, albeit gradually. Although we have described a series of implementation steps for each of them, their successful adoption basically depends on the willingness, openness and flexibility of management to make such drastic change. Yet we described our third major barrier to changing the international orientation of Japanese companies as a parochial management mentality, constrained by ethnocentric biases or conservative inflexibility.

Before the first two recommendations can be achieved, management must deal with any negative or narrow perception of the required changes in organizational processes and strategic roles. Rather than viewing such changes as concessions that will compromise the company's global effectiveness, they should be embraced as important developments that provide an opportunity to build new corporate capabilities, create a more innovative environment and tap into a new and larger pool of managerial and technical talent.

The challenge of changing an entire organizational mentality is one that requires strong and consistent top management leadership over an extended period of time. There are two important approaches that can be effective in achieving the objective: developing a clear vision of the kind of international company the organization wants to become and communicating a commitment to achieve it; and stimulating, guiding and reinforcing the changed mentality to the point it is absorbed into the company's value system.

The backbone of any change in management perceptions and attitudes must be a clearly articulated and well-communicated alternative model and set of assumptions. Matsushita's President Yamashita uses every opportunity he can to communicate to his organization the corporate commitment to change the role and relationship of its foreign operations. Throughout the organization, employees know that the company intends to double the percentage of its offshore manufacturing to 25% by 1990, and that the company's Operation Localization commits it to localizing personnel, technology, materials and capital in all its overseas operations. Sony has made a similar commitment to increase its overseas capacity from 20% in 1986 to 35% by the end of the decade.

But the simple communication of expected change is usually insufficient. Even after new resources are transferred and additional responsibilities are delegated, managers may find it hard to evolve out of their old ways of managing. Mr. Yamashita's frustration at the lack of initiative being taken by managers in the company's Welsh plant illustrates the problem.

Often it takes some kind of major discontinuity or crisis atmosphere to trigger an unfreezing of attitudes and subsequent reorientation of thinking. Where an external threat already exists—and for many companies the 40% appreciation of the yen against the dollar has provided such a problem—management's role is to identify it, focus the organization's attention on it, and use it to galvanize action that will force managers to reevaluate their ideas and approaches. If no such external event exists, management may be able to create internal discontinuities to shake up complacent views and conventional wisdom. Two examples illustrate the approach.

The collective mentality of NEC management was forced to change under pressure of urgent strategic demands in the U.S. The company recognized that after deregulation there would be a five-year window in which to establish a strong presence in the North American public switching market, and thus a viable position as one of the three or four key companies in the global telecommunications industry. The urgent challenge to evolve rapidly from a small, dependent subsidiary of a Japanese company to a competent, responsive company able to meet the very different and fast-changing needs of the U.S. market provided management with a rallying point. The urgency and importance of the task caused managers to become more open in their attitudes and more flexible in their approaches.

When Sony's chief executive, Akio Morita, wanted to change the mentality of his organization toward its overseas operation, he decided to make the bold and dramatic move of relocating to New York and personally taking responsibility for Sony's American operations. This sent two clear messages to his managers—that overseas operations were a vital part of the company, not just foreign appendages, and that the company was prepared to adapt its way of managing in order to accommodate these important entities.[27]

Having jolted management mentality into a state of accepting the need to change, management must then concentrate on stimulating, guiding and reinforcing that change. This involves such operational programs as the ones suggested earlier for the increased rotation of Japanese managers through international assignments to break down parochial views and broaden organizational contacts. Conscious efforts must also be made to publicly reward individuals and groups whose behavior conforms to the ideal of the new international vision.

Conclusion _____

Having used their highly cohesive centralized organizations as the means to penetrate world export markets, many Japanese companies are now faced with the challenge of dismantling the very engine that drove their success and rebuilding it in a different form. Their continued success depends on their ability to respond to new forces in the international environment that are driving them to decentralize concentrated assets, disperse centralized resources and capabilities, and delegate decision making responsibilities from headquarters. The trick will be to overcome the strong cultural influences that constrain such changes without destroying the strength and cohesion they provide. To a large degree, their success in building this new organizational capability overshadows the strategic tasks these companies face.

For western companies, the nature of the challenge and the way in which Japanese managers are able to deal with it are of vital importance. This period of organizational adjustment represents a breathing space in which European and American managers can regroup and prepare for the next stage of the global battle. The timing is fortuitous since many of them need to use the time to establish effective strategic control over their disparate, loosely coordinated worldwide operations. Indeed, in many ways the competitive race has turned into one for effective global organizational capability.

Notes _____

1. Perlmutter (1965) first distinguished between ethnocentric, polycentric and geocentric conception of the MNC. This distinction rests on the differences in the characterization of the international business environment by the MNC: ethnocentrism reflecting a primarily home country view; polycentrism a multi-country view on a country by country basis and geocentrism a global view that recognizes the interdependence of different national contexts.

2. See, for example, Ouchi (1982) and Pascale and Athos (1981).

3. Bartlett and Ghoshal (1987(a); 1987(b)) discuss the development of such organizational capabilities in detail.

4. For a fuller description of the internationalization of Japanese companies, see Yoshihara (1979).

5. Yoshino (1976) correctly predicted that the management processes he described so richly would present an impediment to the internationalization of Japanese organization systems.

6. For an excellent discussion of the role of trading companies and their relationship with manufacturing companies, see Yoshino and Lifson (1986).

7. A fuller account of such Japanese institutional barriers is contained in Encarnation (1986).

8. See Levitt (1983) for a fairly extreme view of the pervasiveness of such forces of globalization.

9. van der Klugt (1985) makes a persuasive case that some approaches to globalization have been simplistic.

10. For a discussion of how the MNCs kept sovereignty at bay, see Vernon (1971). The more recent trend towards a reassertion of sovereignty rights by governments is eloquently discussed by Doz (1986).

11. See Doz (1986).

12. For a more detailed description of these subtle and complex processes, see Yoshino (1976).

13. The use of personnel transfers as a means of coordinating and controlling MNCs was discussed extensively in Edstrom and Galbraith (1977).

14. For a discussion on how the Japanese use this cultural system as a form of control, see Jaeger and Baliga (1985).

15. The aphorism "success breeds failure," has been given theoretical support by the notion of "structural inertia." Thus, Freeman and Hannan (1984) and DiMaggio and Powell (1983) have asserted that organizations often find it difficult to adapt to changed circumstances since they are afraid of losing social and normative legitimacy that exists in successful current practices.

16. As Hedlund (1986) has suggested, the international environment has created a relationship between headquarters and subsidiary that is increasingly reciprocal in nature. That their traditional patterns of subsidiary company dependence require fundamentally different organizational structures (Thompson, 1967) is something that Japanese MNCs are only slowly beginning to realize.

17. For a description of the infamous Tanaka riots, see Ozawa (1979).

18. The dependencia school of political economy has had a powerful influence, particularly in Latin American countries. For a good review of dependencia and post-dependencia perspectives of foreign direct investment, see Greico (1985).

19. The difficulty of changing cognitive frames of reference and the way in which such frames impede strategic adaptation has been discussed by Dutton and Duncan (1987).

20. The importance of viewing the MNC as a distributed pool of geographically dispersed capabilities and information that derives its distinct competitive advantage precisely by leveraging this multinationality has also been stressed by Hedlund (1986).

21. Meyer and Rowan (1977) have commented on the importance of visible myths in sustaining particular organizational forms. Thus the very visible organization practices that are seen as being the very reason for the "Japan as #1" myth are difficult to shed.

22. Van Maanen and Schein (1979) are amongst the pioneers of the view that socialization establishes particular definitions of membership as well as the acceptance of particular organizational processes as a way of life. In as much as these practices are idiosyncratic and unique and rely on certain cultural preconditions (e.g., being Japanese), they present difficult and imposing barriers to entry for the outsider.

23. Steiner (1975), for instance, stresses that being multilingual represents a qualitatively different state than being monolingual and that the former has distinct advantages in terms of adaptation to new situations.

24. This description of an alternate socialization strategy that would move foreigners from the "periphery" to the "core" is consistent with the pat-

terns described by Van Maanen and Schein (1979) in their discussion of socialization strategies.

25. For a more detailed description of how multinational companies are integrating differentiated subsidiary roles into a global strategy, see Bartlett and Ghoshal (1986).

26. See Bartlett (1986) for a more detailed description of the organizational challenges facing MNCs, and the characteristics of the emerging "transnational" organizational form.

27. Symbols and ceremonies can act not only as source of organizational inertia, but also as the means to precipitate quantum change. See Meyer and Rowan (1977) for a discussion of the used symbols and ceremonies and Miller and Freisen (1984) for more detail on strategies for quantum change.

References _____

Bartlett, C. A. "Building and Managing the Transnational: The New Organizational Challenge" in M.E. Porter (Ed.) *Competition in Global Industries*, Boston: Harvard Business School Press, 1986.

Bartlett, C. A. and Ghoshal, S. "Tap Your Subsidiaries for Global Reach," *Harvard Business Review,* Nov-Dec 1986, 87-94.

Bartlett, C. A. and Ghoshal, S. "Managing Across Borders: New Strategic Requirements," *Sloan Management Review*, Summer 1987a, 7-18.

Bartlett, C. A. and Ghoshal, S. "Managing Across Borders: New Organizational Responses," *Sloan Management Review*, Fall 1987b, 43-53.

DiMaggio, P. and Powell, W. (1983). "The Iron Cage Revisited: Institutional Isomorphism and Collective Rationality in Organizational Fields." *American Sociological Review*, 82, 929-964.

Doz, Y. "Government Policies and Global Industries" in M. E. Porter (Ed.), *Competition in Global Industries*, Boston: Harvard Business School Press, 1986.

Dutton, J. and Duncan, R. "Strategic Issue Diagnosis and the Creation of Momentum for Change," *Strategic Management Journal*, 1987, 8, 179-295.

Edstrom, A. and Galbraith, S. R. "Transfers of Managers as a Coordination and Control Strategy in Multinational Organizations." *Administrative Science Quarterly*, June 1977, 248-263.

Encarnation, D. J. "Cross Investment: A Second Front of Economic Rivalry" in T. K. McCraw (Ed.) *American versus Japan*, Boston: Harvard Business School Press, 1986.

Freeman, M. and Hannan, J. "Structural Inertia and Organizational Change." *American Sociological Review*, 1984, 49, 49-64.

Greico, J. "Between Dependence and Autonomy: India's Experience with the International Computer Industry" in T. Moran (Ed.) *Multinational Corporations: The Political Economy of Foreign Direct Investment*, D. C. Heath, 1985.

Hedlund, G. "The Hypermodern MNC—A Heterarchy." *Human Resource Management*, Spring 1986, 9-35.

Jaeger, A. M. and Baliga, B. R. "Control Systems and Strategic Adaptation: Lessons from the Japanese Experience." *Strategic Management Journal*, 1985, 6(2).

Levitt, T. "The Globalization of Markets." *Harvard Business Review*, May/June 1983.

Meyer, J. and Rowan, B. "Institutional Organizations: Formal Structure as Myth and Ceremony." *American Journal of Sociology*, 1977, 83, 340-363.

Miller, D. and Freisen, P. *Organizations: A Quantum View*. Englewood Cliffs, NJ: Prentice-Hall, 1984.

Perlmutter, H. V. "L'enterprise internationale—trois conceptions." *Revere Economique et Sociale*, 1965, 23.

Ouchi, W. *Theory Z*, Reading, Mass: Addison-Wesley, 1982.

Ozawa, T. *Multinationalism, Japanese Style: The Political Economy of Outward Dependency*. Princeton, NJ: Princeton University Press, 1979.

Pascale, R. and Athos, A . *The Art of Japanese Management*, New York: Warner Books, 1981.

Steiner, G. *After Babel*, Oxford University Press, 1975.

Thompson, J. D. *Organizations in Action*, New York: McGraw Hill, 1967.

van der Klugt, C. J. "Penetrating Global Markets: High Tech Companies," speech presented at the "Going Global" conference sponsored by *The Economist* Conference Unit, London, June 17, 1985.

Van Maanen, J. and Schein, E. "Toward a Theory of Organizational Socialization." In B. M. Staw (Ed.) *Research in Organizational Behavior*, Vol. 1, Greenwich, CT: JAI Press, 1979.

Vernon, R. *Sovereignty at Bay*. New York: Basic Books, 1971.

Yoshihara, H. "Japanese Multinational Enterprises: A View from Outside," *Kobe Economic and Business Review*, 25th Annual Report, Kobe University, 1979.

Yoshino, M. Y. *Japan's Multinational Enterprises*, Cambridge: Harvard University Press, 1976.

Yoshino, M. Y. and Lifson, T. B. *The Invisible Link: Japan's Sogo Shosha and the Organization of Trade*, Cambridge, Mass: MIT Press, 1986.

5. CULTURAL CONSTRAINTS ON TRANSFER OF TECHNOLOGY ACROSS NATIONS: IMPLICATIONS FOR RESEARCH IN INTERNATIONAL AND COMPARATIVE MANAGEMENT

BEN L. KEDIA

Ben L. Kedia (Ph.D., Case Western Reserve University) is a Professor of International Management and Chairman of the Department of Management at Louisiana State University in Baton Rouge. Correspondence regarding this article can be sent to him at the Department of Management, College of Business Administration, Louisiana State University, Baton Rouge, LA 70803-6312.

RABI S. BHAGAT

Rabi S. Bhagat (Ph.D., University of Illinois) is a Professor of Organizational Behavior and International Management in the School of Management at the University of Texas, Dallas.

Cultural variations across nations and organizational culture-based differences between organizations that are involved in the transfer of various kinds of technologies are considered two major factors that influence the success of transfer. Relevant contributions from cross-cultural studies on management and organizations are integrated into the literature on organizational culture and diffusion of innovations, and a conceptual model is developed. Implications for research in international and comparative management are discussed.

In the field of international management, issues concerning effective transfer of technology have been regarded as central to the field's mission. A great deal of emphasis has been placed on economic factors that affect transfer of technology (Contractor & Sagafi-Nejad, 1981; Marton, 1986; Pugel, 1978). But there have been almost no theoretical or empirical analyses on the constraining influences of the cultural factors involved in such transactions. Because such transfers

Reprinted from *Academy of Management Review*, Vol. 13, No. 4, 1988, pp. 559-571 by permission of the publisher.

The authors thank Geert Hofstede, Sally McQuaid, and Karen Fontenot for their helpful comments. An earlier version of the paper was presented at the annual meeting of the Academy of Management in Chicago in 1986.

generally involve two organizations located in two distinct cultures for a fairly long period of time, it is surprising to note the absence of emphasis on the role of cultural constraints on such transfers. In this paper, we (a) present a conceptual model of technology transfer across nations that explicitly takes into account the roles of two kinds of cultural factors and receptivity to technological change on the part of the recipient country, (b) advance some research propositions that explain the various links of the model, and (c) examine the relevance these propositions have for future research in international and comparative management.

Before we delineate the conceptual model, we present an analysis of the trends in research in this area. First, there are studies that describe how technology gets transferred, what types of technology are likely to get higher levels of commitment on the part of the managers of the recipient organization, and the nature and the duration of the relationships as a function of the negotiations between the two enterprises (Balasubramanyam, 1973; Marton, 1986; Mason, 1980).

The second group of studies focuses on the absorptive capacity of the recipient organizations and the level of technological development of the host country (Baranson, 1970; Driscoll & Wallender, 1981; Dunning, 1981). Finally, there are case studies that examine the ingredients of the effectiveness of the technology transfer as a function of maturity of the industry, abilities of both the supplier and the recipient organizations, and the life-cycle stage of the technology involved in the transaction (e.g., Baranson & Harrington, 1977; Behrman & Wallender, 1976; Evenson, 1976; Marton, 1986).

Although these studies are helpful to the policy makers of a nation that seeks to lower the economic cost of imported technology by providing industry-specific lessons and negotiating guidance, they offer little in terms of our theoretical understanding of the constraining influences of the cultural factors involved in such transactions. Culture of the recipient organization, strategic management issues, and, perhaps more important, the cultural differences between the two nations involved, play significant roles in determining the efficacy of such transactions.

Many examples show what carefully reasoned economic analyses fail to explain: the failures of those technological transactions that should, indeed, succeed and the successes of those that ought to fail. If we are to better understand the effectiveness of technology transfers across nations, we need a conceptual framework that enhances the role of cultural variations across nations. A scheme depicting the relative importance of cultural variations across nations, organizational culture, and strategic management processes at the level of the enterprise as determinants of the efficacy of technology transfer between nations is presented (Table 1). It shows that the effectiveness of transfer of technology is most affected by variations in societal cultures of the two nations when one of them is an advanced industrialized nation (e.g., West Germany or Japan) and the recipient is a developing country (e.g., India or Brazil). Organizational culture-based differences and related strategic management processes play limited roles in such transfers. In contrast, the transfer of technology from one industrialized country to another industrialized country is most influenced by strategic management-related considerations at the level of the two enterprises involved.

For example, transfer of high technology from IBM of U.S.A. to Siemens of West Germany is likely to be viewed as a strategic issue by both of the transacting organizations. Strategic considerations play greater roles than either the societal culture or the organizational culture-based variations in determining the success of such transfers because of international competitiveness, relative position in the global marketplace, and the critical nature of the technology. On the other hand, transfer of technology from an advanced industrialized to a moderately industrialized nation (e.g., between the United States or West Germany and South Korea or Taiwan) is influenced by all three of the factors, although only moderately. With this framework in mind, we developed a conceptual model (Figure 1) that depicts the role of cultural constraints and other important factors as determinants of efficacy of technology transfers across nations. The model has two causal antecedents (organizational culture-based differences and specific characteristics of the technology involved) and two moderating factors.

Table 1
AN EXAMINATION OF THE RELATIVE IMPORTANCES OF CULTURAL VARIATION AND STRATEGIC MANAGEMENT PROCESSES AS DETERMINANTS OF THE SUCCESSFUL TRANSFER OF TECHNOLOGY ACROSS NATIONS

	From Industrialized to other Industrialized Nations (e.g., U.S. to West Germany)	**From Industrialized to Moderately Industrialized Nations (e.g., U.S. to South Korea)**	**From Industrialized to Developing Nations (e.g., West Germany to India)**
Societal Culture	Least important	Moderately important	Most important
Organizational Culture	Moderately important	Moderately important	Moderately important
Strategic Management Processes	Most important	Moderately important	Least important

Figure 1
A CONCEPTUAL MODEL FOR UNDERSTANDING CULTURAL CONSTRAINTS ON
TECHNOLOGY TRANSFERS ACROSS NATIONS

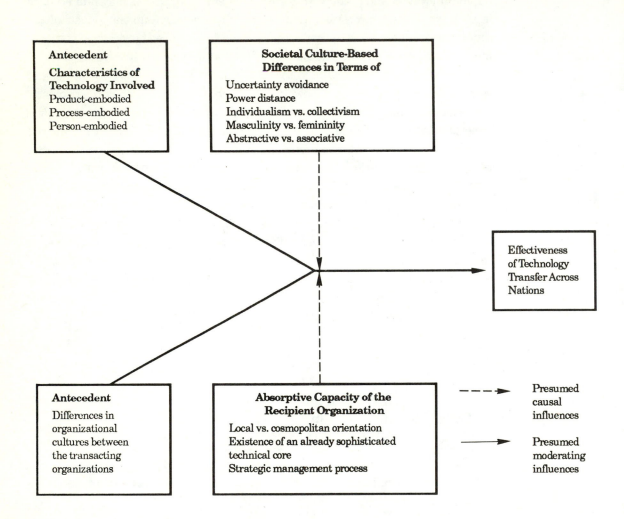

A Conceptual Model _____

The model suggests that the effectiveness of technology transfer is moderated by variations in societal culture-based differences and receptivity to technological change in terms of the absorptive capacity of the recipient organization. First, we consider the specific character of the technology involved.

Type of Technology

Essentially, the process of technology transfer is composed of the transfer of a systematically developed set of organized information, skills, rights, and services from a supplier organization located in a developed country (typically in the West) to a recipient organization located in a developing country (typically, but not always, in one of the third-world nations). In the case of process-embodied technology transfers, concern is with the transfer of blueprints or patent rights of the actual scientific processes and engineering details from the supplier country to a recipient country. Examples include transfer of chemical technology for the manufacture of synthetic fabrics and off-shore petroleum exploration technology. In the case of product-embodied technology transfers, one transfers the physical product itself. Examples would be heavy earth-tilling machinery and sophisticated computer components. Finally, in the case of person-embodied technology transfers, the transfer depends on the efficacy of a mission undertaken by the supplier organization in developing a sophisticated local technical core to implement and diffuse the imported technology.

Hall and Johnson (1970), who recommended the use of this scheme for the classification of technology, clearly recognized that the process of technology transfer in the domain of international commerce is in no way similar to the transfer of a commodity. They imply that the marginal cost of reproducing a technical capability in another foreign location due to transfer is only a small fraction of the original cost of the technology itself. Effectiveness of transfer depends to a large extent on the type or characteristics of the technology involved (i.e., whether it is process-embodied, product-embodied, or person-embodied). We argue that compared to product-embodied technologies, process-embodied and person-embodied technologies are considerably more difficult to transfer across nations because cultural and strategic management factors play larger roles in such transfers and diffusions. The acquisition and generation of industrial technology have become critical aspects of economic planning in the developing countries, and strategic control over foreign technologies, once they have been acquired, becomes an important issue.

Control over dissemination and application of technology is necessary to retain the technological advantage in domestic and foreign markets, and to manage economic growth in a planned fashion (Marton, 1986). Such controls often involve many considerations that are directly related to the prevailing cultural norms and patterns in that country. Product-embodied technologies allow such controls because often there is little room for continued dialogue between the supplier and the recipient organizations involved. However, in the case of both process-embodied and person-embodied technologies, the intrinsic nature of the technology makes it necessary that the supplier organization exercise control through various means, ranging from constraints in the use of technology in the subsidiaries, affiliates, and licensees, to restrictions in the diffusion and utilization of such technologies.

In recent years, almost all types of technology transfers have involved products, processes, and people, even though some are clearly more process-embodied or people-embodied than others. In addition, we should recognize (as Davidson & McFetridge, 1985, and others have shown) the importance of factors such as language, common ancestry, shared history, level of economic development, physical proximity, technical competence of the work force, age of technology at the time of transfer, number of successful prior transfers, and so forth, as determinants of the effectiveness of transfer of technology across nations. Simply stated, although degree of economic development is a major factor, cultural predispositions play an important role.

Culture and Strategic Management Issues

At one point in the history of technology transfer, such transfers took place primarily among Western nations (i.e., transfer of technology from Western Europe to the United States and vice versa). However, this is not the case today. In fact, transfers of technology from the United States to ASEAN (Association of South East Asian Nations) countries and other nations in South America have become important issues in the 1980s (Marton, 1986; McMillan, 1984). Although the technology transfers among developed nations rely greatly on strategic orientations of transacting organizations, the transfers to developing countries depend on the compatibility of the cultures of the nations involved in such transactions. The practice of adopting and implementing Western technologies of the process- and person-embodied types in the context of some of the moderately developing countries has not been a simple case of "borrowing" or imitating, as has been suggested in many popular business periodicals. Indeed, a realistic appraisal of technological diffusion strategy should focus on the structure of preferences that exist in the recipient country at the time of the transfer. In addition, such appraisals also should carefully examine the unique strengths and weaknesses of variations in the societal culture, organizational culture, and strategic management practices between the transacting organizations in two different nations. The primary unit of analysis is at the level of the organization located in the context of its own societal culture. The unrecognized roles that cultural variations (societal and organizational) play on the transfer of process- and person-embodied technologies form the basis of our first proposition.

Proposition 1: Process- and person-embodied technologies are more difficult than product-embodied technologies to transfer and diffuse across nations because cultural differences at the organizational, as well as the societal, level play greater roles in such transfers.

Once the importance of cultural variations on process- and person-embodied technologies is recognized, as emphasized in Proposition 1, it should be noted that technology transfers across national boundaries are predominantly orchestrated and managed by organizations seeking economies of scale and other strategic business advantages. Careful attention should be given to the compatibility of cultures of the organizations involved and compatibility of the societal culture. First, we delineate the moderating role of societal cultural-based differences and compatibility between the transacting organizations.

Compatibility of Societal Cultures

Even though the influences of cultural variations have been recognized (Marton, 1986; McMillan, 1984), we did not discover in our review any specific theoretical analysis or empirical studies that rigorously underscore the importance of cultural variations across nations. What exists in the literature is an implicit recognition of the importance of the societal culture of the developing country as a major determinant of the effectiveness of technology transfers (e.g., Koizumi, 1982). Needless to say, the culture of the society to which technology is being exported makes a significant difference. But so does the culture from which the technology is being imported—a point that has remained surprisingly unrecognized in the literature. In the conceptual model, we have incorporated the work of Hofstede (1980) and Glenn and Glenn (1981) in order to advance research propositions that enable us to better understand the process of technology transfers in the context of cultural differences between the transacting organizations and nations involved. Although there are other relevant dimensions of cultural variations, such as McClelland and Winter's (1969) analysis, that might be potentially useful, we find the four dimensions of Hofstede and the one dimension of Glenn and Glenn to be particularly suited for developing our present analysis and for suggesting the propositions on effectiveness of technology transfer across nations. Such effectiveness depends on cultural compatibility between the two nations. According to Hofstede (1980), national cultures can be mapped according to their fit into a four-dimensional framework of (a) weak versus strong uncertainty avoidance, (b) individualism versus collectivism, (c) small versus large power distance, and (d) masculinity versus femininity.

With uncertainty avoidance, we are concerned with the extent to which people in a society feel the need to avoid ambiguous situations and the extent to which they try to manage these situations by providing explicit and formal rules and regulations, by rejecting novel ideas, and by accepting the existence of absolute truths and superordinate goals in the context of work organizations. In Hofstede's (1980) study, the highest scores on uncertainty avoidance were obtained for countries such as Greece, Japan, and most of the Catholic countries in Latin America, whereas low scores were obtained for Hong Kong, Singapore, and the Scandinavian countries. With individualism versus collectivism, we are concerned with the relationships between individuals and organizations in a society. At the individualistic end of this dimension, ties between individuals are, indeed, very loose, and people are supposed to look after their own self-interests in the domains of both work and non-work. At the collectivist end, we find societies in which social ties or bonds between individuals are very tight, and people learn to distinguish between their own ingroups (e.g., immediate relatives, clans, and members of one's organization) and out-groups (e.g., members from a different community or a foreign country or people with whom one has less frequent contact). In individualistic countries, people are inner-directed, whereas in collectivist countries, individuals are more traditional and other-directed. Examples of individualistic countries are the United States, Great Britain, Australia, Canada, and the Netherlands. Colombia, Venezuela, Taiwan, Singapore, Greece, and Mexico are largely collectivistic in their orientation.

With the dimension of power distance, we are concerned with the extent to which less powerful members of a society accept the unequal distribution of power and rewards as normal features of their society. Hofstede (1980, 1983) has shown that different cultures possess different distributions of power in their organizational and social hierarchies and that the power distance norm can be used as a criterion for characterizing societal cultures. Tannenbaum, Kavcic, Rosher, Viahello, and Wieser (1974), in their analysis of hierarchy in work organizations in five countries, also found that differences in power are associated with significant differences in rewards, privileges, and opportunities among various levels of managements. Large power-distance countries include the Philippines, Mexico, France, Peru, Turkey, Brazil, and India. Small power-distance countries include Austria, Denmark, Sweden, and Israel.

With the fourth dimension, masculinity versus femininity, we are concerned with the extent to which the dominant values in a society emphasize assertiveness, acquisition of money and status, achievement of visible and symbolic organizational rewards (as opposed to an emphasis on quality of life and other less tangible outcomes). In masculine cultures there are sharp distinctions between assertive roles that men perform and service roles that women are expected to fulfill. Hofstede (1983) noted that in a masculine society, the public hero is a successful achiever, an aggressive entrepreneur, and that "big is beautiful" (p. 85). In contrast, feminine societies emphasize quality of life, preservation of the environment, helping others, and putting relationships before money and achievement. The emphasis is on "small is beautiful" (p. 85). Japan is the most masculine country in the world. Also masculine are the German-speaking countries: West Germany, Austria, and Switzerland. Moderately masculine are a number of Latin countries such as Venezuela, Mexico, and Italy. Some former colonies of Anglo countries also are moderately masculine in character, for example, India and the Philippines. The feminine countries are the four Nordic nations, the Netherlands, and some Mediterranean countries like Yugoslavia.

The following four propositions are advanced to reflect the importance of these four distinct cultural variations.

Proposition 2: Transfer of technology is easier between two organizations that are similar in terms of their societal/national culture-based tendencies to either avoid or embrace uncertainty generated in their organizational contexts due to such transfers.

Proposition 3: Technologies that might introduce significant changes in the distributions of power, status (real and symbolic), and rewards in the recipient organization of the developing country that emphasizes power distance are least likely to be effectively transferred.

Knowledge disavowal (Zaltman, 1983) would be fairly common in the organizations of these high power-distance countries despite the fact that the long-term economic implications of such transfers are positive. Knowledge disavowal reflects the tendency to selectively ignore information that might cause important structural as well as programmatic changes in the recipient organization. In India, for example, despite the existence of a rather sophisticated system of technical core and educated personnel, the ownership structure of Indian industry strongly influences the absorption of technology. The impact of regulatory policies and stringent laws on the acquisition and absorption of foreign technology by both public- and private-sector companies makes it difficult to introduce technologies that might affect traditional management and control-related processes (Palhan, 1985).

Individualistic countries generally are more effective in importing technologies than collectivistic countries. However, a closer examination makes this process somewhat less clear. Although there are numerous examples of failures in technology transfers that involve individualistic countries like the United States, Germany, and the United Kingdom, and some collectivistic countries like Venezuela (Marton, 1986), there also are successful examples of technological diffusion in countries that are strongly collectivistic. Japan, Singapore, Hong Kong, and Taiwan are four of the five dragons of economic development in the Asian context. Their ability to absorb Western technology is remarkable, and we cannot cite many parallel examples of modern industrialization in Asia. However, these countries are high in masculinity. One of the consequences of masculinity is that economic growth is seen as more important than social welfare (which is not the case in Scandinavian countries) (Hofstede, 1980). Large-scale enterprises, projects, and performance-driven organizational systems are more popular. This orientation, coupled with collectivism, is, perhaps, responsible for successful transfers of technology to these nations. Otherwise, individualistic cultures are better able both to generate and to import technological advances.

> Proposition 4a: Organizations located in individualistic cultures are more successful than organizations located in collectivistic cultures in their propensity to absorb and diffuse imported technology.

> Proposition 4b: However, collectivistic cultures that are fairly masculine also are effective in such matters.

Collectivism, which sometimes dampens innovation in organizations, is, perhaps, held in check or counterbalanced by an emphasis on masculinity (Triandis, 1987). This tendency of masculine countries to emphasize economic growth and to foster performance-driven criteria in international trade and technology-related transactions leads us to advance our fifth proposition.

> Proposition 5: Masculine cultures are more effective than feminine cultures in absorbing and diffusing imported technology in organizational contexts.

The growth of technology-related advances in these countries, as we have noted earlier, is phenomenal and without parallel in the history of world industrialization. Japan illustrates this pattern remarkably well. In the immediate post-war period, Japanese productivity compared to that of the United States was rather low: 5 percent in coal mining and chemicals, 10 percent in rubber, and 20 percent in rayon. Within a span of less than 40 years, Japan has rivaled the United States in integrated circuits and mainframe computers, and it leads both Europe and the United States in high technology trade to other developing countries (McMillan, 1984). How have Japan and its neighboring countries, such as South Korea (as pointed out by Naisbitt, 1981) and Hong Kong, which are strongly masculine, been able to make these leaps in technology, especially in contrast to countries like the Netherlands, Sweden, and Finland, which are strongly feminine and were left relatively undamaged during World War II? The answers are complex and, perhaps, rooted in economic, historical, and cultural factors. But when we note that these Scandinavian countries are primarily feminine in orientation (Hofstede, 1983, p. 315), a clearer picture emerges. Masculine countries, more driven to compete, are more dynamic and action oriented. To compete successfully in the global economy, one has to rapidly learn strategies for successful implementation of imported technologies. One important caveat is in order. Even though we have illustrated the effectiveness of transfer in terms of Hofstede's dimensions, it should be noted that the idea emphasized here is one of compatibility between nations and receptivity to technological innovation. In future analyses, if more reliable and empirically anchored measures of such dimensions are available, one could use them also in addressing this issue of effectiveness of transfer.

With the final dimension of cultural variation that plays a role in determining the efficacy of technology transfers, we are concerned with the abstractive versus associative tendencies in a given culture (Glenn & Glenn, 1981). In associative cultures, people utilize associations among events that may not have much logical basis, whereas in abstractive cultures, cause-effect relationships or rational Judeo-Christian types of thinking are dominant. Glenn and Glenn (1981), who pioneered this inquiry in differentiating among cultures, clearly stated that associative thinking is not necessarily inferior to abstractive thinking; it is just different. Cognition and behavior in associative cultures often are diffuse. Communication is characterized by face-to-face contact, and it takes place among individuals who share a large body of information based on both historical and contextual modes (Hall, 1976). In contrast, a vast amount of communication in abstractive cultures tends to be conveyed through mass media and related technological mechanisms that are rather dissimilar compared to face-to-face types of communication.

In associative cultures, context is very important (Hall, 1976). The effectiveness of communication and innovation depends on the specific character of the context in which it takes place. Managers of work organizations from associative cultures also tend to be field-dependent (Gruenfeld & MacEachron, 1975) — a tendency to view the world in a somewhat undifferentiated and global fashion. Economic development and technological change foster field independence and abstractive thinking, the dominant mode in the majority of Western countries (Triandis, 1987). Technological changes for the sake of progress per se often are suspect in associative cultures, and smooth transfers, therefore, are bound to be more difficult to manage. The major reason for this is that effective transfer of technology implies that members of a culture are rather sophisticated in terms of their ability to absorb and utilize context-free information. This tendency is difficult to develop in cultures that function primarily by emphasizing context-dependent sources of information (Hall, 1976).

> Proposition 6: Abstractive cultures are more effective than associative cultures in their ability to absorb and diffuse imported technology.

India and some countries in Latin America (e.g., Peru, Colombia, Venezuela) are more associative than European countries in general (Glenn & Glenn, 1981), and a closer examination of the recent literature on technology transfers also reveals that they are less effective in absorbing imported technologies in their organizational contexts (Marton, 1986; Sachs, 1986).

Potential Interaction

Although the above six propositions imply that the five cultural dimensions are distinct, it should be noted that they interact significantly. Theoretically speaking, we could generate additional propositions to reflect the complexity of these interactions. For example, we could suggest that transfer of process- and person-embodied technologies are considerably more difficult from organizations located in cultures that are high in individualism, moderate in masculinity and uncertainty avoidance, low in power distance, and are abstractive (such as the United States) compared with organizations located in cultures that are low in individualism, high in masculinity, uncertainty avoidance, power distance, and are associative (such as Venezuela). However, such propositions are beyond the scope of this paper. Our current research efforts are best directed at testing both the validity and the generalizability of the above-mentioned six propositions. When empirical results on these dimensions become available, research efforts could be redirected toward second or higher-order interactions among these five dimensions. In addition, it must be noted that even though we have utilized specific scores from Hofstede's (1980) data to develop the focused arguments in the propositions, the essential idea is one of compatibility between the cultures involved in the transference of a specific technology in a given situation. This is discussed in the concluding section.

Differences in Organizational Cultures _____

When examining receptivity of countries to technological change, we adopted the concept of negotiated order (Fine, 1984; Strauss, 1982; Strauss, Schatzman, Ehrlich, Bucher, & Sabshin, 1963) in order to understand the role of organizational culture-based differences in technology transfers across nations. Strauss and his colleagues argued that, basically, social order is negotiated, and that organized activity is not possible without some form of continued negotiations. Negotiations are contingent on the structural conditions of the organization, and they reflect patterned, not random, lines of communication in the context of the organization. Negotiations also have temporal constraints, and the structural changes (i.e., the adoption of technological innovations, etc.) might require a revision of the negotiated order. Although formal rules may refer to the transcending features of the organization, the concept of negotiated order focuses on (a) the number of negotiators, their experience, and whom they represent; (b) the sequence and frequency of negotiations; (c) the relative balance of power among the concerned parties; (d) the stakes and visibility of the outcome of negotiations; (e) the complexity of the issues; and (f) the alternatives to avoiding or discontinuing negotiations. We propose that if the negotiated orders in the cultures of the two transacting organizations are significantly different in terms of the above six dimensions, then transfer of technology between them would be a difficult process, and it might be unproductive for both parties. Such differences are conceptualized as one of two major antecedents in the model (Table 1).

> Proposition 7: Differences in the negotiated orders of the cultures of the organizations involved in the transfer and diffusion of technology across nations adversely affect the effectiveness of such transfers.

Potential Interactions

Note that these six dimensions of negotiated order interact with each other much like the societal cultural dimensions. For example, it is likely that the sequence and frequency of negotiations will change the relative balance of power among the parties and the complexity and visibility of the outcomes. Similarity between the two organizations regarding the six cultural dimensions would facilitate the recipient organization's receptivity of the technological diffusion.

Absorptive Capacity

With the final moderating link in the model along with societal culture-based differences we are concerned with (a) local versus cosmopolitan orientation, (b) the existence of a sophisticated technical core in the recipient organization, and (c) the differences in strategic management between the transacting organizations. Some organizations are more innovative despite their small sizes and other resource-related constraints (Kimberly, 1981). An organization's implementation of technical progress by adopting innovative production techniques and changes in design that accommodate these techniques (Child & Kieser, 1981) are dependent on the degree of cosmopolitanism that is inherent in the organization (Merton, 1968). The evolutionary strategies of diffusion of technology are based on the premise that no matter how impressive the performance characteristics of an innovative technology may be (either process- or person-embodied), its adoption and implementation are greatly dependent on the mix of the array of preexisting priorities and conflicting alliances present in the recipient organization.

In a cosmopolitan organization, such conflicts are managed more systematically and routinely, thus ensuring the success of the innovative effort, whereas in local organizations, the array of priorities often succumbs to immediate sociopolitical concerns, thus making it difficult for even or orderly diffusion (Rodgers & Shoemaker, 1971). In a related vein, the lack of a sophisticated technical core makes it harder for the innovation to occur in the first place—a point that, although well recognized, deserves reemphasis. Kiggundu, Jorgensen, and Hafsi (1983) documented and underscored this issue in their examination of the implementation-related issues in developing countries. There could, indeed, be a great deal of interest in utilizing imported technologies in an organization. The cultural factors of the organization and the societal culture-based context of these factors also might be appropriately matched. But the organization must have a sophisticated technical core and a strategic orientation to make this possibility a reality. Developing countries often are caught in situations of rapid change. Often, in such countries more emphasis is put on managing of multiple goals than on developing local talent to monitor the implementation stage of the imported technology (Marton, 1986; Neghandi, 1971). In short, various aspects of strategic management are important in determining the effectiveness of technology transfer.

> Proposition 8: Cosmopolitan organizations in societies that also have a sophisticated technical and an appropriate strategic management orientation are more effective than local organizations in systematically managing technological transfers.

Implications _____

These eight propositions have implications for research in international and comparative management. The following guidelines are offered to stimulate research in this area.

Guide 1. Researchers should explicitly consider the interactions among technology and cultural variations in both societal and organizational contexts.

Our analysis suggests the need to consider the variations in each of these in order to explain the successes of transfers that, in purely economic terms, ought to fail and the failures of those that ought to succeed. The range of situations to which our ideas apply is depicted in Table 1. More specifically, our analysis is most appropriate in explaining transfers of technology from advanced industrialized countries to recently developing ones (e.g., from, say, West Germany to Brazil or Mexico). We used Japan as an example to illustrate the relevance of our theoretical analysis; however, Japan is no longer a developing country, even though it is clearly culturally dissimilar to many countries from which it imported technologies during the 1950s and 1960s. Therefore, variations in strategic management processes and in organizational cultures are superior predictors of efficacy of transfers than the differences in societal culture when we reconsider the Japanese case today. Cultural differences begin to exert much stronger influences when the importing organization is located in a developing country.

Also, researchers should be more explicit regarding the respective cultural profiles of the importing and exporting organizations as well as their respective societal culture-based differences. Empirical findings on propositions reflecting interactions among the Hofstede and Glenn dimensions can aid in extending the significance of their dimensions to other situations.

Guide 2. Researchers should explicitly recognize the absorptive capacity and related organizational context-based variables when considering the transfer of technology. We need to know much more about the dynamics of the absorptive capacity and the negotiated order that exist in the organization importing the technology. Where do ideas for technological innovations come from? How are they developed? How do potential parties remain informed about the new developments that might affect their well being and that of various coalitions?

The processes of absorption and diffusion of technological innovation are by no means linear, and there is evidence that potential adopter enthusiasm would dampen considerably if the parties in key brokerage roles are threatened (Kimberly, 1981). There are examples of innovations that are warmly received by the boundary-spanners of both the organizations in two societies, but when it comes to actual implementation, the idea may either lie dormant for years or get sidetracked by policy vacuums (Louis & Corwin, 1982). The point is that in developing future research designs on technology transfers, researchers should be sensitive to the differences between rhetoric and reality that often accompany some transactions.

Guide 3. Researchers should place greater emphasis on interdisciplinary frameworks. Future research strategies on the effectiveness of various types of technology transfers should not be based only on economic factors. The need for interdisciplinary frameworks to explain the entire process is urgent at this point in theory development. In the past, we have grappled only in a minor way with the *complexity* of technology transfers across nations. Developing countries have many concerns besides economic growth and development. Technologies that do not match the needs of their sociopolitical and cultural contexts are likely to be greeted with more vague rhetoric. Not all countries need to share the individualistic biases that underlie most of our theories of diffusion of technology (Chesanow, 1985; Triandis, 1987, in press). Hofstede (1980) observed that in an eagerness to assist other developing countries to adopt Western methods and techniques, we often forget our ethnocentric biases. Adler (1986) echoed this concern. It would be more effective if significant advances in the field of cross-cultural studies of management and organization were incorporated in future theories and research on technology transfers. Both developed countries and developing countries would benefit from such an interdisciplinary orientation. The ideas presented in this paper are offered to stimulate further research and thinking in this growing and important area in the field of international and comparative management.

References

Alder, N. J. (1986) *International dimensions of organizational behavior.* Boston: Kent.

Balasubramanyam, V. (1973) *International transfer of technology to India.* New York: Praeger Scientific Press.

Baranson, J. (1970, May) Technology transfer through the international firm. *American Economic Review, Papers and Proceedings,* 435-440.

Baranson, J., & Harrington, A. (1977) *Industrial transfers of technology by U.S. firms under licensing arrangements: Policies, practices and conditioning factors.* Washington, DC: Developing World Industry and Technology, Inc.

Behrman, J., & Wallender, H. (1976) *Transfer of manufacturing technology within multinational enterprises.* Cambridge, MA: Ballinger.

Child, J., & Kieser, A. (1981) Development of organizations over time. In P. C. Nystrom & W. H. Starbuck (Eds.), *Handbook of organizational design* (Vol. 1, pp. 28-64). New York: Oxford University Press.

Chesanow, N. (1985) *The world class executive.* New York: Rawson Associates.

Contractor, F. J., & Sagafi-Nejad, T. (1981) International technology transfer: Major issues and policy responses. *Journal of International Business Studies,* 12(2), 113-135.

Davidson, W. H., & McFetridge, D. G. (1985) Key characteristics in choice of international technology transfer mode. *Journal of International Business Studies,* 6(2), 5-21.

Driscoll, R., & Wallender, H. (1981) Control and incentives for technology transfer: A multinational perspective. In R. W. Moxon & H. V. Perlmutter (Eds.), *Controlling international technology transfer: Issues, perspectives and implications* (pp. 273-286). New York: Pergamon Press.

Dunning, J. H. (1981) Alternative channels and modes of international resource transmission. In R. W. Moxon & H. V. Perlmutter (Eds.), *Controlling international technology transfer: Issues, perspectives and implications* (pp. 3-27). New York: Pergamon Press.

Evenson, R. (1976) International transmission of technology in production of sugar cane. *Journal of Development Studies,* 1, 1-13.

Fine, G. A. (1984) Negotiated orders and organizational cultures. *Annual Review of Sociology,* 10, 239-262.

Glenn, E. S., & Glenn, C. G. (1981) *Man and mankind: Conflict and communication between cultures.* Norwood, NJ: Ablex.

Gruenfeld, L. W., & MacEachron, A. E. (1975) A cross-national study of cognitive style among managers and technicians. *International Journal of Psychology,* 10, 27-55.

Hall, E. T. (1976) *Beyond culture.* Garden City, NY: Anchor/Doubleday.

Hall, G., & Johnson, R. (1970) Transfer of United States aerospace technology to Japan. In R. Vernon (Ed.), *The technology factor in international trade* (pp. 305-358). New York: Columbia.

Hofstede, G. (1980) *Culture's consequences: International differences in work-related values.* Beverly Hills, CA: Sage.

Hofstede, G. (1983) The cultural relativity of organizational practices and theories. *Journal of International Business Studies,* 14(2), 75-89.

Kiggundu, M. N., Jorgensen, J. J., & Hafsi, T. (1983) Administrative theory and practice in developing countries: A synthesis. *Administrative Science Quarterly,* 28, 66-85.

Kimberly, J. R. (1981) Managerial innovation. In P. C. Nystrom & W. H. Starbuck (Eds.), *Handbook of organizational design* (Vol. 1, pp. 84-104). New York: Oxford University Press.

Koizumi, T. (1982) Absorption and adaptation: Japanese inventiveness in technological development. In S. B. Lundstedt & E. W. Colglazier, Jr. (Eds.), *Managing innovation: The social dimensions of creativity, invention and technology* (pp. 190-206). New York: Pergamon Press.

Louis, K. S., & Corwin, R. G. (1982) Organizational barriers to utilization of research. *Administrative Science Quarterly,* 27, 4, 623-640.

Marton, K. (1986) *Multinationals, technology, and industrialization.* Lexington, MA: Heath.

Mason, R. H. (1980, January-February) A comment of Professor Kojma's Japanese type vs. American type of technology transfer. *Hototsubashi Journal of Economics.*

McClelland, D. C., & Winter, D. G. (1969) *Motivating economic achievement.* New York: Free Press.

McMillan, C. J. (1984) *The Japanese industrial system.* New York: Water de Gruyter.

Merton, R. K. (1968) *Social theory and social structure.* New York: Free Press.

Neghandi, A. R. (1971) American management abroad: A comparative study of management practices of American subsidiaries and local firms in developing countries. *Management International Review*, 11(4-5), 97-107.

Naisbitt, J. (1981) *Megatrends.* New York: Warner.

Palhan, S. K. (1985) *Technology policy and India's experience in technology transfer.* New Delhi: Government of India, Ministry of Industry.

Pugel, T. (1978) *International technology transfer and neoclassical trade theory: A survey.* Working paper, New York University.

Rodgers, E., & Shoemaker, F. (1971) *Communication of innovations: A cross-cultural approach.* New York: Free Press.

Sachs, J. (1986, February 22) A tale of Asian winners and Latin losers. *Economist*, pp. 63-64.

Strauss, A. (1982) Interorganizational negotiations. *Urban Life*, 11, 350-367.

Strauss, A., Schatzman, L., Ehrlich, D., Bucher, R., & Sabshin, M. (1963) The hospital and its negotiated order. In E. Friedson (Ed.), *The hospital in modern society* (pp. 147-169). New York: Free Press.

Tannenbaum, A. S., Kavcic, B., Rosher, M., Viahello, M., & Wieser, G. (1974) *Hierarchy in organizations.* San Francisco: Jossey-Bass.

Triandis, H. C. (1987) *Collectivism and development.* Paper presented at International Union of Psychological Sciences, Hong Kong.

Triandis, H. C. (in press) Cross-cultural industrial and organizational psychology. In M. D. Dunnette (Ed.), *Handbook of industrial and organizational psychology*. Chicago: Rand McNally.

Zaltman, G. (1983) Knowledge disavowal in organizations. In R. Kilman, K. Thomas, D. Slevin, R. Nath, & S. Jarrell (Eds.), *Producing useful knowledge for organizations* (pp. 173-187). New York: Praeger.

III_____ STRUCTURAL CONSIDERATIONS _____

Strategy and Structure in Multinational Corporations:
A Revision of the Stopford and Wells Model
William G. Egelhoff

Managing across Borders: New Organizational Responses
Christopher A. Bartlett and Sumantra Ghoshal

6. STRATEGY AND STRUCTURE IN MULTINATIONAL CORPORATIONS: A REVISION OF THE STOPFORD AND WELLS MODEL

WILLIAM G. EGELHOFF

Graduate School of Business, New York University, New York, U.S.A.

The Stopford and Wells study of strategy and structure in multinational corporations produced a now familiar model relating certain types of structure to certain elements of a firm's international strategy. This paper re-examines the important relationships expressed by the model, using data from a recent study of 34 large U.S. and European multinationals. While some of the relationships are supported, others are not. A new element of strategy, the relative size of foreign manufacturing, is introduced, and found to be an important predictor of structure. Based on the findings, a revised model for relating strategy and structure in MNCs is proposed.

Introduction

As the international strategies of firms evolve, and become more complex, it is increasingly difficult to know which types of organizational structure facilitate implementing them. While models linking strategy and structure exist, there is a pressing need for further development. The first empirical work which sought to relate structure to the strategy of an organization was Chandler's (1962) study of 70 large U.S. corporations. It tended to show that as a company's product/market strategy changed it was important that the organization's structure also change to support implementation of the new strategy. Additional studies by Pavan (1972), Channon (1973), Rumelt (1974), and Dyas and Thanheiser (1976) further demonstrated that certain strategies need to be supported by certain structures. A number of empirical studies have also attempted to describe the relationship between strategy and structure for multinational corporations (MNCs) (Brooke and Remmers, 1970; Daniels, Pitts and Tretter, 1984, 1985; Fouraker and Stopford, 1968; Franko, 1976; Stopford and Wells, 1972). Of these, the Stopford and

Wells study was the largest and most comprehensive, and it also developed the most explicit theory linking strategy and structure in MNCs.

The Stopford and Wells Model of International Strategy and Structure _____

In their book on strategy implementation, Galbraith and Nathanson (1978) credit Stopford and Wells with having extended the earlier strategy-structure models of Chandler (1962) and Scott (1971) to include international strategy and structure. Figure 1 shows the critical variables and relationships of the Stopford and Wells model, which was empirically derived from data collected on 187 large U.S. MNCs.

Below the international division boundary in Figure 1, foreign product diversity and foreign sales are both relatively low. MNCs employing this strategy tended to support it with an international division structure. As foreign product diversity increased, companies in the sample tended to use product division structures. Similarly, companies pursuing strategies leading to a relatively high percentage of foreign sales tended to use area division structures. When a company's strategy contained both high foreign product diversity and a high percentage of

Figure 1
THE STOPFORD AND WELLS MODEL SHOWING THE RELATIONSHIP BETWEEN STRATEGY AND STRUCTURE IN MULTINATIONAL CORPORATIONS

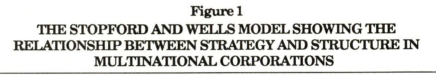

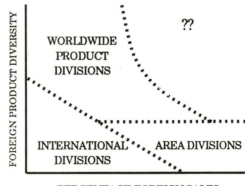

foreign sales, Stopford and Wells hypothesized that MNCs will tend to employ matrix or mixed structures, but the question mark (placed there by Galbraith and Nathanson) indicates there was only weak support for this in Stopford and Wells' data. Although the Stopford and Wells study took place in U.S. MNCs, subsequent research by Franko (1976) in European MNCs tended to confirm the relationships shown in Figure 1.

Recent concerns about international strategy and structure

While recent research has raised some questions about the validity of the international division boundary of the Stopford and Wells Model (Bartlett, 1979, 1983; Daniels *et al.*, 1984; Davidson, 1980; Davidson and Haspeslagh, 1982), the other relationships have essentially gone unchallenged and remain intact. In fact, with the exception of a study by Daniels *et al.* (1985), the upper and right-hand sides of the model (those portions associated with relatively high levels of foreign sales and/or foreign product diversity) have remained largely untested since the original research by Stopford and Wells and Franko. These portions of the model (and especially the portion represented as a question mark) are of growing significance, however, since the strategies of more and more MNCs are moving in this direction.

In fact, recent literature has raised a number of specific questions about strategy-structure relationships in the more strategically complex portions of the Model. First, Galbraith and Nathanson (1978) ask what international strategy fits the matrix structure, since both they and Davis and Lawrence (1977) noted a probable trend toward matrix structures in MNCs. Stopford and Wells suggested that matrix (and mixed) structures might be appropriate for firms in the upper right-hand corner of the model (where both foreign sales and foreign product diversity are high), but their data provided only weak support for this relationship. Since the widespread move to matrix structures expected by Davis and Lawrence has not occurred, despite the fact that many MNC strategies today contain relatively high levels of foreign sales and foreign product diversity, the question about what international strategy fits a matrix structure would still seem to be an open one.

A second issue with strategy-structure implications seems to be raised by Hout, Porter and Rudden (1982). They believe that the increasing growth in global interdependency can best be exploited by global strategies, where the appropriate unit of analysis for strategic planning and management is the global market for a product instead of multiple domestic markets. They point out that global strategies require new, more centralized forms of structure, that can integrate managerial decision-making across many domestic markets that were previously dealt with in a decentralized manner.

A third issue that seems to be influencing international strategy is increasing host government pressure for more national responsiveness in the strategies of MNCs (Doz, 1980; Doz and Prahalad, 1980). This pressure is generally reflected in calls for more local manufacture and R&D, a balance between exports and imports, and sometimes products and technologies that are consistent with national interests. This trend obviously runs counter to the previous trend for global strategies.

These new trends toward global strategies and more national responsiveness have largely come to prominence since the Stopford and Wells study, and subsequent research has not really attempted to integrate these developments into the existing set of strategy-structure relationships for MNCs. This is perhaps not surprising, since the new issues in international strategy seem to be still in the exploratory research phase, while research done under the strategy-structure paradigm has evolved to the point where it requires clearly defined concepts and operational measures. Yet it is important that attempts start to be made to integrate some understanding of the new issues and trends in international strategy into the established set of strategy-structure relationships (as represented by the Stopford and Wells model). Otherwise our understanding of strategy will increasingly outstrip our understanding of how to organize to implement such strategy. In contrast to the decade-long lags between changes in strategy and changes in structure observed by Chandler's study (1962), it is increasingly important for MNC managements to understand strategy-structure relationships and anticipate changes in order to minimize periods of misfit.

The purpose of the present study is to re-examine the key strategy-structure relationships of the Stopford and Wells study and to introduce a new element of international strategy—foreign manufacturing—which Stopford and Wells and other researchers have not considered. The new element is especially important because it seems to capture some of the more recent changes and trends that are altering and complicating the international strategies of MNCs.

Structures for Conducting International Business _____

This section describes the five types of structure that appeared in the Stopford and Wells study, and are presently used to manage international operations: international divisions, worldwide product divisions, area divisions, matrix structures, and mixed structures. With an international division structure, all foreign subsidiaries report to an international division that is separate from the domestic operations. Communications between the international division and the company's domestic operations are usually poor (Brooke and Remmers, 1970), but there is generally considerable flexibility for foreign subsidiaries to develop strategies that vary according to local conditions. Thus an international division structure facilitates implementing strategies that are responsive to local or national concerns, while it hinders carrying out global product/market strategies.

A worldwide product division structure extends the responsibilities of the domestic product divisions to cover their product lines on a worldwide basis. It tends to centralize and integrate strategic decision-making for a product line, since a single subunit (the product division) has global responsibility for the performance of a product line. This structure is especially suited for realizing global specialization and economies of scale in R&D, manufacturing, and even marketing. At the same time this structure will be less sensitive to local political and economic conditions, since it emphasizes optimizing strategic performance on a global basis.

An area division structure divides the world into geographical areas, each with its own HQ. Each HQ is responsible for all of the company's products and business within its geographical area. Consequently this structure tends to coordinate around, and optimize, performance within a geographical area. Coordination between areas is usually poor (Williams, 1967). To the extent that political and economic conditions within an area are more similar than they are between areas, this structure should lead to strategies that are more responsive to local conditions than those of a worldwide product division structure, but less so than those of an international division structure.

A matrix structure is an overlaying of two of the structures already discussed. Foreign operations report in along two different channels to two different kinds of HQs. For example, in a production division × area division matrix structure, a plastics business in Germany would report in to both the worldwide plastics division HQ (the product channel) and the European area HQ (the geographical area channel). Such a structure can simultaneously develop and implement strategy along two different dimensions. The product division hierarchies will each tend to optimize their product line's performance by coordinating R&D, manufacturing, and perhaps certain aspects of marketing on a global basis. The area division hierarchies, on the other hand, will be largely concerned with exports into and out of a region, achieving economies of scale and market share within a region, and conforming to local government, union, and societal conditions within the region. This added flexibility to simultaneously develop and implement strategy along two different dimensions is not without cost (Davis and Lawrence, 1977; Goggin, 1974). Dual hierarchies involve more managers and staffs, and since the goals and strategic concerns of the two often concern the same resources, considerable managerial effort has to be put into constructive conflict resolution.

Mixed structures involve some foreign operations reporting in to one kind of HQ and other foreign operations reporting in to a different kind of HQ. For example, in a product division and area division mixed structure, the German plastics operations may report in to the worldwide plastics division HQ, while the German cosmetics operations report in to the European HQ. Mixed structures are appropriate when one product line requires a global strategy while another needs to be largely responsive to regional or national conditions.

Hypotheses to be Tested

The Stopford and Wells Model can be represented by the following three hypotheses, which the present study will empirically test:

> Hypothesis 1: Companies with worldwide product division structures will tend to have higher levels of foreign product diversity than companies with international division or area division structures.

> Hypothesis 2: Companies with area division structures will tend to have a greater percentage of foreign sales than companies with international division or product division structures.

> Hypothesis 3: Companies with matrix and mixed structures will tend to have relatively high levels of both foreign product diversity and foreign sales.

Not included in these hypotheses is the influence of a new element of strategy on structure, which was included in the present study after preliminary interviews with MNC executives revealed that they thought it significantly affected the parent-foreign subsidiary relationship. This element was what a number of executives saw as a growing shift from exports (from the parent country) to foreign manufacture and the trans-shipment of products within regions. Pressures for more local manufacture and fewer exports from the parent have been discussed by others (Doz and Prahalad, 1980). While there appear to be various reasons for this increase in foreign manufacturing (e.g., host government pressures for local manufacturing, the emergence of tariff-free trading areas such as the Common Market, lower manufacturing costs), they were not *per se* the subject of this study.

Instead it was the influence that this factor seemed to have on the structuring of the parent-subsidiary relationship that argued for its inclusion in the study.

Not only does foreign manufacturing reduce the operating interdependency between the parent's domestic operations and a foreign subsidiary, it seems to frequently increase interdependency among subsidiaries within a region. Since many foreign markets are too small to justify world-class production facilities, there has been a tendency to concentrate production of a product at one point in a region and then trans-ship such products between countries within a region. This kind of regional interdependency appeared to be most strong in Europe (where it is obviously facilitated by the Common Market), but was also apparent in the Far East and to a lesser extent in parts of Latin America. Managers indicated that growth in foreign manufacturing and regional interdependency required regional plans, staffs, and sometimes regional headquarters.

Method

Sample

The sample contained 24 U.S. and 26 European headquartered MNCs and was spread across the following industry groups: auto/truck, electrical/telecommunications equipment, industrial equipment, chemicals, pharmaceuticals, consumer-packaged goods, and tires. From the *Fortune Directories of the 500 Largest U.S. Industrial Corporations* and the *500 Largest Industrial Corporations Outside the U.S.*, the 50 largest companies in these industries (including three not in these industries) were selected. Companies with less than 15 percent foreign sales, or with only minimal foreign manufacturing, were excluded for not being sufficiently multinational. Several companies were also excluded because it was common knowledge they were experiencing major international operating problems. Thus the sample should be representative of the population of large, successful MNCs. This approach is generally similar to that used in the Stopford and Wells study, which also confined itself to firms in the *Fortune* 500.

Data for the present study were collected through structured interviews conducted at each company's headquarters and from published company documents. Type of structure was first discovered during the interviews. Thirty-four companies had one of the structures covered by the Stopford and Wells Model (see Table 1). Of the remaining 16 MNCs, five had a worldwide functional division structure, one a direct reporting structure, one a structure based on size of foreign subsidiary, and nine some form of matrix or mixed structure that was not based on area divisions and product divisions. Since the purpose of this paper is to deal with those structures represented in the Stopford and Wells Model, only the 34 MNCs with similar structures are used in the subsequent analyses.

Table 1 shows considerable relationship between nationality and the type of structure used by a company. MNCs with an international division or area division structure tend to be U.S. companies, while those with worldwide product division structures tend to be European. As a result of differences in goals and environments, European MNCs may consistently possess different international strategies than U.S. MNCs, and, as a consequence, they may frequently require different structures than U.S. companies. Chandler (1962), Stopford and Wells (1972), and other strategy-structure researchers have argued that all organizations must achieve a satisfactory fit or congruence between their strategies and structures if they are to be successful. The present study takes the view that the nature of this fit between strategy and structure should not differ with the nationality of the parent company, even though strategies and their elements (such as the percentage of foreign sales) will clearly vary with nationality.

Studies of U.K. companies (Channon, 1973); French and German companies (Dyas and Thanheiser, 1976); and Italian companies (Pavan, 1972) have tended to find the same relationships between specific elements of strategy (e.g., product diversity) and structure as Chandler and Stopford and Wells found in U.S. companies. Egelhoff (1982) has advanced a conceptual argument for the invariance of critical strategy-structure relationships across cultures. He argues that the information-processing capacities of a structure are essentially the same whether the structure is populated with Germans or Americans, and, consequently, the capacity of a structure to cope with or fit a given strategy can be generalized across nationalities.

Table 1
STRUCTURE AND NATIONALITY OF COMPANIES

	U.S.	Europe	Total
International divisions	6	1	7
Area divisions	8	2	10
Product divisions	2	10	12
PD × AD matrix		2	2
PD & AD mixed	2	1	3
	18	16	34

Note: PD × AD = Product divisions × Area divisions matrix structures;
        PD & AD = Product divisions & Area divisions mixed structures

Measures

The classification of organizational structure was done by either obtaining, or in some cases constructing with the help of organizational members, organization charts for each company. At least 1/2 hour was spent with organization members directly discussing the structure and how it worked. The total interview time spent in each company varied from 5 to 8 hours, and a great deal of additional data, not used in the present study, was also collected. The collection of this additional data generally provided an opportunity to validate the initial classification of structure.

Foreign product diversity was measured by the number of broad product lines a company offered for sale in two designated foreign countries. In all but a few cases, one was the company's largest European subsidiary and the other was Brazil. Since both tended to be large, actively developed markets for most companies in the sample, the product offerings in these two markets were considered representative of the company's total foreign product offering. Correlation between these two measures was high ($R = 0.87$), and the highest of these two measures was used to represent the company's foreign product diversity.

The number of broad product lines in a subsidiary was measured during interviews with knowledgeable company executives. In order to be considered a separate broad product line, products had to have either a different manufacturing technology (i.e., cannot be made with the same manufacturing facility) or different customers and end uses, or both. For example, in a pharmaceutical company, pharmaceuticals, veterinary supplies and cosmetics are considered separate broad product lines. This approach led to eight categories of foreign product diversity, where the final category was "eight or more" broad product lines (four companies fell into this final category).

The concept of product diversity as an important contingency variable for organizational structure was first defined and operationalized by Chandler (1962). Although he did not develop a quantitative measure of product diversity, he identified its impact on organizational structure in terms of the different kinds of technical knowledge and customer characteristics with which the organization had to cope. The present study's attempt to measure product diversity in terms of technological and market differences is consistent with Chandler's original notion about why product diversity creates pressures for new organizational structures.

The Stopford and Wells study used a different operational measure of foreign product diversity. It measured the number of two-digit SIC codes which were represented by a company's foreign manufacturing. Using this method, Stopford and Wells identified three levels of foreign product diversity, ranging from none (all products in one SIC code) to high (products in three or more SIC codes). Generally, it appears the SIC codes reflect technology and market differences, although the linkage has not been made as explicit as with the broad product line measure used in the present study.

The percentage of foreign sales was measured by the percentage of a company's sales occurring outside the parent country. In instances where a U.S. company's Canadian operations were organizationally treated as a part of U.S. operations and management for the two was integrated, Canadian sales were considered to be domestic rather than foreign. The Stopford and Wells study treated all Canadian sales as domestic sales for U.S. firms.

Some have also wondered whether European countries should not be treated as a part of the domestic market for European MNCs. This is a debatable issue, but at the present time we think European managers tend not to view Europe as a single national market. While European MNCs often treat neighboring countries as markets they understand very well and can depend upon, both strategically and organizationally they tend to respect and distinguish between the national differences more than U.S. or Canadian firms generally do with the North American market. Among the sample companies, the only exception was the way some German MNCs tended to treat the Austrian market.

The size or percentage of foreign manufacturing was operationalized as the percentage of foreign sales accounted for by foreign manufacturing rather than exports from the parent country. This was measured by dividing the value of foreign manufacturing (adjusted by the gross profit margin to make it equivalent to sales volume rather than cost of goods sold) by foreign sales. In a few instances where this information was not available, it was calculated by using foreign manufacturing assets to estimate the percentage of total company manufacturing occurring outside of the parent country, which was then divided by the percentage of foreign sales. This concept has not been previously measured and, of course, was not included in the Stopford and Wells Model.

It is important to notice how the concept of a firm's strategy has been operationally measured in the study. Mintzberg has defined strategy as "consistent patterns in streams of organizational decisions" (1979: 25). If various decisions made in a firm have led it to diversify into many different product areas (as measured by the number of broad product groups or SIC codes in its product line), we say it is pursuing a diversified product strategy. Similarly, if decisions in a firm have led it to develop many foreign manufacturing facilities (as measured by the percentage of foreign manufacturing), we say it pursues a strategy of sourcing foreign sales from local manufacturing rather than from parent country exports. Thus we tend to operationally measure a strategy with its trail of outcomes, because it is too difficult to directly measure the "streams of organizational decisions" in order to discern the "patterns", which actually comprise the strategy. Other research studies that have attempted to quantitatively measure strategy have also tended to measure outcomes rather than decisions (Daniels *et al.*, 1984; Franko, 1976; Stopford and Wells, 1972).

Table 2 shows the correlation among the three contingency variables. As might be expected in relatively mature, successful MNCs, there is a significant positive correlation between foreign product diversity and the percentage of foreign sales, but they are still sufficiently independent elements of a company's strategy to be considered separately.

Results _____

Several types of analyses were performed on the data. First, one-way ANOVA was used to directly test the first two hypotheses developed from the Stopford and Wells Model. The third hypothesis had to be examined visually, since there are not enough firms with matrix and mixed structures in the sample to support statistical analysis. Finally, a multivariate discriminant analysis was used to simultaneously examine the relationship between structure and all three of the contingency variables (elements of strategy).

Testing the Stopford and Wells hypotheses

Table 3 shows the mean levels of the three elements of strategy by type of structure. One-way ANOVA contrasts were used to determine the significance of the differences between international division, area division, and product division structures. Since there are only two firms with matrix structures and three with mixed structures in the sample, significance of difference involving these types of structure could not be measured. Hypothesis 1 stated that MNCs with worldwide product division structures will tend to have more foreign product

Table 2
CORRELATION AMONG THE CONTINGENCY VARIABLES
(N = 28-33)

		1	2
1	Foreign product diversity		
2	Percentage foreign sales	0.49[*]	
3	Percentage foreign manufacturing	−0.16	−0.25

[*]$p < 0.01$

diversity than firms with either an international division or area division structure. The sample data clearly support this hypothesis.

Hypothesis 2 stated that MNCs with area division structures will tend to have a greater percentage of foreign sales than firms with either international division or product division structures. This hypothesis is only partially supported by the data. Companies with area division structures do have a significantly greater percentage of foreign sales than companies with international division structures, but less than companies with worldwide product division structures. The Stopford and Wells study found that companies with area division structures tended to have a greater percentage of foreign sales than companies with product division structures. This was reflected in the model, which further implied that if companies possess both high product diversity and a high percentage of foreign sales, they should tend to have matrix or mixed structures. In the present study, however, the group of MNCs operating with worldwide product division structures tend to possess both high foreign product diversity and a high percentage of foreign sales.

Hypothesis 3 stated that MNCs with matrix and mixed structures will tend to have relatively high levels of both foreign product diversity and foreign sales. While this cannot be tested with any statistical measure, we can examine whether the few matrix and mixed structures in the sample tend to support or contradict this hypothesis. Clearly the two MNCs with matrix structures tend to support it. Their mean foreign product diversity is 6 (ranging from 5 to 7) and their mean percentage of foreign sales is 92 (ranging from 88 to 96).

The three MNCs with mixed product and area division structures provide a somewhat different picture. Their mean foreign product diversity is 4.3 (ranging

Table 3
MEAN VALUES OF ELEMENTS OF STRATEGY BY TYPE OF STRUCTURE

	Mean Values of Elements of Strategy				
	International divisions	Area divisions	Product divisions	PD × AD matrix	PD & AD mixed
Foreign product diversity	1.7	3.4	5.8[a]	6.0	4.3
Percentage foreign sales	34[b]	47	61	92	52
Percentage foreign manufacturing	76	91[c]	61	86	82

[a]Different from area divisions at $p < 0.01$ and international divisions at $p < 0.001$.
[b]Different from area divisions at $p < 0.05$ and product divisions at $p < 0.01$.
[c]Different from product divisions at $p < 0.001$.

from 2 to 7). Their mean percentage of foreign sales is 52 (ranging from 36 to 71). The high variances would seem to indicate that it is impossible to generalize about the levels of foreign product diversity and foreign sales that are or should be associated with mixed structures. Actually, mixed structures are some weighted average of product division and area division structures (i.e., some percentage of an MNC's foreign operations are organized under worldwide product divisions and the remaining percentage is organized under area divisions). Since the weighting will vary from company to company, there is no conceptual basis for specifying a unique set of contingency conditions for mixed structures.

Thus the results support some parts of the Stopford and Wells Model, but raise questions about other parts of the model. Hypothesis 1 is fully supported, while hypotheses 2 and 3 are partially supported. Where the present study primarily differs from the Stopford and Wells study is in how to distinguish between the strategic domains of MNCs with product division structures and those with area division structures. Stopford and Wells concluded that high levels of foreign product diversity lead to product division structures while high levels of foreign sales lead to area division structures. The present study finds that both structures tend to be associated with relatively high percentages of foreign sales, and that only foreign product diversity distinguishes in a significant way between the strategic domains of the two.

Stopford and Wells also suggested that strategies involving high levels of both foreign product diversity and foreign sales could best be addressed with matrix and mixed structures. The present study finds that this particular strategic domain seems to be occupied by MNCs with product division and matrix structures. The present findings also suggest that mixed structure companies can vary widely in their strategic domains (as measured by foreign product diversity and foreign sales) and that they should be excluded from the kind of contingency model Stopford and Wells have attempted to construct.

The influence of size of foreign manufacturing

Table 3 shows how the third element of strategy, percentage of foreign manufacturing, varies across the five structures in the sample. MNCs with area division structures tend to be associated with significantly higher levels of foreign manufacturing than MNCs with worldwide product division structures. As previously discussed, strategies which provide for a high level of foreign manufacturing create high interdependencies between foreign subsidiaries within a region and reduce interdependency between foreign subsidiaries and the parent's domestic operations. The area division structure fits this kind of interdependency. It provides a high level of coordination and information processing between subsidiaries within a region. A lower percentage of foreign manufacturing and more exports means there is less opportunity for economies of scale through regional coordination and integration. Following this strategy implies less interdependency among subsidiaries within a region, and more interdependency between a subsidiary and the parent. The worldwide product division structure provides the kind of coordination and information processing which fits this kind of interdependency. Thus, foreign manufacturing, the third element of strategy, seems to provide a meaningful way of distinguishing between the strategic domains of MNCs with area division structures and those with worldwide product division structures.

A multivariate analysis

In order to examine the fit between structure and the three elements of strategy simultaneously, a multiple discriminant analysis was run using the four types of structure as the groups and the three elements of strategy as the independent variable. Mixed structures were excluded from the analysis, since their high variance along the dimensions of strategy makes them indistinguishable as a separate group or category. The results of the discriminant analysis appear in Table 4. The standardized discriminant coefficients indicate the relative contributions of the independent variables to the discriminant function. Both foreign product diversity and the percentage of foreign sales load heavily on the first function. The second discriminant function can largely be associated with the percentage of foreign manufacturing. It is statistically significant at the $p = 0.11$

Table 4
MULTIPLE DISCRIMINANT ANALYSIS OF THE THREE ELEMENTS OF STRATEGY ON TYPE OF STRUCTURE

Dependent variable: Type of structure

Independent variable	Discriminant function			F-value
	1	2	3	
Foreign product diversity	0.72	0.08	0.70	8.76[***]
Percentage foreign sales	0.59	0.38	−0.71	7.18[**]
Percentage foreign manufacturing	−0.35	0.93	0.14	3.76[*]
Canonical correlation	0.84	0.50	0.27	
Wilks lambda	0.21[***]	0.69[†]	0.93	

[†]$p=0.11$; [*]$p < 0.05$; [**]$p < 0.01$; [***]< 0.001
Note: All values under the three discriminant functions are standardized discriminant coefficients.

level. The third discriminant function is neither meaningful nor statistically significant.

Table 5 shows how successful the discriminant model is in predicting the structure of each company, given knowledge of the three elements of strategy. The discriminant model could predict the actual structure of a company in 74 percent of the cases, which is significantly better than the chance probability of predicting only 31 percent of the cases correctly.

Table 6 shows the centroids of each of the four groups (types of structure) measured along the three discriminant functions. The first discriminant function, which most heavily reflects foreign product diversity, clearly separates product division and product division × area division matrix structures from international division and area division structures. This can be viewed as another test of hypothesis 1. The second discriminant function, which largely reflects the percentage of foreign manufacturing, separates area division and product division × area division matrix structures from international division and product division structures. While the second discriminant function is only significant at the $p = 0.11$ level, it is consistent with the previous significant finding in Table 3, that level of foreign manufacturing (and not level of foreign sales, as hypothesized by Stopford and Wells) best distinguishes between the strategic domains of area division and worldwide product division structures. It is also clear from the analysis of centroids that the strategic domain of the product division × area division matrix structure resembles that of the product division structure when it comes to foreign product diversity (discriminant function 1), and resembles that of the area division structure when it comes to percentage of foreign manufacturing (discriminant function 2). Thus the multivariate

Table 5
PREDICTED TYPE OF STRUCTURE FROM COEFFICIENTS OF DISCRIMINANT FUNCTIONS

Actual group membership	Predicted group membership			
	International divisions	Area divisions	Product divisions	PD × AD matrix
International divisions	6	1	0	0
Area divisions	2	7	1	0
Product divisions	1	1	8	2
PD × AD matrix	0	0	0	2

Note: Structures of MNCs correctly classified = 74 percent.

Table 6

**CENTROIDS OF THE FOUR STRUCTURAL GROUPS MEASURED
ALONG THE DISCRIMINANT FUNCTIONS**

	Discriminant function		
Group	1	2	3
International divisions	−1.90	−0.55	−0.13
Area divisions	−0.63	0.68	0.13
Product divisions	1.47	−0.29	0.09
PD × AD matrix	1.82	0.79	−1.16

discriminant analysis tends to support and extend the conclusions which were drawn from the earlier bivariate analysis.

Discussion and Revision of the Stopford and Wells Model_____

The sample data of the present study have supported some of the hypotheses underlying the Stopford and Wells Model, but failed to support others. Stopford and Wells observed that the strategic domain of international division companies can be characterized by relatively low levels of foreign product diversity and foreign sales. This is confirmed by the present study.

Product divisions versus area divisions

Stopford and Wells further hypothesized that the strategic domains of area division and product division MNCs differed by level of foreign product diversity and level of foreign sales, since these differences occurred in their sample. The present study confirms the hypothesized difference in foreign product diversity, but fails to find a significant difference in terms of percentage of foreign sales. Both area division and product division structures seem to fit strategies that involve relatively high percentages of foreign sales (the mean being 47 percent for area structures and 61 percent for product division structures). This is a highly significant deviation from the Stopford and Wells findings and Model.

The reason why MNCs in the present study with product division structures possess such a high percentage of foreign sales undoubtedly lies in the fact that the majority are European-headquartered, while those in the Stopford and Wells study were all U.S.-headquartered. It is difficult for European companies to become large, prominent MNCs without having a high percentage of foreign sales, due to the limited size of most home country markets. While this explains the relatively higher percentage of foreign sales in European MNCs, it does not explain why these companies operate with worldwide product division structures instead of matrixing or mixing product divisions with area divisions as the Stopford and Wells Model would predict. It would appear that Stopford and Wells have found part of the answer, but not all of it. Clearly worldwide product division structures can and do support international strategies containing high percentages of foreign sales.

The reason this was not apparent in the Stopford and Wells study is because it was confined to U.S. MNCs and did not measure the percentage of foreign manufacturing (a third important element for defining the strategic domain of MNCs). The MNCs with area division structures in both the Stopford and Wells study and the present study tend to have high percentages of foreign sales. The present study, however, found that while this strategic condition is necessary, it is not sufficient to specify an area division structure. Large European MNCs with worldwide product divisions also tend to have a high percentage of foreign sales. It is possible that the Stopford and Wells companies with area division structures also had a high percentage of foreign manufacturing—and that it was this strategic condition along with a high percentage of foreign sales that led to the selection of an area division structure. It is also possible that the Stopford and Wells companies with product division structures possessed relatively lower levels of foreign manufacturing, insufficient to require the kind of coordination and information processing necessary to realize area synergies and economies of scale. Thus, the empirical findings of both the Stopford and Wells study and the present study might be consistent and reconcilable, if all of the data were available.

When MNCs support foreign sales with exports from the parent, the primary interdependency is between a foreign subsidiary and the parent's domestic operations. The worldwide product division structure provides the kind of information processing and integration required to coordinate this kind of interdependency. When the strategy is to support foreign sales with extensive foreign manufacturing, important interdependencies usually develop between foreign subsidiaries within a region or area, as the company now attempts to realize area economies of scale to replace the economies of scale which were formerly provided by centralizing production of the product in the parent. The area division structure provides the kind of information processing and integration required to coordinate this kind of interdependency.

Matrix structures

A second major area where the present study differs from the Stopford and Wells Model deals with matrix structures. Here the difference is not so much contradiction as extension of the model. Both the Stopford and Wells study and the present study observed very few product division × area division matrix structure companies (three and two respectively). This part of the Model must therefore rely more on the logic underlying it, and the consistency of the limited empirical data with that logic, than upon any significant empirical testing. Davis and Lawrence (1977) have argued that matrix structures tend to fit situations requiring a dual focus (e.g., equal pressures to organize around products and areas) and high information processing within the organization. The present study found that product division × area division matrix structures tend to occur when there is both high foreign product diversity and a high percentage of foreign manufacturing. These two elements of strategy require a dual focus and different kinds of information processing. They require the kind of information processing and integration that can only be provided by the simultaneous existence of product divisions and area divisions.

The product division × area division matrix companies in the sample also tend to have a high percentage of foreign sales, as hypothesized by Stopford and Wells. Unlike the Stopford and Wells Model, however, the present study found a high percentage of foreign sales and high foreign product diversity to be necessary but not sufficient conditions for a product division × area division matrix structure. A high percentage of foreign manufacturing is also required. It is, again, quite possible that the three Stopford and Wells matrix companies had a high percentage of foreign manufacturing, but this was not measured. Thus the present study extends the Stopford and Wells Model to include a third precondition for product division × area division matrix structures.

A revised model

Based on the above findings, Figure 2 shows a revised model linking strategy and structure in MNCs. International strategies which involve a relatively low percentage of foreign sales and low foreign product diversity tend to fit international division structures. Such strategies and structures facilitate responsiveness to national interests. Both the Stopford and Wells and the present study supported this relationship.

Strategies involving high foreign product diversity and a low percentage of foreign sales probably tend to be transitional strategies for successful companies, as they attempt to increase their percentage of foreign sales by introducing more product lines. The Stopford and Wells study found these strategies to be associated with worldwide product division structures. The present study, which observed only the largest MNCs, found no companies in this strategic domain and, therefore, could not test this relationship.

Figure 2
REVISED MODEL SHOWING THE RELATIONSHIP BETWEEN STRATEGY AND STRUCTURE IN MULTINATIONAL CORPORATIONS

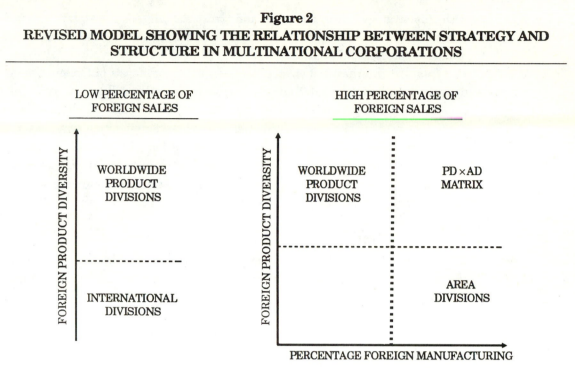

When international strategies involve relatively high percentages of foreign sales, supporting structures tend to be those which provide higher levels of coordination and information processing between a foreign subsidiary and other sectors of the company. It is in this area that the revised model based on the present study alters and extends the Stopford and Wells Model. Worldwide product division structures provide a high level of coordination and information processing between a company's foreign operations and its domestic product operations. This tends to fit strategies involving high foreign product diversity and substantial exports from the parent to the foreign subsidiaries. This is a global strategy that requires a global structure with less potential for national or even regional responsiveness.

When the strategy involves manufacturing a high percentage of the goods needed to support foreign sales abroad, foreign subsidiaries become relatively more interdependent with each other, and interdependency between the foreign and domestic operations of the company decreases for operational matters. The revised model shows that area division structures provide the type of coordination and information processing needed to handle the interdependency associated with this strategy. Such strategies and structures are not global, but regional, and therefore more responsive to regional and national interests than global product strategies and structures.

When the international strategy involves both high levels of foreign product diversity and foreign manufacturing, foreign subsidiaries will tend to be highly dependent on the parent for product and technical knowledge, and highly interdependent with neighboring subsidiaries in the area for operating synergies and economies of scale. This requires the dual coordination and information processing provided by worldwide product divisions and area divisions. The model shows that matrix structures containing both product divisions and area divisions fit such strategies.

Managerial implications

There are a number of managerial implications which follow from this revision of the Stopford and Wells Model. The first is that MNCs do not have to abandon worldwide product division structures when the size of foreign operations becomes large, as Stopford and Wells suggest. There are numerous successful European MNCs with worldwide product division structures. A second implication is that MNCs should not adopt an area division structure if they still rely largely on exports from the parent country to supply foreign operations. Most large U.S. MNCs have developed large foreign manufacturing operations to support their foreign sales, but many European MNCs still rely heavily on exports from the parent country. If these European MNCs move to supply more of their foreign sales with foreign manufacturing, one would expect that ultimately they will also change their structures to either area division or product division × area division matrix structures, to restore good fit between strategy and structure.

Research implications

The primary implication for researchers of strategy and structure in MNCs is the importance of foreign manufacturing as an element of international strategy. This variable appears to significantly modify the impact of the size of foreign operations on structure, and in the present study was the most important discriminator between area division and product division structures. It is possible that foreign manufacturing is operationally measuring some of the difference between global product strategies and more regionally and nationally responsive strategies. Doz (1980), Doz and Prahalad (1980), and Hamel and Prahalad (1983) have generally defined the forces favoring such responsiveness in terms of political and cultural factors. While this is undoubtedly true, the potential for area synergies and economies of scale, as reflected in the size of foreign manufacturing, probably combines with political and cultural factors to encourage regional strategies and structures.

By revising and extending the original Stopford and Wells model, the present study has sought to advance our understanding of critical relationships between strategy and structure in MNCs. The revised model is unfortunately more complex than the original model. It uses a three-dimensional instead of a two-dimensional framework to partition the strategic domains of MNCs. Yet this complexity seems warranted, since it allows the model to identify and take into account increasingly important trends toward globalism and regionalism in international strategies.

Both the recent Daniels *et al.* (1985) study and the present study reveal a strong need for additional research on the more strategically complex portions of the strategy-structure relationship. The present study has suggested that foreign manufacturing is an important aspect of the recent trends toward global strategies and more national and regional responsiveness. Other contingency variables need to be identified and operationalized that will tap other dimensions of these trends. Examples would include the role of international versus domestic R&D in a firm's strategy, and the need to globally transfer technology within and between firms. As mentioned earlier, exploratory research seems to be uncovering increasingly complex forms of international strategy, and extending the strategy-structure paradigm and model to address it is a major challenge facing those who seek to better understand the multinational corporation.

Our bias is to study strategy-structure fit in multinational samples of MNCs. As was the case in the present study, this tends to widen both the range of available international strategies and the number of structural alternatives employed. Both of these encourage the development of more comprehensive strategy-structure models. As international competition has become increasingly multinational (i.e., involving MNCs from different countries) there is an accompanying need to understand both strategy and strategy-structure relationships from a more comprehensive or multinational perspective.

References _____

Bartlett, C. A. "Multinational structural evolution: the changing decision environment in international divisions." Doctoral dissertation, Harvard Business School, Boston, MA, 1979.

Bartlett, C. A. "MNCs: get off the reorganization merry-go-round." *Harvard Business Review,* **61**(2), 1983, pp. 138-146.

Brooke, M. Z. and H. L. Remmers. *The Strategy of Multinational Enterprise.* American Elsevier, New York, 1970.

Chandler, A. D. *Strategy and Structure: Chapters in the History of Industrial Enterprise.* MIT Press, Cambridge, MA, 1962.

Channon, D. F. *The Strategy and Structure of British Enterprise.* Division of Research, Graduate School of Business Administration, Harvard University, Boston, MA, 1973.

Daniels, J. D., R. A. Pitts and M. J. Tretter. "Strategy and structure of U.S. multinationals: An exploratory study." *Academy of Management Journal,* **27**(2), 1984, pp. 292-307.

Daniels, J. D., R. A. Pitts and M. J. Tretter. "Organizing for dual strategies of product diversity and international expansion." *Strategic Management Journal,* **6**, 1985, pp. 223-237.

Davidson, W. H. *Experience Effects in International Investment and Technology Transfer.* UMI Research Press, Ann Arbor, MI, 1980.

Davidson, W. H. and P. Haspeslagh. "Shaping a global product organization." *Harvard Business Review,* **60** (4), 1982, pp. 125-132.

Davis, S. M. and P. R. Lawrence. *Matrix.* Addison-Wesley, Reading, MA, 1977.

Doz, Y. L. "Strategic management in multinational companies." *Sloan Management Review,* Winter 1980, pp. 27-46.

Doz, Y. L. and C. K. Prahalad. "How MNCs cope with host government intervention." *Harvard Business Review,* March-April 1980, pp. 149-157.

Dyas, G. P. and H. T. Thanheiser. *The Emerging European Enterprise: Strategy and Structure in French and German Industry.* Macmillan, London, 1976.

Egelhoff, W. G. "Strategy and structure in multinational corporations: An information-processing approach." *Administrative Science Quarterly,* **27**, 1982, pp. 435-458.

Fouraker, L. E. and J. M. Stopford. "Organizational structure and multinational strategy." *Administrative Science Quarterly,* **13**, 1968, pp. 47-64.

Franko, L. G. *The European Multinationals: A Renewed Challenge to American and British Big Business.* Greylock Publishing, Stamford, CT, 1976.

Galbraith, J. R. and D. A. Nathanson. *Strategy Implementation: The Role of Structure and Process.* West Publishing, St. Paul, MN, 1978.

Goggin, W. C. "How the multidimensional structure works at Dow Corning." *Harvard Business Review,* January-February 1974, pp. 54-65.

Hamel, G. and C. K. Prahalad, "Managing strategic responsibility in the MNC," *Strategic Management Journal,* **4**, 1983, pp. 341-351.

Hout, T., M. E. Porter and E. Rudden. "How global companies win out." *Harvard Business Review,* September-October 1982, pp. 98-108.

Mintzberg, H. *The Structuring of Organizations: A Synthesis of the Research.* Prentice-Hall, Englewood Cliffs, NJ, 1979.

Pavan, F. D. J. "The strategy and structure of Italian enterprise." Doctoral dissertation, Harvard Business School, Boston, MA, 1972.

Rumelt, R. P. *Strategy, Structure, and Economic Performance.* Division of Research. Graduate School of Business Administration, Harvard University, Boston, MA, 1974.

Scott, B. R. Stages of corporate development. 9-371-294. BP.988. Intercollegiate Case Clearinghouse. Harvard Business School, Boston, MA, 1971.

Stopford, J. M., and L. T. Wells, Jr. *Managing the Multinational Enterprise,* Basic Books, New York, 1972.

Williams, C. R. "Regional management overseas," *Harvard Business Review*, **45**, 1967, pp. 87-91.

7. MANAGING ACROSS BORDERS: NEW ORGANIZATIONAL RESPONSES

CHRISTOPHER A. BARTLETT

Christopher A. Bartlett is Associate Professor of Business Administration at the Graduate School of Business Administration, Harvard University. Dr. Bartlett holds the B. Econ. degree from the University of Queensland, Australia, and the M.B.A. and D.B.A. degrees from Harvard University. Prior to his academic career, Dr. Bartlett had extensive management experience in Alcoa, McKinsey and Co., and Baxter Travenol, where he was general manager of the French subsidiary. His research has focused on the strategic and organizational problems facing multinationals.

SUMANTRA GHOSHAL

Sumantra Ghoshal is Assistant Professor of Business Policy at the European Institute of Business Administration (INSEAD) in Fontainebleau, France. Dr. Ghoshal holds the undergraduate degree from the University of Delhi, India. He also holds the S.M. and Ph.D. degrees from the Sloan School of Management, M.I.T., and the D.B.A. degree from the Graduate School of Business Administration, Harvard University. He is co-author of Strategic Control *and has written articles for* Sloan Management Review *and* Harvard Business Review. *He has teaching or consulting relationships with a number of U.S. and European companies.*

The authors have argued that limited organizational capability is the most critical constraint facing international companies that attempt to respond to new strategic demands ("Managing across Borders: New Strategic Requirements," *SMR*, Summer 1987). Here, they describe how companies have overcome this constraint by building a "transnational" organization able to cope with the increasing complexity of the international environment. *Ed.*

In a companion article (Summer 1987), we described how recent changes in the international operating environment have forced companies to optimize *efficiency, responsiveness,* and *learning* simultaneously in their worldwide operations. To companies that previously concentrated on developing and managing one of these capabilities, this new challenge implied not only a total strategic reorientation but a major change in organizational capability, as well.

Implementing such a complex, three-pronged strategic objective would be difficult under any circumstances, but in a worldwide company the task is complicated even further. The very act of "going international" multiplies a company's organizational complexity. Typically, doing so requires adding a third dimension to the existing business- and function-oriented management structure. It is difficult enough balancing product divisions that bring efficiency and focus to domestic product-market strategies with corporate staffs whose functional expertise allows them to play an important counterbalance and control role. The thought of adding capable, geographically oriented management—and maintaining a three-way balance of organizational perspectives and capabilities among product, function, and area—is intimidating to most managers. The difficulty is increased because the resolution of tensions among product, function, and area managers must be accomplished in an organization whose operating units are often divided by distance and time and whose key members are separated by culture and language.

From Unidimensional to Multidimensional Capabilities _____

Faced with the task of building multiple strategic capabilities in highly complex organizations, managers in almost every company we studied made the simplifying assumption that they were faced with a series of dichotomous choices.[1] They discussed the relative merits of pursuing a strategy of national responsiveness as opposed to one based on global integration; they considered whether key assets and resources should be centralized or decentralized; and they debated the need for strong central control versus greater subsidiary autonomy. How a company resolved these dilemmas typically reflected influences exerted and choices made during its historical development. In telecommunications, ITT's need to develop an organization responsive to national political demands and local specification differences was as important to its survival in the pre- and post-World War II era as was NEC's need to built its highly centralized technological manufacturing and marketing skills and resources in order to expand abroad in the same industry in the 1960s and 1970s.

When new competitive challenges emerged, however, such unidimensional biases became strategically limiting. As ITT demonstrated by its outstanding historic success and NEC showed by its more delayed international expansion, strong *geographic management* is essential for development of dispersed responsiveness. Geographic management allows worldwide companies to sense, analyze, and respond to the needs of different national markets.

Effective competitors also need to build strong *business management* with global product responsibilities if they are to achieve global efficiency and integration. These managers act as champions of manufacturing rationalization, product standardization, and low-cost global sourcing. (As the telecommunications switching industry globalized, NEC's organizational capability in this area gave it a major competitive advantage.) Unencumbered by either territorial or functional loyalties, central product groups remain sensitive to overall competitive issues and become agents to facilitate changes that, though painful, are necessary for competitive viability.

Finally, a strong, worldwide *functional management* allows an organization to build and transfer its core competencies—a capability vital to worldwide learning. Links between functional managers allow the company to accumulate specialized knowledge and skills and to apply them wherever they are required in the worldwide operations. Functional management acts as the repository of organizational learning and as the prime mover for its consolidation and circulation within the company. It was for want of a strongly linked research and technical function across subsidiaries that ITT failed in its attempt to coordinate the development and diffusion of its System 12 digital switch.

Thus, to respond to the needs for efficiency, responsiveness, and learning *simultaneously*, the company must develop a multidimensional organization in which the effectiveness of each management group is maintained *and* in which each group is prevented from dominating the others. As we saw in company after company, the most difficult challenge for managers trying to respond to broad, emerging strategic demands was to develop the new elements of multidimensional organization without eroding the effectiveness of their current unidimensional capability.

Overcoming Simplifying Assumptions

For all nine companies at the core of our study, the challenge of breaking down biases and building a truly multidimensional organization proved difficult. Behind the pervasive either/or mentality that led to the development of unidimensional capabilities, we identified three simplifying assumptions that blocked the necessary organizational development. The need to reduce organizational and strategic complexity has made these assumptions almost universal in worldwide companies, regardless of industry, national origin, or management culture.

- There is a widespread, often implicit assumption that roles of different organizational units are uniform and symmetrical; different businesses should be managed in the same way, as should different functions and national operations.

- Most companies, some consciously, most unconsciously, create internal interunit relationships on clear patterns of dependence or independence, on the assumption that such relationships *should* be clear and unambiguous.
- Finally, there is the assumption that one of corporate management's principal tasks is to institutionalize clearly understood mechanisms for decision making and to implement simple means of exercising control.

Those companies most successful in developing truly multidimensional organizations were the ones that challenged these assumptions and replaced them with some very different attitudes and norms. Instead of treating different businesses, functions, and subsidiaries similarly, they systematically *differentiated* tasks and responsibilities. Instead of seeking organizational clarity by basing relationships on dependence or independence, they built and managed *interdependence* among the different units of the companies. And instead of considering control their key task, corporate managers searched for complex mechanisms to *coordinate and coopt* the differentiated and interdependent organizational units into sharing a vision of the company's strategic tasks. These are the central organizational characteristics of what we described in the earlier article as transnational corporations—those most effective in managing across borders in today's environment of intense competition and rapid, often discontinuous change.

From Symmetry to Differentiation _____

Like many other companies we studied, Unilever built its international operations under an implicit assumption of organizational symmetry. Managers of diverse local operating companies in products ranging from packaged foods to chemicals and detergents all reported to strongly independent national managers, who in turn reported through regional directors to the board. In the post-World War II era, the company began to recognize a need to supplement this geographically dominated structure with an organizational ability to capture potential economies and to transfer learning across national boundaries. To meet this need, a few product-coordination groups were formed at the corporate center. But the assumption of organizational symmetry ensured that all businesses were similarly managed, and the number of coordination groups grew from three in 1962 to six in 1969 and to ten by 1977.

By the mid-1970s, however, the entrenched organizational symmetry was being threatened. Global economic disruption caused by the oil crisis dramatically highlighted the very substantial differences in the company's businesses and markets and forced management to recognize the need to differentiate its organizational structures and administrative processes. While standardization, coordination, and integration paid high dividends in the chemical and detergent businesses, for example, important differences in local tastes and national cultures impeded the same degree of coordination in foods. As a result, the roles, responsibilities, and powers of the central product-coordination groups eventually began to diverge as the company tried to shake off the constraint of the symmetry assumption.

But as Unilever tackled the challenge of managing some businesses in a more globally coordinated manner, it was confronted with the question of what to coordinate. Historically, the company's philosophy of decentralized capabilities and delegated responsibilities resulted in most national subsidiaries' becoming fully integrated, self-sufficient operations. While they were free to draw on product technology, manufacturing capabilities, and marketing expertise developed at the center, they were not required to do so, and most units chose to develop, manufacture, and market products as they thought appropriate. Thus functions, too, tended to be managed symmetrically.

Over time, decentralization of all functional responsibilities became increasingly difficult to support. In the 1970s, for example, when arch-competitor Procter & Gamble's subsidiaries were launching a new generation of laundry detergents based on the rape seed formula created by the parent company, most of Unilever's national detergent companies responded with their own products. The cost of developing thirteen different formulations was extremely high, and management soon recognized that not one was as good as P&G's centrally developed product. For the sake of cost control and competitive effectiveness, Unilever had to break with tradition and begin centralizing European product development. The company has since created a system in which central coordination is more normal, although very different for different functions such as basic research, product development, manufacturing, marketing, and sales.

Just as they saw the need to change symmetrical structures and homogeneous processes imposed on different businesses and functions, most companies we observed eventually recognized the importance of differentiating the management of diverse geographic operations. Despite the fact that various national subsidiaries operated with very different external environments and internal constraints, they all traditionally reported through the same channels, operated under similar planning and control systems, and worked under a set of common and generalized mandates.

Increasingly, however, managers recognized that such symmetrical treatment can constrain strategic capabilities. At Unilever, for example, it became clear that Europe's highly competitive markets and closely linked economies meant that its operating companies in that region required more coordination and control than those in, say, Latin America. Little by little, management increased the product-coordination group's role in Europe until they had direct line responsibility for all operating companies in their businesses. Elsewhere, however, national management maintained its historic line management role, and product coordinators acted only as advisers. Unilever has thus moved in sequence from a symmetrical organization to a much more differentiated one: differentiating by product, then by function, and finally by geography.

Recently, within Europe, differentiation by national units has proceeded even further. Operations in "key countries" such as France, Germany, and the United Kingdom are allowed to retain considerably more autonomy than those in "receiver countries" such as Switzerland, Sweden, Holland, and Denmark. While the company's overall commitment to decentralization is maintained, "receiver countries" have gradually become more dependent on the center for direction and support, particularly in the areas of product development and competitive strategy.

Figure 1 is a schematic representation of the different ways in which Unilever manages its diverse businesses, functions, and markets.[2] The vertical axis represents the global integration, and hence of central coordination; the horizontal axis represents the extent of national differentiation, and consequently of the desired influence of subsidiaries in strategic and operational decisions.

The detergent business must be managed in a more globally integrated manner than packaged foods, but also needs a more nationally differentiated strategy than the chemicals business. But not all tasks need to be managed in this differentiated yet coordinated manner: there is little need for national differentiation in research or for global coordination of sales management. And even those functions such as marketing that exhibit the more complex simultaneous demands need not be managed in this way in all national markets. Marketing strategy for export sales can be highly coordinated, while approaches taken in closed markets like India and Brazil can be managed locally. Only in key strategic markets like Germany, the U.K., and France is there a need for differentiated yet coordinated marketing strategies. This flexible and differentiated management approach stands in marked contrast to the standardized, symmetrical approach implied in Unilever's earlier blanket commitment to decentralized responsibility.

But Unilever is far from unique. In all of the companies we studied, senior management was working to differentiate its organizational structure and processes in increasingly sophisticated ways.[3] For example, Philips's consumer electronics division began experimenting with an organization differentiated by

Figure 1
UNILEVER'S DIFFERENTIATED ORGANIZATION

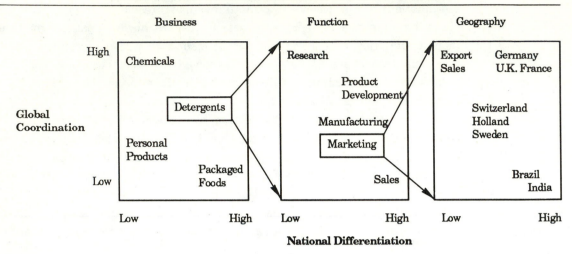

product life-cycle stage—high-tech products like CD players being managed with very different strategies and organization processes from those for stable high-volume products like color TVs, which, in turn, were managed differently from mature and declining products like portable radios. Procter & Gamble is differentiating the roles of its subsidiaries by giving some of them responsibilities as "lead countries" in product strategy development, then rotating that leadership role from product to product.[4] Matsushita differentiates the way it manages its worldwide operations not on the basis of geography, but on the unit's strategic role. (Single-product, wholly owned manufacturing units, the A Group, are managed differently from multiproduct, multifunction companies, the B Group, and from simple sales and marketing subs, the C Group.) L.M. Ericsson, which had centralized most of the basic research on its digital switch, is now decentralizing development and applications responsibilities to a few key country subsidiaries that have the capability to contribute.[5]

Thus, instead of deciding the overall roles of product, functional, and geographic management on the basis of simplistic dichotomies such as global versus domestic businesses or centralized versus decentralized organizations, many companies are creating different levels of influence for different groups as they perform different activities. Doing this allows the relatively underdeveloped management perspectives to be built in a gradual, complementary manner rather than in the sudden, adversarial environment often associated with either/or choices. Internal heterogeneity has made the change from unidimensional to multidimensional organization easier by breaking the problem up into many small, differentiated parts and by allowing for a step-by-step process of organizational change.

From Dependence or Independence to Interdependence _____

The limitations of the assumption of clarity in organizational relationships eventually confronted top managers in the Japanese soap and detergent company Kao. In the early 1980s they began to recognize that their foreign subsidiaries' strong dependence on the parent company provided significant benefits of global efficiency only at the cost of less sensitivity and responsiveness to local market needs. For example, when investigating the reason for the company's slow penetration of the shampoo market in Thailand despite offering a technologically superior product, headquarters managers found that the subsidiary had adopted the product positioning, packaging, and pricing policies developed for the Japanese domestic market. Since local management had been unable to make the necessary local adaptations, managers were brought in from headquarters to identify the source of the problem and to make necessary changes in the marketing mix.

In other companies we studied—Unilever and ITT, for example—clarity of organizational relationships was achieved by giving foreign subsidiaries substantial independence. But, as our earlier discussion of Unilever illustrated, such organizational clarity was achieved at the cost of substantial inefficiency; individual subsidiaries often reinvented the wheel or operated at suboptimal scale.

New strategic demands make organizational models of simple interunit dependence *or* independence inappropriate. The reality of today's worldwide competitive environment demands collaborative information sharing and problem solving, cooperative support and resource sharing, and collective action and implementation. Independent units risk being picked off one-by-one by competitors whose coordinated global approach gives them two important strategic advantages—the ability to integrate research, manufacturing, and other scale-efficient operations, and the opportunity to cross-subsidize the losses from battles in one market with funds generated by profitable operations in home markets or protected environments.[6] The desire to capture such strategic benefits was one of Philips's main motivations as it attempted to coordinate the competitive responses of historically independent national organizations.

On the other hand, foreign operations totally dependent on a central unit must deal with problems reaching beyond the loss of local market responsiveness described in the Kao example. They also risk being unable to respond effectively to strong national competitors or to sense potentially important local market or technical intelligence. This was the problem Procter & Gamble's Japan subsidiary faced in an environment where local competitors began challenging P&G's previously secure position with successive, innovative product changes and novel market strategies, particularly in the disposable diapers business. After suffering major losses in market share, management recognized that a local operation focused primarily on implementing the company's classic marketing strategy was no longer sufficient; the Japanese subsidiary needed the freedom and incentive to be more innovative. Not only to ensure the viability of the Japanese subsidiary, but also to protect its global strategic position, P&G realized it had to expand the role of the local unit and change its relationship with the parent company to enhance two-way learning and mutual support.

But it is not easy to change relationships of dependence or independence that have been built up over a long history. Many companies have tried to address the increasing need for interunit collaboration by adding layer upon layer of administrative mechanisms to foster greater cooperation. Top managers have extolled the virtues of teamwork and have even created special departments to audit management response to this need. In most cases these efforts to obtain cooperation by fiat or by administrative mechanisms have been disappointing. The independent units have feigned compliance while fiercely protecting their independence. The dependent units have found that the new cooperative spirit implies little more than the right to agree with those on whom they depend.

Yet some companies have gradually developed the capability to achieve such cooperation and to build what Rosabeth Kanter calls an "integrative organization."[7] Of the companies we studied, the most successful did so not by creating new units, but by changing the basis of the relationships among product, functional, and geographic management groups. From relations based on dependence or independence, they moved to relations based on formidable levels of explicit, genuine interdependence. In essence, they made integration and collaboration self-enforcing by making it necessary for each group to cooperate in order to achieve its own interests. Companies were able to create such interdependencies in many ways, as two brief examples will illustrate.

- NEC has developed reciprocal relationships among different parts of its organizations by creating a series of internal quasi markets. It builds cooperation between the R&D function and the different product groups by allocating only a part of the R&D budget directly to the company's several central laboratories. This portion is used to support basic and applied research in core technologies of potential value to the corporation as a whole. The remaining funds are allocated to the product groups to support research programs that reflect their priorities. In response to the product divisions' proposed projects, each research group puts forward proposals that it feels will lead to the desired product or process improvements. What follows is a negotiation process that results in the product divisions' "buying" some of the proposals put up by the laboratories, while different R&D groups adopt some of the projects demanded by the product managers. In other words, NEC has created an internal market for ensuring that research is relevant to market needs. (A similar process seems to have had comparable success at Matsushita.)[8]

- Procter & Gamble employs an entirely different approach to creating and managing interdependencies. In Europe, for example, it formed a number of Eurobrand teams for developing product-market strategies for different product lines.[9] Each team is headed by the general manager of a subsidiary that has a particularly well-developed competence in that business. It also includes the appropriate product and advertising managers from the other subsidiaries and relevant functional managers from the company's European headquarters. Each team's effectiveness clearly depends on the involvement and support provided by its members and, more important, by the organizational units they represent. Historically, the company's various subsidiaries had little incentive to cooperate. Now, however, the success of each team—and the reputation of the general manager heading it—depends on the support of other subsidiaries; this has made cooperation self-enforcing. Each general manager is aware that the level of support and commitment he can expect from the other members of the Eurobrand team depends on the support and contribution the product managers from his subsidiaries provide to the other teams. The interdependencies of these Eurobrand teams were able to foster teamwork driven by individual interests.

In observing many such examples of companies building and extending interdependence among units, we were able to identify three important flows that seem to be at the center of the emerging organizational relationships. Most fundamental was the product interdependence that most companies were building as they specialized and integrated their worldwide manufacturing operations to achieve greater efficiency, while retaining sourcing flexibility and sensitivity to host country interests.[10] The resulting *flow of parts, components, and finished goods* increased the interdependence of the worldwide operations in an obvious and fundamental manner.

We also observed companies developing a resource interdependence that often contrasted sharply with earlier policies that had either encouraged local self-sufficiency or required the centralization of all surplus resources. Systems such as NEC's internal quasi markets were designed to develop a greater *flow of funds, skills, and other scarce resources* among organizational units.

Finally, the worldwide diffusion of technology, the development of international markets, and the globalization of competitive strategies have meant that vital strategic information now exists in many different locations worldwide. Furthermore, the growing dispersion of assets and delegation of responsibilities to foreign operations have resulted in the development of local knowledge and expertise that has implications for the broader organization. With these changes, the need to manage the *flow of intelligence, ideas, and knowledge* has become central to the learning process and has reinforced the growing interdependence of worldwide operations, as P&G's Eurobrand teams illustrate.

It is important to emphasize that the relationships we are highlighting are different from the interdependencies commonly observed in multiunit organizations. Traditionally, MNC managers have attempted to highlight what has been called "pooled interdependence" to make subunit managers responsive to global rather than local interests. (Before the Euroteam approach, for instance, P&G's European vice president often tried to convince independent-minded subsidiary managers to transfer surplus generated funds to other more needy subsidiaries, in the overall corporate interest, arguing that, "Someday when you're in need they might be able to fund a major product launch for you.")

As the example illustrates, pooled interdependence is often too broad and amorphous to affect day-to-day management behavior. The interdependencies we described earlier are more clearly reciprocal, and each unit's ability to achieve its goals is made conditional upon its willingness to help other units achieve their own goals. Such interdependencies more effectively promote the organization's ability to share the perspectives and link the resources of different components, and thereby to expand its organizational capabilities.[11]

From Control to Coordination and Cooption _____

The simplifying assumptions of organizational symmetry and dependence (or independence) had allowed the management processes in many companies to be dominated by simple controls—tight operational controls in subsidiaries dependent on the center, and a looser system of administrative or financial controls in decentralized units.[12] When companies began to challenge the assumptions underlying organizational relationships, however, they found they also had to adapt their management processes. The growing interdependence of organizational units strained the simple control-dominated systems and underlined the need to supplement existing processes with more sophisticated ones. Furthermore, the differentiation of organizational tasks and roles amplified the diversity of management perspectives and capabilities and forced management to differentiate management processes.

As organizations became, at the same time, more diverse and more interdependent, there was an explosion in the number of issues that had to be linked, reconciled, or integrated. The rapidly increasing flows of goods, resources, and information among organizational units increased the need for *coordination* as a central management function. But the costs of coordination are high, both in financial and human terms, and coordinating capabilities are always limited. Most companies, though, tended to concentrate on a primary means of coordination and control—"the company's way of doing things." (At ITT it was through "the system," as Harold Geneen used to call his sophisticated set of controls, while at Kao it was primarily through centralization of decisions.) Clearly, there was a need to develop multiple means of coordination, to rank the demands for coordination, and to allocate the scarce coordinating resources. The way in which one of our sample companies developed its portfolio of coordinative processes illustrates the point well.

During the late 1970s and early 1980s, Philips had gradually developed some sophisticated means of coordination. This greatly helped the company shape its historically evolved, nationally centered organization into the kind of multidimensional organization it needed to be in the 1980s. Coordinating the flow of goods in a global sourcing network is a highly complex logistical task, but one that can often be formalized and delegated to middle and lower-level management. By standardizing product specifications and rationalizing sourcing patterns through designating certain plants as international production centers (IPCs), Philips facilitated goods-flow coordination. By making these flows reasonably constant and forecastable, the company could manage them almost entirely through formal systems and processes. These became the main coordination mechanisms in the company's attempt to increase the integration of worldwide sourcing of products and components.

Coordinating the flow of financial, technical, and human resources, however, was not so easily routinized. Philips saw the allocation of these scarce resources as a reflection of key strategic choices and therefore managed the coordination process by centralizing many decisions. The board became heavily involved in major capital budgeting decisions; the product divisions reasserted control over product development, a process once jealously guarded by the national organizations; and the influential corporate staff bureau played a major role in personnel assignments and transfers.

But while goods flows could be coordinated through formalization, and resource flows through centralization, critical information flows were much more difficult to manage. The rapid globalization of the consumer electronics industry in the 1970s forced Philips to recognize the need to move strategic information and proprietary knowledge around the company much more quickly. While some routine data could be transferred through normal information systems, much of the information was so diverse and changeable that establishing formal processes was impossible. While some core knowledge had to be stored and transferred through corporate management, the sheer volume and complexity of information—and the need for its rapid diffusion—limited the ability to coordinate through centralization. Philips found that the most effective way to manage complex flows of information and knowledge was through various socialization processes: the transfer of people, the encouragement of informal communication channels that fostered information exchange, or the creation of forums that facilitated interunit learning.

Perhaps most well known is the company's constant worldwide transfer and rotation of a group of senior managers (once referred to internally as the "Dutch Mafia," but today a more international group) as a means of transferring critical knowledge and experience throughout the organization. Philips also made more extensive use of committees and task forces than any other company we studied. Although the frequent meetings and constant travel were expensive, the company benefited not only from information exchange but also from the development of personal contacts that grew into vital information channels.

In other companies, we saw a similar broadening of administrative processes as managers learned to operate with previously underutilized means of coordination. Unilever's heavy reliance on the socialization of managers to provide the coordination "glue" was supplemented by the growing role of the central product-coordination departments. In contrast, NEC reduced central management's coordination role by developing formal systems and social processes in a way that created a more robust and flexible coordinative capability.

Having developed diverse new means of coordination, management's main task is to carefully ration their usage and application. As the Philips example illustrates, it is important to distinguish where tasks can be formalized and managed through systems, where social linkages can be fostered to encourage informal agreements and cooperation, and where the coordination task is so vital or sensitive that it must use the scarce resource of central management arbitration.[13]

While the growing interdependence of organizational units forces the development of more complex administrative processes, the differentiation of roles and responsibilities forces management to change the way it uses the new coordination and control mechanisms. Even though they recognize the growing diversity of tasks facing them, a surprising number of companies have had great difficulty in differentiating the way they manage products, functions, or geographic units. The simplicity of applying a single planning and control system across businesses and the political acceptability of defining uniform job descriptions for all subsidiary heads were often allowed to outweigh the clear evidence that the relevant business characteristics and subsidiary roles were vastly different.

We have described briefly how companies began to remedy this situation by differentiating roles and responsibilities within the organization. Depending on their internal capabilities and on the strategic importance of their external environments, organizational units might be asked to take on roles ranging from that of strategic leader with primary corporatewide responsibility for a particular business or function, to simple implementer responsible only for executing strategies and decisions developed elsewhere.

Clearly, these roles must be managed in quite different ways. The unit with strategic leadership responsibility must be given freedom to develop responsibility in an entrepreneurial fashion, yet must also be strongly supported by headquarters. For this unit, operating controls may be light and quite routine, but coordination of information and resource flows to and from the unit will probably require intensive involvement from senior management. In contrast, units with implementation responsibility might be managed through tight operating controls, with standardized systems used to handle much of the coordination—primarily of goods flows. Because the tasks are more routine, the use of scarce coordinating resources could be minimized.

Differentiating organizational roles and management processes can have a fragmenting and sometimes demotivating effect, however. Nowhere was this more clearly illustrated than in the many companies that unquestioningly assigned units the "dog" and "cash cow" roles defined by the Boston Consulting Group's growth-share matrix in the 1970s.[14] Their experience showed that there is another equally important corporate management task that complements and facilitates coordination effectiveness. We call this task *cooption*: the process of uniting the organization with a common understanding of, identification with, and commitment to the corporation's objectives, priorities, and values.

A clear example of the importance of cooption was provided by the contrast between ITT and NEC managers. At ITT, corporate objectives were communicated more in financial than in strategic terms, and the company's national entities identified almost exclusively with their local environment. When corporate management tried to superimpose a more unified and integrated global strategy, its local subsidiaries neither understood nor accepted the need to do so. For years they resisted giving up their autonomy, and management was unable to replace the interunit rivalry with a more cooperative and collaborative process.

In contrast, NEC developed an explicitly defined and clearly communicated global strategy enshrined in the company's "C&C" motto—a corporatewide dedication to building business and basing competitive strategy on the strong link between computers and communications. For over a decade, the C&C philosophy was constantly interpreted, refined, elaborated, and eventually institutionalized in organizational units dedicated to various C&C missions (e.g., the C&C Systems Research Laboratories, the C&C Corporate Planning Committee, and eventually the C&C Systems Division). Top management recognized that one of its major tasks was to inculcate the worldwide organization with an understanding of the C&C strategy and philosophy and to raise managers' consciousness about the global implications of competing in these converging businesses. By the mid-1980s, the company was confident that every NEC employee in every operating unit had a clear understanding of NEC's global strategy as well as of his or her role in it. Indeed, it was this homogeneity that allowed the company to begin the successful decentralization of its strategic tasks and the differentiation of its management processes.

Thus the management process that distinguished transnational organizations from simpler unidimensional forms was one in which control was made less dominant by the increased importance of interunit integration and collaboration. These new processes required corporate management to supplement its control role with the more subtle tasks of coordination and cooption, giving rise to a much more complex and sophisticated management process.

Sustaining a Dynamic Balance: Role of the "Mind Matrix" _____

Developing multidimensional perspectives and capabilities does not mean that product, functional, and geographic management must have the same level of influence on all key decisions. Quite the contrary. It means that the organization must possess a differentiated influence structure—one in which different groups have different roles for different activities. These roles cannot be fixed but must change continually to respond to new environmental demands and evolving industry characteristics. Not only is it necessary to prevent any one perspective from dominating the others, it is equally important not to be locked into a mode of operation that prevents reassignment of responsibilities, realignment of relationships, and rebalancing of power distribution. This ability to manage the multidimensional organization capability in a flexible manner is the hallmark of a transnational company.

In the change processes we have described, managers were clearly employing some powerful organizational tools to create and control the desired flexible management process. They used the classic tool of formal structure to strengthen, weaken, or shift roles and responsibilities over time, and they employed management systems effectively to redirect corporate resources and to channel information in a way that shifted the balance of power. By controlling the ebb and flow of responsibilities, and by rebalancing power relationships, they were able to prevent any of the multidimensional perspectives from atrophying. Simultaneously, they prevented the establishment of entrenched power bases.

But the most successful companies had an additional element at the core of their management processes. We were always conscious that a substantial amount of senior management attention focused on the *individual* members of the organization. NEC's continual efforts to inculcate all corporate members with a common vision of goals and priorities; P&G's careful assignment of managers to teams and task forces to broaden their perspectives; Philips's frequent use of conferences and meetings as forums to reconcile differences; and Unilever's extensive use of training as a powerful socialization process and its well-planned career path management that provided diverse experience across businesses, functions, and geographic locations—all are examples of companies trying to develop multidimensional perspectives and flexible approaches at the level of the individual manager.

What is critical, then, is not just the structure, but also the mentality of those who constitute the structure. The common thread that holds together the diverse tasks we have described is a managerial mindset that understands the need for multiple strategic capabilities, that is able to view problems from both local and global perspectives, and that accepts the importance of a flexible approach. This pattern suggests that managers should resist the temptation to view their task in the traditional terms of building a formal global matrix structure—an organizational form that in practice has proven extraordinarily difficult to manage in the international environment. They might be better guided by the perspective of one top manager who described the challenge as "creating a matrix in the minds of managers."

Our study has led us to conclude that a company's ability to develop transnational organizational capability and management mentality will be the key factor that separates the winners from the mere survivors in the emerging international environment.

References

1. The findings presented in this article are based on a three-year research project on the organization and management of multinational corporations. A description of the three-phase study and of the nine American, European, and Japanese MNCs that made up the core of the clinical research stage is contained in the companion article, "Managing across Borders: New Strategic Requirements" (Summer 1987). Complete findings will be presented in the forthcoming book, *Managing across Borders: The Transnational Solution* (Boston: Harvard Business School Press, forthcoming).

2. This global integration/national responsiveness framework was first applied to the analysis of MNC tasks by Prahalad. See C. K. Prahalad, "The Strategic Process in a Multinational Corporation" (Boston: Harvard Business School, unpublished doctoral dissertation, 1976).

3. Working with a group of Swedish companies, Hedlund has come to similar conclusions. He describes MNCs with dispersed capabilities and differentiated operations as "heterarchies." See G. Hedlund, "The Hypermodern MNC—A Heterarchy?" *Human Resource Management*, Spring 1986, pp. 9-35.

4. Rugman and Poynter have observed a similar phenomenon in the trend toward assigning mature national subsidiaries worldwide responsibility for products with worldwide markets. See A. M. Rugman and T. A. Poynter, "World Product Mandates: How Will Multinationals Respond?" *Business Quarterly*, October 1982, pp. 54-61.

5. This issue of differentiation in the roles and responsibilities of MNC subsidiaries has been discussed and a normative framework for creating such differentiation has been proposed in C. A. Bartlett and S. Ghoshal, " Tap Your Subsidiaries for Global Reach," *Harvard Business Review*, November-December 1986, pp. 87-94.

6. Such global competitive strategies have been described extensively by many authors. See, for example, T. Hout, M. E. Porter, and E. Rudden, "How Global Companies Win Out," *Harvard Business Review*, September-October 1982, pp. 98-108; and G. Hamel and C. K. Prahalad, "Do You Really Have a Global Strategy?" *Harvard Business Review*, July-August 1985, pp. 139-148.

7. See R. M. Kanter, *The Change Masters* (New York: Simon & Schuster, 1983).

8. The use of such internal quasi market mechanisms as a means of managing interdependencies has been richly described by Westney and Sakakibara. See D. E. Westney and K. Sakakibara, "The Role of Japan-Based R&D in Global Technology Strategy," *Technology in Society* 7 (1985): 315-330.

9. For a full description of the development of Eurobrand in P&G, see C. A. Bartlett, "Procter & Gamble Europe: Vizir Launch" (Boston: Harvard Business School, Case Services #9-384-139).

10. Kogut provides an excellent discussion on how multinational corporations can develop operational flexibility using a worldwide configuration of specialized resource capabilities linked through an integrated management system. See B. Kogut, "Designing Global Strategies: Profiting from Operational Flexibility," *Sloan Management Review,* Fall 1985, pp. 27-38.

11. The distinction among sequential, reciprocal, and pooled interdependencies has been made in J. D. Thompson, *Organizations in Action* (New York: McGraw-Hill, 1967).

12. The role of headquarters management in establishing control over worldwide operations and the means by which it is done have been richly described in Y. L. Doz and C. K. Prahalad, "Headquarters Influence and Strategic Control in MNCs," *Sloan Management Review*, Fall 1981, pp. 15-30.

13. The use of centralization, formalization, and socialization as means of coordination has been discussed by many authors, including P.M. Blau and R. A. Schoenherr, *The Structure of Organizations* (New York: Basic Books, 1971); and W. G. Ouchi, "Markets, Bureaucracies, and Clans," *Administrative Science Quarterly* 25 (March 1980): 129-141.

   In the specific context of the multinational corporation, the process implications of these mechanisms were described by Bartlett in a model that distinguished "substantive decision management," "temporary coalition management," and "decision context management" as alternative management process modes in MNCs. See C. A. Bartlett, "Multinational Structural Evolution: The Changing Decision Environments" (Boston: Harvard Business School, unpublished doctoral dissertation, 1979).

   See also the contributions of G. Hedlund, T. Kogono, and L. Leksell in *The Management of Headquarters—Subsidiary Relationships in MNCs,* ed. L. Otterbeck (London: Gower Publishing, 1981); and Doz and Prahalad (Fall 1981).

14. See P. Haspeslagh, "Portfolio Planning: Uses and Limits," *Harvard Business Review*, January-February 1982, pp. 58-73.

IV ____ OWNERSHIP AND CONTROL_____

Control and Coordination in Multinational Corporations
David Cray

Expatriate Reduction and Strategic Control in American Multinational Corporations
Stephen J. Kobrin

Joint Ventures as Self-Organizing Systems: A Key to Successful Joint Venture Design and Implementation
Peter Lorange and Gilbert J. B. Probst

Common Mistakes of Joint Venture Experienced Firms
Marjorie A. Lyles

8. CONTROL AND COORDINATION IN MULTINATIONAL CORPORATIONS

DAVID CRAY

David Cray is Assistant Professor of Human Resource Management at the Carleton University School of Business, Ottawa, Canada. He is currently co-authoring a book based on the Bradford Studies of Strategic Decision Making. He is also engaged in extending the concepts outlined in this paper through a study of Canadian subsidiaries of U.S.-based multinationals.

The integration of French and British subsidiaries into U.S.-based multinationals is examined. A theory linking the use of control and coordination mechanisms to the need for predictability, flexibility, and the cost of achieving them is investigated by relating organizational structure, technology, foreign commitment, financial performance, and nationality to the use of coordination and control.

Introduction

For any large complex organization the problem of ensuring that its constituent parts act in accordance with overall policy is a central and continuing concern. The specialization of subunits which allows the organization to undertake complicated tasks requires an equally developed system of integration to bond them into an operational whole [Lawrence and Lorsch 1967, pp. 8-13; Blau and Schoenherr 1971, p. 8]. In addition to the differentiation stemming from functional specialization, the organization is subject to divisive tendencies in the form of departmental interests, competing functional goals, and differential demands from the environment that lead subunits to pursue their own strategies [Karpik 1978; Pfeffer 1978, pp. 6-7]. To overcome these centrifugal forces the leaders of the organization must maintain a system of integration that minimizes overlap and conflict among its varied subunits while allowing them the necessary flexibility to adapt to their particular environments.

Reprinted from *Journal of International Business Studies*, Fall 1984, pp. 85-98 by permission of the publisher.

Thanks to Michael Aiken, Peter Frost, Moses Kiggundu, David Hickson, Geoff Mallory, and David Wilson for their comments on earlier versions of this paper. This research was supported by a grant from the National Science Foundation and a grant by the Social Science Research Council.

When the organization in question is a multinational corporation (MNC), the centrifugal forces tend to be more acute, increasing the problems of integration [Stopford and Wells 1972, pp. 18-19]. The foreign subsidiary is subject to the laws of the country in which it is located (the host country) as well as certain statutes of the nation in which the parent is domiciled (the home country). The foreign subsidiaries must be differentiated enough to confront cultures, markets, and customs that contrast markedly with those of the home country, but this flexibility has to be accommodated within a structure that will provide the maximum contribution to corporate performance. Given these difficulties, the integration system of the multinational corporation has grown correspondingly complex [Wilkins 1974, p. 419].

The issue of integration of multinational corporations is of interest not only to managers within the firm but to policy makers in home and host countries as well [United Nations 1978, pp. 19-28]. The degree to which control is retained by the center of the MNC, the supranational hierarchical levels above the foreign subsidiary, conditions the impact the host country may have on its foreign investors. The voluminous literature on the multinational corporation contains a wide range of assumptions as to how closely foreign subsidiaries are controlled, but there is little empirical work to support any of these assertions [Goehle 1980, p. 8]. In this paper the results of an empirical study of the integration processes in multinational corporations are reported. A number of factors that have been associated with the degree of integration are examined, and the relationship between 2 processes of integration—coordination and control—is explored.

Processes of Integration _____

The integration of subunits into large organizations depends mainly on the manipulation of 2 processes: control and coordination [Katz and Kahn 1966, pp. 94-95, 201; Hage, Aiken, and Marrett 1971]. Both processes are central to the organizational literature and have formed, implicitly or explicitly, key elements in theories of organizational behavior. Although there has been some overlap in their usage, they have acquired distinct and generally consistent definitions. Control is seen as a process which brings about adherence to a goal or target through the exercise of power or authority [Etzioni 1965]. Coordination is seen more as an enabling process which provides the appropriate linkage between different task units within the organization [Van de Ven, Delbecq, and Koenig 1976; Tuggle 1978, p. 150]. The relationship between control and coordination in organizations has been subject to some theoretical conjecture but virtually no empirical investigation [Hage, Aiken, and Marrett 1971].

With few exceptions (Lawrence and Lorsch [1967] and Thompson [1967] are the most notable) the study of organizational control and coordination has centered on the behavior of individuals in organizations. As a number of theorists have observed, however, the control of the individual is carried out in a framework of organizational control that exists on several connected levels [Edwards 1978; Clegg 1979, pp. 125-143]. For the multinational corporation, integration is clearly more than the sum of relationships between individuals at adjoining levels in the hierarchy. Control and coordination of specific individuals are part of the integration system, but patterns exist that will persist despite changing personal relationships and that will change while the personnel remain the same. By conceptualizing integration at this level, the larger problems of integration that confront the manager can be more clearly understood.

Control

Within the organizational literature, research has focused mainly on the use of different types of control. Some of the typologies generated have been purely speculative [Etzioni 1965] while others have been linked to empirical studies. In many of these studies the use of a particular type of control has depended on the availability of that control mechanism [Hage 1974, pp. 29-36; Ouchi 1977]. For the multinational manager attempting to control foreign subsidiaries the issue is not one of availability. There are any number of functions that the subsidiary must perform in concert with the parent that may serve as avenues of control. Although the degree to which control of functions or groups of functions is used to integrate subsidiaries is an important research issue, the prior question from both a policy and a theoretical standpoint is the degree of total control exerted over the subunit. This, in turn, is but half of the larger question of the level of integration that is maintained between parent and subsidiary.

The purpose of control is to minimize idiosyncratic behavior and to hold individuals or groups to enunciated policy, thus making performance predictable [Tannenbaum 1968, p.3]. That the parent firm does not attempt to maximize predictability through control is due to 2 considerations that are apt to be overlooked when control is conceptualized at the individual level. The first of these is flexibility. That an organization must maintain freedom of action when faced with a changeable environment has become an accepted tenet of organizational theory [Burns and Stalker 1961; Lawrence and Lorsch 1967]. When the subunit's environment is substantially different from that of the parent corporation, flexibility becomes even more necessary. The subsidiary itself is a complex organization, and if every action must be cleared with a higher level, reaction time is slowed and resources are wasted in endless communication.

The second constraint on predictability is the cost of control. When control of individuals is considered, the marginal cost of increased control is assumed to be negligible. In his discussion of the integration of subunits in an organization, however, Thompson [1967, pp. 57-59] makes cost one of the primary considerations. He argues that by grouping complementary functions, the cost of communication can be minimized and the cost of integration lowered. For the multinational corporation the cost of communication for an increment of control may involve anything from a personal visit across thousands of miles to a fully integrated computer system linking several countries. The costs associated with such control efforts are hardly trivial. The level of control exerted over a subunit will therefore represent a compromise between the desire for predictability, the need for flexibility, and the cost of maintaining control.

Coordination

Although coordination has also been the subject of some theoretical attention, very little empirical work has been attempted. Most of the work of both types is based on a few observations by March and Simon [1958, pp. 160]. Thompson [1967] considerably expanded on these observations and modified them into 3 types: coordination by plan, by mutual adjustment, and by standardization. His formulation has the advantage of being oriented toward the subunit level but the disadvantage of being extremely difficult to operationalize. In one of the few empirical studies of coordination, Van de Ven and his colleagues [1976] proposed 3 types of coordination at the individual level. They distinguished among an impersonal type—planning—and 2 personal types—personal and groups.

For the multinational corporation the issue is not so much the type of coordination utilized, but the amount or degree of coordination. The primary consideration for the multinational firm (or any large, dispersed organization) is that the subunits be successfully integrated into the larger organization. As with control there are a number of functions, the coordination of which leads to a higher level of integration. The actual mechanism used is largely irrelevant since the important issue is the degree to which the subsidiary is tied into the overall structure of the firm. It makes relatively little difference whether the delivery of raw materials from subsidiary A to subsidiary B is accomplished through personal or impersonal coordination; the important thing for both subsidiaries and for their integration into the total organization is that this relationship exists.

Coordination's contribution to integration has 2 dimensions. First, with how many other units does the subsidiary coordinate functions? The more extensive the network of reciprocal obligations, the greater will be the burden of coordination, the more integrated the subsidiary will be, and the less room for independent maneuver it will enjoy. Similarly, if the subsidiary coordinates a number of different functions with a given number of other units, it will be more enmeshed in the coordination network than if the coordination were confined to a single function. The breadth of coordination (the number of units in the coordination network) and the diversity of coordination (the number of functions coordinated) will be important aspects of the degree to which the subsidiary is integrated into the multinational corporation.

The attempt to integrate through coordination is subject to the same cost and flexibility constraints as control. The more complicated the coordination network, the less flexibility the subsidiary has to react to local events. For example, a producing subsidiary that supplies goods to several other units for resale cannot quickly change its product mix. It would first have to negotiate with these subsidiaries to accept a supply of new products or find a new source. Similarly, increased coordination will involve increased costs. Coordination networks require communication among the coordinating parties to maintain an even flow of goods, services, and information. The more extensive the network, the more communication is required and the greater its cost.

The Relationship Between Control and Coordination _____

The 2 integration processes described in the preceding sections provide very different solutions for the problem of binding subunits into the larger organization. Control is a more direct intervention into the operations of the subsidiary. It can be very specific and limited to the short term. As such it has a tendency to be more costly because of the direct forms of communication that are required. There are control mechanisms, such as the annual budgeting with monthly reporting system that characterizes most American firms, which do not require direct intervention for their success. To agree upon a budget generally necessitates a great deal of communication, however, often culminating in face-to-face meetings. To change a budget or the monitoring and reporting system associated with it can be equally expensive. Control, as it is conceptualized for this paper, tends to be direct, costly, and episodic when compared to coordination. Coordination is distinguished not by direct intervention but by situating the subsidiary in a network of responsibilities to other parts of the firm. The pattern of coordination can be imposed through an act of control, but the resulting responsibilities are rooted in coordination. Coordination is generally less costly because the communication required is minimal and routine. At the same time it is a less precise method of integration than control in the sense that a change in any part of the coordination network is likely to have reverberations throughout that network.

Compared to control the coordination is less direct, less costly, and has a longer time horizon.

Given the distinction between coordination and control, what is the relationship between them and how is it associated with other aspects of the organization? To some extent they must act as substitutes for one another in that each can integrate the subsidiary into the firm. This would imply that for a given level of integration the 2 processes would likely be negatively related. At the same time it seems unlikely that over a wide range of integration one or the other process would tend to dominate. The cost of a high level of control would argue for a substitution of coordination where possible. The limited flexibility of coordination would require control to complement its integrative function. Over a wide range of integration, from subunits that are closely integrated to those which are relatively autonomous, the 2 processes should be positively related because they serve complementary roles in the overall integration strategy. Because the subsidiaries examined in this study do show such a wide range, it is predicted that the overall relationship will be positive.

Hypotheses

From the description given above, one would expect that control would be more apt to be used when the subsidiary is likely to deviate from overall organizational policy or when the need for predictability is high. For multinational corporations this will occur when the subsidiary is seen to be in danger of capture by local political, cultural, or economic forces. Because control is seen to be vertical, specific, and costly, this tendency will be blunted by factors that make control efforts too expensive. Control efforts become more expensive when they must cope with the need for increased flexibility, that is, when the contingencies which face the subsidiary are numerous, complex, and expensive. The general hypothesis then is that control will increase with the possibility of external influence but decrease as the subsidiary faces more contingencies.

This does not mean that a parallel set of hypotheses hold for coordination. It is more useful to look at coordination as responding to the properties of the organizational system in which the subsidiary is embedded because coordination is primarily a means of integration through horizontal associations. One would expect then that a more complex corporate system would be bound together by more systems of coordination and hence the coordination experienced by each subsidiary would be greater. The overall cost of integration would be lower, as would the predictability and flexibility of the system.

One may use these general hypotheses to derive more specific ones which relate particular variables from the literature to coordination and control. For example, the negative relationship between size of the organization and the centralization of control is well established. This would indicate that a larger organization would tend to use less control than a smaller one over its subunits, providing, of course, that these findings at the individual or group level can be translated to the subunit level. A larger organization is most generally a more complex one so that while the amount of control will be less, the amount of integration is likely to be higher. At the subunit level, increasing size is likely to be associated with more contingencies facing a more complex subunit so the amount of control would tend to be negatively related to subsidiary size. The effect on coordination is less clear because the subsidiary may be embedded in a complex or simple organizational system.

Similarly, one can take the observation by many researchers that a more complex technology creates more contingent situations for an organization [Perrow 1967; Hage 1980, pp. 387-388]. Given the reasoning in this paper, integration for a unit with a complex technology is more likely to take the form of coordination than control. The contingencies associated with complex technologies make the provision of close control too costly both directly and in terms of decreased flexibility. To the extent that complex technologies are the hub of complex organizational systems, coordination will be used to attain the required level of integration.

One could generate a series of such hypotheses, but given the number of variables in the literature linked to integration, such an exercise would be tedious. It is more useful to proceed from the general hypotheses to an examination of several categories of factors which may be associated with variance in levels of integration. Variables in 5 general categories—structure, technology, foreign commitment of the corporation, profitability, and location of the subsidiary—will be examined below. Some of these variables are drawn from the organizational literature, while others are taken from the literature focusing on the performance of multinational corporations. The specific importance of each will be discussed in the results section.

Sample and Methods _____

The sample of organizations included in this study consists of 57 subsidiaries of 34 American multinational corporations. The firms were chosen from 83 companies listed in the *Fortune* directory of the top 500 industrial firms. The original sample of 83 represented all the firms that had sales of between $500 million and

$1 billion for the base year and had at least one subsidiary in both France and Great Britain. Thirty-nine of the 83 firms were chosen to represent a wide range of technologies and products. Eventually data were collected from all but 5 of them. Where the MNC had multiple subsidiaries in a country, the flagship subsidiary, if it was identifiable, or the largest subsidiary in the country was chosen. In some cases, especially when different product groups had separate reporting structures in the country, more than one subsidiary was approached. The final sample consisted of 27 subsidiaries of 25 corporations in England and 30 subsidiaries of 28 firms in France. No firm supplied more than 3 subsidiaries for the final sample.

The bulk of the data for the study was collected in interviews with the managers of the foreign subsidiaries and their superiors and colleagues in the United States. In Great Britain 57 percent of the subsidiaries contacted eventually provided the necessary information; for France the figure was 79 percent. In the subsidiaries approximately two-thirds of the interviewees were managing directors of the subsidiary with the bulk of the remaining third coming from the personnel department. The positions of the 38 respondents located in the United States were quite varied, ranging from the vice-president of the international division to a manager in charge of technical information for a division. Most were from the staff of the vice-president of the division in which the subsidiary is located.

The data were collected in a semi-structured interview that began with 3 general questions about the subsidiary and its personnel, and proceeded to more specific topics including the items that make up the control index. After the European interviews were completed, a round of interviews with the informants in the United States was held to confirm and amplify the information received, especially the data comprising the control index. Additional data on the financial performance of the subsidiaries and parents were gathered from a number of sources, including *Fortune*, *Moody's*, the Securities and Exchange Commission's form 10-K, and public records available in Great Britain. Where possible, financial data supplied by the managers of the subsidiaries were confirmed, but this was difficult, especially for the French subsidiaries.

The index of control was constructed from a series of questions as to the location of certain important decisions. Each question asked to what extent the particular function or process was controlled by the subsidiary or by units outside the subsidiary. It is important to note that no distinction was made as to where the control was located in the corporate environment of the subsidiary. For this study it was not important to determine whether the control resided in the division, corporate headquarters, or at some intermediate level. The index was designed to tap the extent to which the subsidiary was able to control its own destiny in regard to specific functions. Each question had 3 possible responses, the lowest indicating more subsidiary control, the highest, more parent control. Thus, a high score on the control index indicates that the parent corporation, through its various administrative levels, exercises a great deal of control over the subsidiary. The only deviation in this system was the item which tapped the control of production. If a subsidiary had no production facilities, it received a score of 4 instead of the usual maximum of 3. It was decided that the complete absence of production functions reduced the contingencies that faced the subsidiary so severely that it represented an important increment of control for the parent firm. The items comprising the control index are given in the appendix.

The measures of diversity and breadth of coordination were gathered by asking the manager what functions were regularly coordinated with other units in the corporation and how many units were included in this network of coordination. Diversity was measured by asking managers, "Which of the following 10 functions do you regularly share with other units in the corporation?" The 10 functions are listed in the appendix. Breadth was measured through the question, "How many other units in the firm do you work with on a regular basis?" The measure did not include the unit that was administratively responsible for the focal subsidiary because all subsidiaries must coordinate with their headquarters. As would be expected, the 2 measures of coordination were highly correlated, $r = .58$.

Results

The 2 measures of coordination were, as hypothesized, positively related to control, but only coordination diversity achieved significance. It is not surprising that coordination diversity is more closely related to control because both variables tap the sharing of decisions among units. What is more important for this discussion is the relative weakness of the relationships between control and coordination. This implies that the 2 processes, while generally increasing with the overall level of integration, may vary substantially in the degree to which each changes in response to other factors. In the following sections, some of these important factors affecting integration will be examined.

Integration and Structure

One group of factors that has been extensively investigated for its relationship with integration processes is that of the structural variables. In this study 3 types of structural variables were examined: size, subsidiary function, and location in the organizational structure. The most pervasive explanatory variable in the structure pantheon has been organizational size. The positive relationship between the size of the organization and decentralization of control is well documented [Pugh, et al. 1968; Blau and Schoenherr 1971; Child 1973]. As the results given in Table 1 show, this same relationship was not found for this sample of multinational corporations. Larger size, as measured by the number of employees in the parent corporation, was positively associated with all three measures of integration. Although only the measure with breadth of coordination was significant, the association between size and control narrowly missed significance at the .05 level.

The marked difference between these and previous findings is probably due to a difference in what was measured. In most previous work, decentralization referred to the degree to which certain decisions were moved down the hierarchy away from top management. In this study the measure was the degree to which the subunit was controlled. The results would seem to imply that moving decisions away from the peak of the hierarchy may actually increase the amount of control exerted on subunits by giving more power to managers at intervening levels. This was certainly the case in one subsidiary in which the devolution of control over advertising expenditures from the divisional to the regional level gave the regional manager the opportunity to introduce a coordinated advertising scheme for all subsidiaries under his jurisdiction. The significant correlation between coordination breadth and size points up the role that coordination can play in integrating the subsidiary into a large corporation.

For the size of the subsidiary, neither measure of coordination is important, but control is strongly and negatively related to both the absolute and relative size of the subsidiary. This supports the original hypothesis and indicates the contradictory processes that take place as the organization gets larger. As the parent grows, tasks become specialized and are devolved to lower levels which, in turn, allows for greater integration of subunits. To the extent that the subsidiary shares in this growth, it takes on more functions and faces more contingencies. Thus, despite the greater importance of the subsidiary to the parent, the cost of integration becomes excessive, and levels of integration are lowered by the diminution of control over specific decisions.

The growth of the organization can also result in a more complex administrative structure that utilizes a multilevel hierarchy. The number of levels between the manager of the subsidiary and the top of the corporate hierarchy, the administrative distance, may affect the level of integration. Greater administrative distance means that the lines of communication will be longer, incurring greater costs and increasing the probability of distortion of messages. Administrative dis-

Table 1
CORRELATIONS BETWEEN CONTROL AND COORDINATION
AND STRUCTURAL VARIABLES

Structural variables	Control	Coordination diversity	Coordination breadth
Size			
Parent employees	.21	.13	.39***
Subsidiary employees	−.30*	.01	.04
Relative size	−.35**	.04	.01
Location			
Administrative distance	.33**	.00	.08
International division (dummy)	.15	.02	−.01
Product division (dummy)	−.28*	−.14	−.30*
Function			
Production function (dummy)	−.27*a	.18	−.04

*** p < .001 (One-tailed test of significance.)
** p < .01 (One-tailed test of significance.)
* p < .05 (One-tailed test of significance.)
N = 57
[a]Control of production item deleted from the index for this correlation.

tance shows no significant association with either dimension of coordination, but is significantly and positively associated with control. This may reflect the existence of more layers of administration, each of which may exert some control on the subsidiary. However, since these are the subsidiaries that are most likely to be at some risk of capture precisely because they are at the end of long lines of communication, the parent is willing to incur the higher price to insure the necessary predictability for the subsidiary.

Because multinational corporations are large complex organizations, the subunits may be integrated into the larger structure in a number of different ways. The structural form that integration takes—that is, the type of division in which the subsidiary is located—can have an impact on the level of integration that the subsidiary experiences. Of the several structures that were used for integration,

2—the international division and the worldwide product division—were important for this study. The international division consists of all the firm's subsidiaries outside the home country. Usually it is formed in an attempt to rationalize the company's international business and to coordinate the activities of foreign subsidiaries [Stopford and Wells 1972, pp. 21-25]. With the formation of the product division the entire firm is divided into product groups that have worldwide responsibility for specific products. This type of division is usually associated with a strategy of product diversification [Stopford and Wells 1972, pp. 39–43].

The correlations presented in Table 1 indicate that the 22 subsidiaries that were found in international divisions did not experience significantly different levels of integration from those in other structures. The location of the 23 subsidiaries in product divisions has a much more dramatic impact. The dummy variable for product division was negatively related to all 3 measures of integration, significantly so for control and coordination breadth. The strategy of product diversification that gives rise to worldwide product divisions introduces complexity which makes close integration of foreign subsidiaries difficult. Such close supervision would also go against the spirit of such divisions because they are usually charged with the active pursuit of new opportunities to exploit old products or develop new ones. To give the subsidiaries the autonomy to accomplish this task, some measure of integration must be sacrificed.

The last structural aspect of the firm to be examined is the function played by the subsidiary. Because almost all the subsidiaries in the sample had a significant sales force as part of their complement, it was not possible to compare sales subsidiaries against purely production subsidiaries. Instead those subsidiaries that had production functions as well as sales functions were entered in a dummy variable against those that were limited to sales. The subsidiaries that included production facilities did not show a significant difference in levels of coordination when compared to purely sales subsidiaries. This is somewhat surprising since the production subsidiaries presumably must distribute their goods to other subsidiaries to sell. Control is significantly lower when the production function is present, indicating that the more complex contingencies that the production function entails would make the cost of a level of control equivalent to that over sales subsidiaries too high. Sales subsidiaries can be controlled through the imposition of programming devices such as detailed budgets which break down both expenditures and expected income into numerous categories. When production is included such close control becomes too limiting and too expensive.

Integration and Technology _____

The technology of the organization has long been argued to have an important impact on the level of integration necessary for a subunit. From the general remarks of Woodward [1965] and Perrow [1967] to the more specific formulations of Lawrence and Lorsch [1967] and Ouchi [1977], technology has been allotted an important role in the structuring of organizational systems of integration. Complex techniques are thought to require structures which allow more flexibility in order to deal with the many contingencies that may arise. Too rigid a structure of integration may inhibit the reactions of managers and blunt the competitive edge gained from more complex technology. The effect of complexity, defined as the number and integration of steps in the production process, is often exacerbated by rapid change in the technical process and the introduction of new, more sophisticated products. The need for flexibility is enhanced by the need for frequent adaptations to new products. In this case the need for flexibility outweighs the need for predictability so that more complex technologies should be associated with lower levels of integration.

As can be seen from Table 2, the level of control exerted on the subsidiary depends on the complexity of the technology of the parent but not on that of the subsidiary itself. The greater importance of the parent technology for the control relationship supports Thompson's [1967] argument that the demands of the technical system shape the structure of the control system. It is evident, however, that technology has a much larger and more pervasive impact on the system of coordination. Both dimensions of coordination are significantly associated with parent and subsidiary technology as well as with the rate of technological change represented by expenditures on research and development.

The large increase in coordination and the decrease in control can be seen as a solution to the twin imperatives that a corporation with more complex technology faces. On the one hand the imposition of control is expensive and inhibits flexibility. Yet technologically complex subsidiaries represent large investments that must somehow be integrated, especially if the parent company is similarly complex and devoted to the production of new products. By increasing both the number of units with which the subsidiary coordinates and the number of functions thus coordinated, the subsidiary can be bound into a network of reciprocal relationships that serve to integrate at a lower overall cost. Flexibility is, to some extent, inhibited by the obligations thus incurred by the subsidiary, but renegotiation is possible to accommodate changes in technology or product. More importantly, these adjustments are carried out between the focal subsidiary and those with which it coordinates activities, a more parsimonious solution than imposing

Table 2
CORRELATIONS BETWEEN CONTROL AND COORDINATION
AND TECHNOLOGY VARIABLES

Technology variables	Control	Coordination diversity	Coordination breadth
Parent complexity	$-.26^*$	$.31^{**}$	$.40^{***}$
Subsidiary complexity	.06	$.41^{***}$	$.47^{***}$
R & D expenditures	.13	$.47^{***}$	$.60^{***}$

[***] p < .001 (One-tailed test of significance.)
[**] p < .01 (One-tailed test of significance.)
[*] p < .05 (One-tailed test of significance.)
N = 57

such coordination from a higher hierarchical level through direct control. This undoubtedly explains why corporations with high overall complexity have lower levels of control. If the subsidiary is complex but the entire firm is not, then the cost of ordering such coordination can be accepted. Thus, as predicted, it is the complexity of the entire organizational system that is important for the level of coordination employed.

Integration and Foreign Commitment

The original overseas investment of American multinational corporations has almost inevitably been a small tentative venture which had little initial impact on the firm as a whole. As the foreign business becomes more important, specialist groups are established to manage it and integrate it into the firm [Wilkins 1974, pp. 416-422]. The logical conclusion is that the more that multinational corporations were committed to foreign business, the more they would exert control and coordination over their subsidiaries.

The results shown in Table 3 indicate that this hypothesis is supported strongly for coordination breadth and diversity, but only weakly for control. The control that is exerted over the subsidiaries increases significantly with the number of countries in which the multinational corporation has establishments, but is not associated with the number of subsidiaries or the percentage of sales outside the home country. This would seem to indicate that it is not the simple growth of overseas operations that leads to increased control, but the inclusion of more countries with differing business environments. It is not the financial weight of the network that is important, but the degree to which the network is dispersed.

The importance of network complexity for determining the shape and level of integration processes is underlined by the strong relationship between the 3 measures of foreign commitment and the 2 dimensions of coordination. As predicted, a more complex network requires more efforts at coordination. Clearly this holds true even more strongly for the foreign network of subsidiaries than it does for the organization as a whole. Although the increase in parent size shows a significant relationship only with coordination breadth, the more complex foreign network also shows a significant association with diversity. To be sure, the very presence of more subsidiaries offers more opportunities for coordination, but the size of the correlations and the marginally stronger associations with the number of countries with subsidiaries and percentage of foreign sales indicate that it is not simply the number of subsidiaries that leads to greater coordination.

Integration and Financial Performance

Because the whole point of integration of subsidiaries is to ensure that they accomplish their specified tasks, the degree to which a subsidiary has been successful should affect the closeness of integration. If the subsidiary has been unsuccessful, that is, unprofitable, then higher levels of control and coordination should be expected. An attempt to increase predictability and hence profits would entail increased costs for integration and decreased flexibility for the subsidiary. Because the parent is such an important part of the economic environment of the subsidiary, its success should also affect the amount of integration. The impact that poor parent performances would have is more difficult to predict. In times of economic stringency the parent would wish to ensure close compliance with policies but might be reluctant to increase expenditures for integration.

Table 3
CORRELATIONS BETWEEN CONTROL AND COORDINATION
AND FOREIGN COMMITMENT VARIABLES

Foreign commitment variables	Control	Coordination diversity	Coordination breadth
Number of foreign subsidiaries	.12	.36**	.47***
Countries with subsidiaries	.23*	.44***	.57***
Percentage of sales abroad	−.16	.40***	.58***

***p < .001 (One-tailed test of significance.)
** p < .01 (One-tailed test of significance.)
* p < .05 (One-tailed test of significance.)
N = 57

The results reported in Table 4 show that this hypothesis is not upheld and that it looks much more probable that the reverse is true. Subsidiary profitability has no association with control but is significantly and positively related to diversity of coordination. Thus, a subsidiary which coordinates more functions with other parts of the organization usually shows a greater return on investment. The coefficient for coordination breadth is also substantial, but because it was impossible to obtain reliable financial data for over half the subsidiaries, the number of cases is reduced and the coefficient does not reach significance.

For parent performance, control and coordination both show significant positive associations. More profitable corporations tend to have more closely integrated foreign subsidiaries. This finding can be interpreted in a number of ways depending on the direction of causality one wishes to assume. One could argue that greater financial success allows the firm to devote more of its resources to the process of integration. Because financial success is positively associated with increased coordination but not with control at the subsidiary level, it would seem that there is some tentative evidence to support this view. The possibility that those firms which maintain higher levels of integration are thereby more successful, however, cannot be ruled out. A longitudinal study of the relationship between profitability and integration is needed to provide a definitive answer.

Integration and Nationality

The final factor to be examined for its association with integration is the country in which the subsidiary is located. This research was designed to allow a comparison between subsidiaries located in France and Great Britain. While it was not possible to obtain a precisely matched sample with one subsidiary of each

Table 4
CORRELATIONS BETWEEN CONTROL AND COORDINATION
AND PROFITABILITY VARIABLES

Profitability variables	Control	Coordination diversity	Coordination breadth
Subsidiary's average percentage profit (n = 29)	.01	.41*	.31
Parent's average percentage profit (n = 57)	.34**	.38**	.34**

**p < .01 (One-tailed test of significance.)
*p < .05 (One-tailed test of significance.)

firm in each country, the distribution was approximately equal with 27 of the subsidiaries located in Great Britain and 30 in France. These 2 countries were chosen because they demonstrate very different legal and managerial attitudes toward the operation of a business [Granick 1972, pp. 357-362]. If the business practices of the host country were to have an impact on the integration of subsidiaries, then a comparison between these 2 countries would be likely to show it.

As expected, there was no significant association between the dummy variable for location in France and either dimension of coordination. There was, however, a significant association with control. Subsidiaries located in France were significantly more likely to operate under high levels of control. It would be tempting to attribute this difference to language difficulties or other problems of communication that prompted the American managers to impose more direct control over French subsidiaries. However, several measures of rates of communication between the subsidiary and other parts of the corporation failed to show a single significant difference between subsidiaries in France and England. Since all but a few of the French managers spoke excellent English there is no evidence to support this explanation.

It is probably more useful to look to the American managers' perception of France as a business environment for an explanation of these results. Although the direct effects of government policy on multinational corporations have not been noticeably different in France than in Great Britain, there had been a number of nationalizations (predating the current socialist government) that raised questions about the government's attitude toward large foreign-owned businesses. This probably did not translate directly into a perceived need for more control but contributed to a general uneasiness that is shown up in efforts to maintain greater predictability through direct control.

Discussion and Conclusions _____

Taken together, these results help to illuminate the relationship between control and coordination as 2 components of the integration process. The significant correlation between coordination diversity and control indicates that they do vary together, but the failure to find a significant correlation with coordination breadth indicates that this association is not overwhelming. What is of more interest is the way in which the 2 processes respond to the different variables that have been suggested in the literature as affecting integration.

Control and coordination respond to sets of organizational variables in different ways and with differential strength. For the structural characteristics of size and location in the corporate structure, control seems to be more reactive, although coordination breadth does show some association. For the technology variables, the associations with both dimensions of coordination are strong and consistent while for control they are weak and generally in the opposite direction. For foreign commitment, the pattern is much the same except that control is generally in the same direction as coordination. For profitability, the associations are of nearly equal strength and in the same direction.

This variety of associations indicates that few of the variables thought to affect patterns of integration actually affect coordination and control in the same way. This lends credence to the initial assertion that they represent separate, if related, solutions to the integration problem. A subsidiary which is large, technologically complex, located in a product division, and highly profitable will very likely be integrated through extensive coordination with other parts of the organization while retaining a good deal of control over its own affairs. A small subsidiary, located at a long administrative distance from the center of the organization, and sharing a simple technology with its parent, will be subject to higher levels of control and lower levels of coordination.

These results also support the general propositions that control will be more responsive to the contingencies faced by the subsidiary and the danger of capture by the environment, while coordination responds to the complexity of the overall system. One implication of this difference can be seen in the way that coordination and control are associated with factors that apply at both the subsidiary and parent level. With the exception of the relationship between coordination breadth and parent size, coordination has consistent effects at the 2 levels. Control is much more likely to have effects with opposite signs at the organization and subunit levels as with size and technological complexity, or large versus trivial coefficients as with profitability. Because coordination seems to be more responsive to the complexity of the network in which the subsidiary is embedded, its consistency is to be expected. Control, being the more specific mechanism of integration, may react in different ways to parallel developments such as increasing corporate and subsidiary size.

The results of this study also hold implications for countries in which subsidiaries are located. For example, many countries, especially those in Western Europe, would like to attract subsidiaries that are large enough to offer substantial employment opportunities. They would also like to attract firms that have access to advanced technology so that local firms can gain from the contact and local workers can acquire new skills. These results indicate that large subsidiaries tend to be controlled less than their smaller counterparts. Assuming that less corporate control allows room for local negotiation, this should make them more responsive to local control. Similarly, parents with complex technologies exert less control over their subsidiaries, making them more responsive to local influence. At both the parent and subsidiary levels, however, technological complexity is associated with dense networks of integration. The choice, thus, seems to be between large, technologically complex subsidiaries that have more direct control over their own functions but are tightly tied to other subsidiaries, or small, technologically simple firms that are subject to a greater degree of direct control.

The degree to which these results would hold for organizations other than MNCs is a question that awaits further research. Although multinational corporations clearly face more diverse environments than purely domestic firms, there is no reason why the theory should not apply to any organization with geographically dispersed subunits. It may be, however, that a more uniform environment would alter the results reported here. The finding that coordination and control represent methods of integration that are differentially affected by organizational characteristics provides a framework within which these issues can be investigated.

Appendix _____

Control Index Items

1. Who initiates the budget process?
2. How frequent and detailed are the financial reports which are sent to headquarters?
3. Does the subsidiary have computer links with headquarters?
4. How quickly are financial results available to the subsidiary?
5. To what extent can budgeted funds be shifted?
6. What personnel can the subsidiary's managing director appoint without prior approval?
7. How much influence does the subsidiary have over acquisitions?
8. What legal matters must be referred to higher levels?
9. Which personnel can the subsidiary's managing director promote without prior approval?
10. Where are the transfer prices set?
11. Where is the subsidiary's sales plan set?
12. Where is the subsidiary's production plan set?
13. Who does the purchasing for the subsidiary?
14. What access does the subsidiary have to research and development facilities?
15. Who markets the subsidiary's products?
16. Who approves advertising for the subsidiary?

Items for Coordination Measures

1. Do you regularly (at least once a year) coordinate any of the following activities with other units of the corporation?
   a. Supply finished products to other units.
   b. Receive finished products from other units.
   c. Receive raw materials or partially processed goods from other units.
   d. Send raw materials or partially processed goods to other units.
   e. Coordinate sales programs with other units.
   f. Coordinate research and development programs with other units.
   g. Coordinate purchasing with other units.
   h. Coordinate marketing with other units.
   i. Coordinate advertising with other units.
   j. Have a regular exchange of personnel with other units.
2. With how many other subsidiaries and units, excluding your immediately superior headquarters, do you coordinate at least one of these functions?

References

Blau, Peter M., and Schoenherr, Richard A. *The Structure of Organizations.* New York: Basic Books, 1971.

Burns, Thomas, and Stalker, G. M. *The Management of Innovation.* London: Tavistock, 1961.

Child, John. "Predicting and Understanding Organization Structure," *Administrative Science Quarterly*, June 1973, pp. 168-185.

Clegg, Stewart. *The Theory of Power and Organization.* London: Routledge & Kegan Paul, 1979.

Edwards, Richard C. "The Social Relations of Production at the Point of Production." *The Insurgent Sociologist*, Fall 1978, pp. 109-125.

Etzioni, Amitai. "Organizational Control Structure." In *Handbook of Organizations*, edited by James G. March. Chicago: Rand McNally, 1965, pp. 650-677.

Goehle, Donna G. *Decision Making in Multinational Corporations.* Ann Arbor: U.M.I. Research Press, 1980.

Granick, David. *Managerial Comparisons of Four Developed Countries: France, Britain, United States, and Russia.* Cambridge, MA: The M.I.T. Press, 1972.

Hage, Jerald. *Communication and Organizational Control: Cybernetics in Health and Welfare Settings.* New York: John Wiley and Sons, 1974.

_____. *Theories of Organizations: Form, Process, and Transformation.* New York: John Wiley and Sons, 1980.

Hage, Jerald; Aiken, Michael; and Marrett, Cora Bagley. "Organization Structure and Communications." *American Sociological Review*, October 1971, pp. 860-871.

Karpik, Lucien. "Organizations, Institutions and History." In *Organization and Environment,* edited by Lucien Karpik. Beverly Hills: Sage, 1978, pp. 15-68.

Katz, Daniel, and Kahn, Robert L. *The Social Psychology of Organizations*. New York: John Wiley and Sons, 1966.

Lawrence, Paul R., and Lorsch, Jay. *Organization and Environment: Managing Differentiation and Integration*. Boston: Harvard University Press, 1967.

March, James G., and Simon, Herbert A. *Organizations*. New York: John Wiley and Sons, 1958.

Ouchi, William G. "The Relationship between Organizational Structure and Organizational Control." *Administrative Science Quarterly*, March 1977, pp. 95-113.

Perrow, Charles. "A Framework for the Comparative Analysis of Organizations." *American Sociological Review*, April 1967, pp. 194-208.

Pfeffer, Jeffrey. *Organizational Design*. Arlington Heights, IL: A.H.M. Publishing, 1978.

Pugh, D. S.; Hickson, D. J.; Hinings, C. R.; and Turner, C. "Dimensions of Organization Structure." *Administrative Science Quarterly*, June 1968, pp. 65-105.

Stopford, John M., and Wells, Louis T. Jr. *Managing the Multinational Enterprise*. New York: Basic Books, 1972.

Tannenbaum, Arnold S. *Control in Organizations*. New York: McGraw-Hill, 1968.

Thompson, James D. *Organizations in Action*. New York: McGraw-Hill, 1967.

Tuggle, Francis D. *Organizational Processes*. Arlington Heights, IL: A.H.M. Publishing, 1978.

United Nations Commission on Transnational Corporations. *Transnational Corporations in World Development: A Re-examination*. New York: United Nations, 1978.

Van de Ven, Andrew H.; Delbecq, André L.; and Koenig, Richard Jr. "Determinants of Coordination Modes Within Organizations." *American Sociological Review*, April 1976, pp. 322-338.

Wilkins, Mira. *The Maturing of Multinational Enterprise*. Cambridge, Mass.: Harvard University Press, 1974.

Woodward, Joan. *Industrial Organization: Theory and Practice*. London: Oxford University Press, 1965.

9. EXPATRIATE REDUCTION AND STRATEGIC CONTROL IN AMERICAN MULTINATIONAL CORPORATIONS

STEPHEN J. KOBRIN

Stephen J. Kobrin is a Professor of Management at The Wharton School of The University of Pennsylvania. His research interests involve the intersection of international business and international politics and the impact of global strategies on multinationals and nation states. He has published in such journals as International Organization, *the* Journal of International Business Studies, *and the* Journal of Conflict Resolution. *He is the author of* Managing Political Risk Assessment, *published by the University of California Press (1982).*

The significant reduction in the use of home country expatriates abroad by American multinationals is generally taken positively, reflecting internationalization, the environmental competence of host country nationals, equity, and the cost of maintaining Americans abroad. In this article I dissent, arguing that the phase-out of expatriates has gone too far, much further in fact than European or Japanese competition and that the dominant reason for the cutback is the difficulty Americans have in adapting to overseas assignments and the high failure rate they have experienced. I conclude that expatriate reduction has significant consequences for the strategic management of multinational corporations: reduced identification with the worldwide organization and its objectives, difficulty exercising control through personnel, and a lack of opportunities for Americans to gain information expertise through assignments abroad. Although I do not advocate returning to the ineffective and inequitable over-reliance on home country nationals, I argue that a corps of expatriates performs a function valuable to the MNC and that a means must be found to develop a group of managers who identify with the organization as a whole and provide overseas experience to home country managers.

Twenty years ago a visitor to an overseas subsidiary of an American firm was likely to find U.S. expatriates in most significant managerial positions. The Chief Executive and Financial Officers, as well as the heads of marketing and manufacturing, were typically Americans and it was not unusual to find expatriates in the second and third levels of management. A return to the same subsidiary today would find the situation radically changed. The visitor would have to look long and hard to find an American expatriate, and when (s)he did, the employee might well be on a very short term assignment. There has been a dramatic and significant replacement of American expatriates abroad by local (or third country) nationals. Both managers and academics note a number of good business reasons for the replacement of expatriates by local nationals, including environmental competence and cost reduction. The sharp decrease in their number is taken positively as one more indication of the internationalization or globalization of American firms. In this article I dissent, arguing that the replacement of expatriates has gone too far, much further in fact than in European and Japanese competitors. Although all of the reasons given for the phasing out of expatriates are valid, I suggest one that is not discussed actually dominates: the difficulty many Americans have had adapting to overseas assignments and the abysmally high failure rates they have experienced. Put simply, Americans have not been able to handle working and living in other cultures and U.S. MNCs have found it easier to replace them with foreign nationals than to make an effort to solve the underlying problem. I conclude that the cutback of expatriates has important implications for the strategic management of American multinational firms. First, if most employees are local then there are precious few who either have an encompassing knowledge of the worldwide organization or identify with it and its objectives. Second, in many diversified MNCs, personnel are a critical instrument of headquarters' strategic control and the virtual elimination of expatriates affects control adversely. Last, at least in American firms, managers have gained their international expertise on the job through overseas assignments in one or more countries. The significant reduction in these opportunities raises important questions about future sources of such expertise, and indeed whether Americans who spend their careers at home will be competent to run their own worldwide corporations.

The Replacement of American Expatriates_____

The evidence indicates a marked reduction in the assignment of American expatriates abroad. In a 1984 study of large U.S. based international firms (industrials and banks), I found that half of the companies surveyed indicated a significant reduction in expatriates in the past decade, 26 percent reported no change, and only 23 percent an increase. When asked about trends over the next ten years, 41 percent projected a continued reduction, 40 percent no change, and 18 percent an increase (Kobrin, 1984:43).

Interviews confirmed the survey results; many respondents who said that their firms used expatriates heavily in the past could count those currently abroad on the fingers of one hand and noted that most were there short-term, to fill a specific need. (Banks, and to a lesser extent petroleum and construction firms, are exceptions as they still tend to use significant numbers of expatriates abroad.)

Tung (1982) found that well under half of the senior management positions in U.S. subsidiaries were staffed by Americans and that the Middle and Far East aside, less than 10 percent of middle management positions were held by home country nationals. A Conference Board Study (Berenbeim, 1983:v) reported that 80 percent of U.S. firms surveyed employed a local national as head of a majority of country operations. In the main, expatriates have been replaced with local nationals, although there are significant numbers of third country (neither home nor host) nationals in the managerial ranks of many MNCs.

It should be absolutely clear that past over-reliance on American expatriates was neither effective nor efficient; there are a number of good reasons for their wholesale replacement with local nationals. As managerial and technical competence in many countries (developing as well as industrialized) increased, a large number of proficient managers became available. All things equal, a local national who speaks the language, understands the culture and the political system, and is often a member of the local elite should be more effective than an expatriate alien.

The cost of maintaining an American (and an American family) abroad is often prohibitive. U.S. salary levels—and often incentives—must be paid in countries where local pay scales may be considerably lower. Furthermore, other costs such as private schooling, trips home, benefits, living allowances, club memberships, and the like can become excessive very quickly. One estimate of the direct costs of expatriates is three times the domestic salary plus relocation expense (Harvey, 1983).

In many countries there is pressure (explicit or implicit) to "nationalize" management. There may be regulatory limits on the number of expatriates that can be employed, difficulties in obtaining visas or work permits, or more subtle government pressures to train and promote local nationals. Last, over-reliance on expatriates can cause severe morale problems in subsidiaries due to home country managers' inability to deal with culturally different employees or simply because local managers feel that they are discriminated against when it comes to promotion.

On the whole, the replacement of expatriates with local nationals has been seen as a positive trend: lowering costs; increasing managerial effectiveness; minimizing conflict with both employees and environmental groups; and contributing to host country managerial and technical development. Berenbeim concludes that, ". . . there is a near unanimity of opinion as to the desirability of using local nationals to manage local operations," (1983:24). It is seen as a reflection of the maturation of American multinationals; indeed the number of foreign employees is often taken as an index of internationalization. A firm that has operations in a large number of countries and competes globally should reflect its geographical composition in its employees. In summary, the reduction in expatriates can be seen as an appropriate response to changed environmental conditions.

The Failure of Americans Abroad_____

There is another, less appealing explanation for the drastic reduction in U.S. expatriates: corporate experience with overseas assignments has been disastrous. Zeira and Banai (1985) summarize eight studies of failure rates of expatriates abroad that range from 30-70 percent, with higher failure rates in developing countries or relatively distant cultures such as Japan. Harvey (1983:72) notes that "depending on the source, from 33 to 80 percent of expatriated families return to the United States before their contract expires." Although it is difficult to define failure precisely and the estimates should not be taken as hard data, it is very clear that the overseas assignment of Americans has been a difficult and costly process and one that cannot be deemed successful.

There is a large literature on expatriate selection and performance that deals with reasons for the failure of American managers abroad (see Edwards, 1978; Harvey, 1983; Mendenhall and Oddou, 1985; Tung, 1982, 1987; and Zeira and Banai, 1985). Although it is not to my purpose to discuss reasons for failure here, it is attributed to selection procedures—typically domestic performance (Miller, 1973), inadequate preparation, and the general difficulty that individuals from an isolated environment have in adapting to different cultures.

The costs of expatriate failure are enormous in terms of direct expenses, management time, and most important, human misery. Although it is certainly a hypothesis rather than a conclusion, I argue that the high failure rate and its attendant costs have played a major role in the decision of many multinationals to reduce drastically the number of Americans assigned abroad. In the short run, it is easier to train and promote host and third country nationals than it is to select high potential candidates and expend the resources necessary to give them the attitudes and cultural skills they need to function effectively abroad. It must be noted that the problem is exacerbated by the scandalously low levels of international awareness and language competence found in graduates of American universities and business schools.

The European and Japanese Experience

Tung's extensive studies of European and Japanese multinationals provide data on both expatriate usage and failure rates that are at least consistent with the hypothesis I suggest above. In Western Europe, U.S. deployment of expatriates in senior management slots is only marginally below that of European firms: 33 vs. 38 percent. Both are well below the Japanese average of 77 percent. Once one moves to the developing countries—where there generally are lower levels of managerial and technical competence and where the cross-cultural adjustments are more difficult for Americans—the differences are considerably more striking.

In Latin America, 44 percent of senior management positions in U.S. subsidiaries were filled by home country nationals, compared to 79 percent in European firms and 83 percent for the Japanese. In the Mid-East the numbers are 42, 86, and 67 percent; in the Far East 55, 85, and 65 percent; and in Africa 36, 75, and 50 percent (see Tung, 1982:61; the data are for the early 1980s).

Two points must be made. First, the comparison must take differences in managerial systems into account, particularly when comparing U.S. and European firms with Japanese. Second, I am not arguing that levels of expatriate staffing found in European or Japanese firms are correct; rather that the U.S. reduction may be excessive and a response to difficulty in cross-cultural adjustment rather than changed business conditions.

In a later paper (based on the same data) Tung (1987) compares American, European, and Japanese failure rates. More than half of her American respondents had failure rates of 10 to 20 percent and for an additional seven percent of the sample, a failure rate of 30 percent was reported. (She concludes that, "these statistics are consistent with the findings of others that approximately 30 percent of overseas assignments within U.S. multinationals are mistakes;" Tung, 1987:117). In contrast, she found that 59 percent of the European MNCs had failure rates of under five percent, an additional 38 percent of 6-10 percent, and three percent of 11-15 percent. Seventy-six percent of the Japanese firms had failure rates of under five percent, 10 percent of the sample 6-10 percent, and 14 percent of 11-19 percent.

Tung attributes the lower failure rates among European and Japanese firms to a combination of: selection procedures; career planning; better preparation for overseas assignments; expatriate support; and in the European case, a more developed international orientation and language capability (Tung, 1987). Summarizing the study, U.S. MNCs appear to have reduced use of home country expatriates to a much greater extent than their European and Japanese competitors (especially outside of Western Europe) and have had significantly greater "failure rates" in the past.

Although the evidence is much too limited to draw any general conclusions, it is consistent with my—admittedly speculative—argument. U.S. MNCs may have gone too far in substituting local (and third country) nationals for expatriates and they may have done so in response to the difficulties that Americans have had in adjusting to other cultural environments rather than for the usual reasons of effectiveness and efficiency cited above. Put directly, Americans may not have been able to handle international assignments and many U.S. firms may have "solved" the problem by virtually getting out of the expatriate business.

Replacing expatriates with local nationals certainly has a number of important benefits to both the firm and the host country. The overuse of expatriates is dysfunctional from the firm's point of view and stunts the development of local nationals as managers and of the host country economy. On the other hand, a multinational firm comprised primarily of employees who identify with the local subsidiary rather than the worldwide organization raises some major issues for strategic management and control. I now turn to those questions.

Consequences for the Global Firm _____

In the past few years there has been a good deal of academic and managerial attention given to the global firm and global competition (see Porter, 1986 for a summary). As Porter notes, "Competing internationally is a necessity rather than a matter of discretion for many firms" (1986:1). The pressures for international integration of strategy and operations flow from the increases in the scale of production and technology and from the need to exploit new sources of competitive advantage.

In many industries (automobiles are an example) the minimal scale of production has increased to the point where few national markets are large enough to support efficient operations. In others, (such as computers) technological demands are so great that returns from even the largest domestic markets are insufficient to support adequate research and development efforts. In both instances firms must integrate transnationally to compete; they must link operations in a number of national markets to achieve the minimal scale required to produce efficiently or to remain in the race technologically. Put another way, the geographic territory required for efficient business operations is larger than that of most nation states.

Even in industries where most national markets are large enough to support efficient operations — consumer products and processed food are prime examples — there are competitive pressures for some degree of international coordination or integration; to exploit knowledge gained in one market in others and save time and lower costs (Porter, 1986). Thus, many multinationals face competitive pressures to coordinate and integrate operations transnationally: they face global competition.

The world, however, is not multinational and firms must compete in an environment comprised of over 160 sovereign, territorially defined, independent nation states with very different objectives, political systems, cultures, languages, and modes of social organization. That, in turn, puts pressure on all MNCs to respond to political and socio-cultural differences between markets by fragmenting strategy and operations.

The critical challenge facing managers of multinational firms is trading off pressures for integration and fragmentation: responding to what Prahalad and Doz (1981a) call the economic and political imperatives of global business. An appropriate balance must be struck between reaping the benefits of integration and responding to local conditions and objectives. I agree with Bartlett (1986) that forces for both integration and fragmentation are likely to increase in strength in the future and that firms must be able to respond to both simultaneously. That requires accurate and up to date knowledge of a large number of local environments, an understanding of how local conditions affect the worldwide system, and centralized integration and coordination of strategy and operations. It requires the ability to develop a global strategy, strong local management operating in a global context, and the exercise of sufficient control to insure the strategy is implemented.

A MNC is a paradox in that even the most integrated strategy must be executed by national subunits. Effective management of a diversified MNC entails exploiting the strengths and knowledge of the subsidiary within the context of the global system. Furthermore, optimization at the system level is more complex than a simple sum of local optima; the subsidiary's role is to maximize its contribution to worldwide objectives rather than local returns. Given the complex environment of the MNC, there may well be a conflict between achieving local and systemwide objectives.

That implies that at least a core of managers simultaneously understand and identify with the global organization and are knowledgeable about, and sensitive to, local differences. It also implies some means of exerting control over geographic and (often) culturally diverse subsidiaries.

The reduction in expatriate assignments by U.S. MNCs means that most employees of the firm are part of, and identify with, a single local unit. The exceptions are headquarters managers who, at least in theory, identify with the corporation as a whole. However, to the extent that they are home country nationals with limited international experience, their outlook is likely to be ethnocentric and narrow. That may be the case in many U.S. MNCs, as data from the early 1980s indicates that only about one-third have even one foreigner who is a top manager and that the median percentage of top executives with foreign experience is only 15 percent (Berenbeim, 1983:16, 19).

The sharp reduction in expatriate assignments in U.S. MNCs raises four issues for strategic management and control: (1) identification with firm-wide rather than local objectives; (2) knowledge of, and identification with, the global organization; (3) corporate control of local subsidiaries; and (4) acquisition of international expertise by home country nationals.

Identification with Firm Wide Strategic Issues_____

To a local national who works in a subsidiary the corporation as a whole is an abstraction. The manager's task environment is immediate and it is local performance that matters. As noted above, corporate-subsidiary strategic conflict is not exceptional in an MNC, particularly one that is integrated transnationally. A subsidiary, for example, may want to export but be prohibited from doing so by headquarters because of potential intra-organizational conflict, underutilization of other facilities, or the like. Sourcing decisions, may be systemwide, even though they conflict with established relationships with local suppliers or involve a higher cost to a given local unit. Manufacturing may be rationalized, limiting a subsidiary to component production or it may even be shifted entirely to meet the more important demands of another host country.

Corporate-subsidiary conflict can be exacerbated by local government demands for control and autonomy; it may well object to shifts in the locale of manufacturing or from final product to component assembly. Although the conflicts are unavoidable, and any manager—regardless of his or her experience—has some tendency to identify with the immediate task environment, it is critical that some core of managers in the MNC, who influence subsidiaries' strategic decisions, identify with the global task environment: with the corporation as a whole.

It is obvious that home country expatriates are only one means of accomplishing this end. Furthermore, I am not suggesting that U.S. MNCs return to the practice of staffing all of the important managerial posts in subsidiaries with Americans. Rather, I am trying to point out some of the costs of the sharp reduction in use of expatriates by U.S. firms. I will deal with these points in more detail below.

Identification with the Worldwide Organization

The replacement of expatriates with local nationals increases the difficulties MNCs face in creating informal organizational links across subunits. Although any diversified corporation serving a large geographic area faces problems of this sort, the MNCs are exacerbated by larger geographic distances, time changes that make direct social communication via telephone more difficult, and especially cultural and linguistic differences.

To the extent managers are hired by, and spend most—if not all—of their careers in the local subsidiary, there is a greater tendency to see managers from other subsidiaries or headquarters as alien, as "they." Although many American expatriates were not well integrated into subsidiaries and were perceived as alien, they formed a core of international managers who had personal links worldwide. While that network tended to exclude local employees, it did serve as a corporate-wide informal organization. Its function—without its discrimination against local nations—is essential in a MNC.

This problem takes on particular importance as MNCs attempt to organize in ways that facilitate formulation and implementation of global strategies. Bartlett (1982) argues that the complex strategic problem facing MNCS — the need to be simultaneously globally competitive and nationally responsive —makes a single structural solution problematic. Rather, he views organization of the MNC "... as an adaptive evolutionary process rather than as a series of powerful, and sometimes traumatic, reorganizations" (1982:26).

He argues for open and flexible cooperative arrangements that are difficult to achieve through formal organization. " The subtlety and complexity of a flexible multidimensional decision-making process appears difficult to achieve solely (or even primarily) through formal organizational change" (1982: 32). Rather, by focusing on transfers, assignments, careers, and meetings, senior management shifts its means of influence from the formal to the informal structure.

Several points are relevant. First, MNCs have had a great deal more difficulty with global organization than with global strategy. Second, one does not have to go as far as Bartlett to accept that informal organizational links are critical in MNCs and that there are very significant barriers to establishing them. Extensive direct social contact is required to overcome organizational conflicts and cultural/linguistic differences.

Personnel moves and assignments within the firm, including temporary assignment of host country nationals to other units and short term transfers or significant and repeated travel, are critical. Managers within the MNC must get to know and trust one another, despite the very real barriers to doing so. However, it is also critically important that home country nations — who for better or worse are more likely to rise to the senior corporate ranks — develop informal linkages through the corporation. Again, assignment of home country expatriates abroad *alone* is not a sufficient, effective, or fair solution to this problem. However, by drastically reducing expatriates—to the point where they are rare in many firms—management has given up an important instrument of policy and control.

Control

The control problems faced by any large diversified organization are exacerbated in the MNC. First, as noted above, the geographic and cultural distances between subunits are significantly greater in the international firm. Second, differences in political and legal jurisdictions may well place limits on subsidiary responsiveness. Third, subsidiaries tend towards autonomy: many MNCs built up international organizations through acquisition of previously independent firms, and even where subsidiaries have always been owned by the parent there was typically a polycentric period with little headquarters control exercised.

Prahalad and Doz (1981a) address control problems in MNCs arguing that as subsidiaries mature, resources such as capital, technology, and access to markets no longer provide an adequate basis for headquarters control. Rather, MNCs must create an organizational context that blends structure, information systems, measurement and reward systems, career planning, and a common organizational culture.

As do others, they argue that managers in a global firm must balance conflicting pressures for integration and fragmentation (in their terms economic and political imperatives). They suggest three organizational mechanisms that substitute for resource based control: data management, managers' management, and conflict resolution (1981b). The second concerns managerial selection, career paths, development, and socialization. The third, mechanisms for integration and coordination mechanisms. In short, strategic control in a mature multinational depends on control over personnel and the informal organization.

It is difficult for any manager in a MNC to strike an appropriate balance between integration and national responsiveness. Headquarters managers may well underestimate the importance of local social and political factors and place too much emphasis on standardization and rationalization. On the other hand, local nationals may well feel caught between conflicting corporate and local interests. It may be hard for them to transcend their cultural and political background and strike an appropriate balance between integration and national responsiveness. They may find themselves allied with local policy makers against corporate headquarters.

There are mechanisms other than home country expatriates that allow head-quarters to gain control: career planning, development, and assignment of local nationals can certainly play a role as can other socialization mechanisms. However, a core of international employees—third as well as home country na-tionals—simplifies problems of strategic control through personnel and facilitates the socialization needed to build a common organizational culture worldwide. Ex-patriates will not (and should not) automatically identify with home vs. host country: rather at their best, they should be able to assess local interests in the context of global strategy and identify with the worldwide organization. One can-not deny, however, that they are more likely to be responsive to the objectives of headquarters management than host country nationals who spend their entire careers in a subsidiary. They are clearly a more effective vehicle to exercise con-trol through personnel.

Acquiring International Expertise

Most American managers who become internationalized do so on the job; they ac-quire cross-cultural expertise, language skills, and knowledge about other countries' social, political, and cultural systems as a result of travel and overseas assignment. A mailed survey and interviews of managers in large, U.S. based in-ternational firms (Kobrin, 1984) indicates that very few managers with interna-tional responsibilities began their careers as internationalists. When asked to evaluate sources of their international expertise, less than 16 percent said that Peace Corps, government, military, or religious service abroad was an important factor, and less than 15 percent felt that education— graduate or under-graduate—was important.

The vast majority of managers said that they acquired their international ex-pertise from either business travel or assignment abroad. Many, if not most, of the managers I spoke with who were committed internationalists had served tours of duty abroad. It is important to note that over half were not "volunteers;" they went abroad at the request of the company. A surprising number recalled how their first expatriate assignment had changed their lives: how living and working abroad had enlarged their horizons and generated excitement about other cultures and languages.

In summary, very few managers in American MNCs were internationalists as a result of pre-career experience. The vast majority gained their commitment and knowledge on the job, particularly through assignment abroad.

American managers can gain international expertise through university or mid-career education, travel that involves serious intercultural interaction and a systematic attempt to learn, or in a number of other ways. To this point, however, the primary vehicle for doing so has been assignment abroad. As the decline in expatriate assignments has resulted in a significant reduction in opportunities for medium- or long-term tours abroad, the typical manager (in all but a few industries) will not have that opportunity during his or her career.

Conclusions

In this paper I have argued that: (1) there has been a sharp reduction in use of expatriates by American MNCs; (2) the abysmally high failure rate among Americans assigned abroad—reflecting the difficulties of many managers in making cultural adjustments—is as, if not more, important an explanation than the positive reasons usually cited; (3) the cut back has gone further than in European and Japanese firms; and (4) the reduction in expatriates has resulted in costs in terms of identification with the global strategy and organization, control, and the internationalization of managers.

The multinational firm is a paradox; regardless of how globally integrated the strategy, it must be executed by local units that are inherent parts of a given social, cultural, political, and economic system. A core of expatriate managers can offset this centrifugal tendency, as their primary identification is corporate rather than local. Furthermore, they can have a "multiplier" effect as they can help internationalize local management, develop knowledge of and identification with the corporation as a whole, and help spread and institutionalize the corporate culture.

In theory, there is no reason that home country nationals have to participate in this process. As the firm's sales and profits become increasingly international, one would expect employees from an increasingly large group of nations to play an important managerial role. The core of expatriates could be comprised of third country nationals assigned to headquarters often enough to assimilate corporate culture and objectives and develop the contacts necessary for the informal organization to develop.

In practice, I wonder if American MNCs and the U.S. economy would be willing to tolerate the logical results of that strategy. To the extent that international expertise is a requisite for top managerial jobs—and it is far from clear that all managers agree that it is—fewer and fewer Americans would qualify. U.S. MNCs would face the choice of having top management dominated by foreign nationals or promoting unqualified individuals on the basis of citizenship.

I would hope that as U.S. firms become global competitors that managerial selection would take place on the basis of qualifications regardless of nationality; that any individual joining the company in any country in the world would have the same chance of becoming CEO. However, unless the expertise obtained from overseas assignments is gained in other ways, Americans may simply become unqualified for top management roles in the future.

I am not recommending that the old model of a quasi-permanent corps of long term U.S. expatriates be resurrected. Rather, that the corps of expatriates served a number of important functions and their placement on the endangered species list leaves a vacuum that must be filled. I do feel that there is increasing value to expatriate assignment as firms become global competitors and that a means must be found to provide this experience to as many managers as possible. That would probably involve shorter term expatriate assignments whose purpose is avowedly developmental—for both the individual and the organization.

References

Bartlett, C. A. Building and managing the transnational: The new organizational challenge, in Michael E. Porter (Ed.), Competition in global industries, pp. 367-404, 1986.

Bartlett, C. A. How multinational organizations evolve. *Journal of Business Strategy*, Summer 1982, 20-32.

Berenbeim, R. E. *Managing the international company: Building a global perspective*, New York: The Conference Board, 1983.

Edwards, L. (1978) Present shock and how to avoid it abroad. *Across the Board*, February 1978, 36-43.

Harvey, M. G. The multinational corporation's expatriate problem: An application of Murphy's Law. *Business Horizons*, January-February 1983, 71-78.

Kobrin, S. J. *International expertise in American Business*. New York: Institute of International Education, 1984.

Mendenhall, M., and Oddou, G. The dimensions of expatriate acculturation: A review. *Academy of Management Review*, 1985, 39-47.

Miller, E. L. The international selection decision: A study of some dimensions of managerial behavior in the selection decision process. *Academy of Management Journal*, 1973, 239-252.

Porter, M. E. Competition in global industries: A conceptual framework, in Michael E. Porter (Ed.), *Competition in global industries*. Boston: Harvard Business School Press, 1-60, 1986.

Prahalad, C. K., and Doz, Y. L. An approach to strategic control in MNCs. *Sloan Management Review*, Summer 1981a, 5-13.

Prahalad, C. K., and Doz, Y. L. Headquarters influence and strategic control in MNCS. *Sloan Management Review*, Fall 1981b, 15-29.

Tung, R. L. Selection and training procedures of U.S., European, and Japanese multinationals. *California Management Review*, Fall 1982, 57-71.

Tung, R. L. Expatriate assignments: Enhancing success and minimizing failure. *Academy of Management Executive*, Summer 1987, 117-126.

Zeira, Y., and Banai, M. Selection of expatriate managers in MNCs: The host country point of view. *International Studies of Management and Organization*, 1985, 33-51.

10. JOINT VENTURES AS SELF-ORGANIZING SYSTEMS: A KEY TO SUCCESSFUL JOINT VENTURE DESIGN AND IMPLEMENTATION

PETER LORANGE

Peter Lorange is the William H. Wurster Professor of Multinational Management and Professor of Management at The Wharton School, and Director of Wharton's Center for International Management Studies. Dr. Lorange has written extensively on the subjects of corporate planning and strategic management. He is a strategic management consultant to major corporations in the US, Europe, South America and the Far East.

GILBERT J. B. PROBST

Dr. Probst is a Professor at the University of Geneva and holder of the Chair of Organization at the University which is located in Switzerland. He is also a faculty member of the International Management Institute (IMI), also located in Geneva.

This paper proposes that joint ventures have self-organizing properties that can be designed and managed to ensure success. These properties, related issues, and recommendations for joint ventures and parent relationships are discussed.

Joint ventures have received a great deal of attention from managers and researchers over the last few years, primarily because of their importance as a strategic alternative. Joint ventures and other forms of cooperative arrangements, are increasingly seen as options that organizations have at their disposal to develop novel, innovative strategies to compete in today's business environment (Fusfeld and Haklish 1985; Killing 1983; Harrigan 1985; Hagg and Johanson 1983; Lorange 1985, 1986; Contractor and Lorange 1987).

Much discussion has been focused on how to make joint ventures more successful. Typically, these discussions have been focused on developing traditional substantive competitive strategies directed at both the parent and child. A second set of approaches for delineating strategic success has focused on how to apply more appropriate management *processes* to the joint venture, with particular emphasis on how to delineate plans, how to control the joint venture, how to come up with appropriate human resource management processes, etc. (Lorange 1986).

Reprinted from *Columbia Journal of World Business,* Vol. XXII, No. 2, Summer 1987, pp. 71-78 by permission of the publisher.

Appropriately conceived strategic processes can represent an important compliment to well delineated strategies—strategic content *and* process go hand-in-hand.

This article takes a somewhat different approach. Properly conceived strategies and processes may often be inadequate if they cannot be adjusted to meet changing circumstances. A dynamic, evolutionary view of the cooperative venture's development may be needed. Consequently, we shall claim that any organization, in order to be successful, must possess self-organizing properties in order to cope with evolutionary pressures (Probst 1985, 1987). An organization must adapt and evolve on its own to meet new environmental circumstances. Joint ventures must be similarly flexible. However, the reason for many joint venture failures seems to be that they have not been designed with sufficient adaptive properties to cope with emerging environmental turbulences.

The article will first delineate four critical criteria for establishing self-organizing systems and discuss how these principles apply to three joint venture archetypes. These will emerge from a discussion of the so-called organizational boundary delineation issue that is faced by joint ventures. Is a joint venture a "free-standing organization"? How can the structuring of a joint venture be delineated for each of these three archetypes so as to incorporate the four characteristics of self-organization that have been proposed? Is the joint venture in each case organized so that it designs and regulates itself as an entity? The article will conclude by delineating management processes for the joint venture so that they adhere to the four proposed organizing principles. If the choice of strategies, structure and process exclude self-organizing properties, the result over time is likely to be confusion, stress, or failure.

The issues, arguments and recommendations raised by this article should be of particular interest to joint ventures in multinational corporations, although they also apply to domestic joint ventures.

Self-Organization: A Key Premise _____

Self-organizing organizations have been studied extensively by Ulrich/Probst (1984), Probst (1987), Ben-Eli/Probst (1986), Morgan (1986) and others. This stream of research has its source in system theory, and has been applied extensively to biological systems (Ried 1984). Recently, however, there has been an increased emphasis on *social* systems applications. In this article we shall focus on four partly interrelated properties that may enhance social systems' self-organizing potential (cf. Probst, 1987).

Complexity

To label a system as complex is not the same as implying that it is complicated. The question is not only how many elements there are in a system. Rather, the issue is a matter of understanding the nature of the *relatedness* between the parts, when putting together a highly interrelated network, such as a joint venture. It is the *dynamics* that grow with the interrelations and interactions that create complexity.

Complexity is neither good nor bad. Rather, the question is handling complexity, and developing processes of managing it. Building models may be one approach to learning more about complexity. Unfortunately, however, complex systems are often modeled as if they were "trivial machines." Since reality typically is far from this, designing and controlling processes based on such triviality assumptions may have disastrous consequences. Complex systems are analytically indeterminable and unpredictable. Still they are history-dependent and deterministic, and can thus be constructed and designed. However, they change their internal states in response to environmental behavior and corresponding internal control action (v. Foerster, 1984).

The critical question arises: How complex is the context within which a joint venture is supposed to be functioning? For instance, how many owners are there in the joint venture, and how many different and potentially irreconcilable strategies do these parents have? How interrelated are the various parts of the value-creating process: manufacturing, the R&D function, distribution, marketing, etc.? How many different strategies is the joint venture itself supposed to carry out? How many physical locations are there? How many previously autonomous and thus different types of organizational cultures have been put together into a joint venture? To what extent must they interact? How turbulent is the environment with which the joint venture interacts?

The more complex the situation is the more difficult it will be for a joint venture to become an effective self-organizing system. Consequently, "respect" for, and sensitivity to, complexity is critical. A joint venture's strategies are designed to cope with the complexity of its competitive environment. The joint venture's structure and organization consequently need to be designed in such a way that it can execute its strategy and realistically be able to cope with its environment. To build in sufficient flexibility in a joint venture is a crucial factor. How *complex* the joint venture *system* will need to be to achieve this depends on the *requisite variety* in its environment. The challenge will be to make the system complex enough to adapt to its environment, but simple enough to be managed.

Self-Reference

Self-organizing systems are "operationally closed." All behaviour of the system feeds back on itself and becomes the basis for the system's behaviour. Operationally closed networks must create and maintain their own boundaries on a continuously evolving basis. Similarly, in social systems the symbolic, less tangible aspects of the system need to be re-aligned relative to the environment. An argument raised by one of IBM's founding fathers illustrates what self-reliance and maintenance of systems boundaries means in a joint venture context: ". . . if an organization is to meet the challenge of a changing world, it must be prepared to change everything about itself except those beliefs, as it moves through corporate life" (Watson, 1965, p. 4). The boundaries drawn may well be a manifestation of the corporate culture, and of shared beliefs. What this implies is that while certain aspects of the boundaries always should be changed, others should be seen as so "well set on the map" that changing them would question the basic rationale of the organization.

What does self-reference and boundary reassessment mean in the context of a joint venture? The ongoing viability of a joint venture will depend significantly on its ability to maintain a degree of internal coherence while it readjusts to the environment. What the system does, how it reacts as a consequence of its structuring must be considered. The ability to develop feedback properties in the joint venture organization so that its members can learn from its own past is also key. It must develop plans and control mechanisms which allow it to adapt to changes in environmental circumstances. Thus, a manager must build on "experience" regarding the initial business strategy's execution, so as to make further refinements and redirection as needed.

However, the mechanisms for adjusting the system's boundaries must function to maintain internal cohesion and agreement among the key stakeholders. They must provide a shared, agreed-upon sense of self-referencing.

A critical design issue is whether the joint venture is able to develop its own plans and to monitor progress against these plans, so that necessary boundary adjustments may be made and necessary experiential competencies developed. If the joint venture's planning function is "split" among the various partners in such a way that less realistic learning and adaptive feedback measures are generated, then the joint venture will face disadvantages due to this lack of self-reference. Similarly, if the control process is delineated so it is not self-corrective, needed changes due to dysfunctional design aspects imposed by the partners' realistic feedback and adaptation measures may be impossible. The management system may be too fragmented and bureaucratized, and have too many irreconcilable parts to create a self-referencing organization. Is the joint venture organization complete, stable and flexible enough to interpret the experiences from its initial actions, and build up a learning process, adapt and evolve over time? Or, are the managers so fragmented in their loyalties, and are organizational tasks carried out on such an ad-hoc basis, that learning will not occur? Thus, self-reference, in the form of ability to develop corrective and innovative boundary redefinition, based on creative feedback, learning and development, is critical in order to make a joint venture successful. As the joint venture evolves, the roles of various stakeholders involved will change —some may become more active, visible and powerful — others may eventually withdraw. Moreover, these realignments must be commonly shared, understood and accepted through the self-referencing process.

Autonomy

Self-organizing systems must be autonomous. The interrelations and interactions defining a system as an entity should only involve the system in question and no other system. Even free standing self-regulating systems with self-referential abilities, may not necessarily be independent (cf. Susman 1976). No real-life system that is part of a larger encompassing whole can be totally independent. To a greater or lesser degree, it will be dependent on resources, markets, technologies and values. To operationalize the meaning of autonomy therefore, "why the system does what it does" as a quasi-independent entity should be concentrated on, instead of the contingent factors "determining" limits of the system's autonomy. Autonomous systems produce their limits and the limits define the system.

Research should emphasize the search for sources and rules that impact the internal delineation, maintenance and transformation of the value-creating coherences. A joint venture will have to depict a certain degree of free-standing independence within its environment to survive in the long run. If it totally relies on reacting to environmental demands, on behalf of the parents and using resources "borrowed" from them, it becomes dependent and has no control over its destiny. Autonomy in the sense of controlling sufficient resources to act and react independently, thus, becomes a key factor for survival (cf. Peters and Waterman 1982, p. 322, Gomez and Probst 1984). In this context, autonomy therefore means whether the joint venture is sufficiently "complete" organizationally and with respect to its resource composition to be able to be a sufficiently free-standing, self-regulating entity. Is the management of the joint venture given enough holistic authority to carry out its tasks in a reasonably independent way, or are responsibility patterns so fragmented that no autonomy can exist? To the extent that that autonomy is maintained, it becomes another important source for making joint ventures more successful.

Redundancy

Self-organizing systems are redundant. There are potentially more resources, management capacities and processes embedded in the system than strictly are needed. This gives the system added flexibility to adapt and evolve. Often this redundancy stems from being able to design and control something in time and at the right place, in the face of unexpected opportunities. Resources may, therefore, be found in "one" centralized locus but may also be distributed throughout the system. This redundancy of functions gives the system flexibility. This is a purposeful redundancy of functions and not a wasteful redundance of the "same" parts (see Trist 1981, Morgan 1986). Redundancy is built into a system in the sense that the whole is organized into parts, with a minimal specification (cf. Herbst 1976) of the structuring of a part. It is, of course, a difficult question to determine how many parts, and how much overlap one should settle for. Here again the answer lies in the law of requisite variety, creating enough behavioral states for the system to adapt and develop.

A joint venture should be set up to have alternative ways of carrying out its value creation tasks if something should go wrong. For otherwise, it will have little or no flexibility to deal with emergencies. It may be obliged to be dependent on its parent organizations in very specific ways which, in essence, makes it very unadaptive in coping with emergencies. Therefore, redundancies up to a limit, in the form of a certain amount of built-in flexibility, is another necessary precondition for developing successful self-organizing joint ventures.

Joint Venture Self-Organizing Archetypes _____

It is critical to understand what the strategies of each of the parent organizations are when delineating the design of a joint venture. For instance, do each of the parents have a strong interest in the business that the joint venture is engaged in, or are the parents more passive regarding their own future in the area where joint venture is engaged? As a variant, does one of the parents expect to continue to be active strategically in the same business area as the joint venture, while the other parent expects to become more passive in the future?

The task of adapting to new environmental circumstances is intimately related to answering questions such as the ones just posed. If both parents expect to be strategically active in the same business as the joint venture, many adaptive responsibilities and initiatives will have to be executed by the parents, and the joint venture might be relatively dependent on the parents and might not adapt on its own fully. If, on the other hand, none of the parents expect to remain strategically active in the business, then the joint venture organization must be largely responsible for adapting to new environmental circumstances. In this case, a more autonomous joint venture organization which possessed a range of resources would be needed to carry out these adaptive tasks.

A third and intermediate alternative would be that one parent intends to be highly involved in the same business as the joint venture, but the other parent does not. In this case, the adaptive responsibilities should be shared between the active parent and the joint venture, yielding sufficient integration between this parent and the joint venture to allow for effective adaptation.

The implication of this discussion is that three types of joint venture archetypes emerge, as are illustrated by Charts 1, 2 and 3. For each of these archetypes, we now explore what would be necessary to develop effective self-organizing capabilities.

Chart 1 illustrates that none of the parents intend to continue to have a strong direct operating future strategic interest in the strategy that the joint venture is pursuing. Rather, these activities are "transferred" to the joint venture by each partner. To make the joint venture a self-organizing system, able to adapt on its own, might be relatively straightforward in this case.

The complexity of the joint venture itself does not have to be excessive, given that the structuring of the various subtasks in the value-creating process can be done as if the joint venture was a free-standing, independent company. The self-referencing task of redefining boundaries for the joint venture's activities might

Chart 1
A FREESTANDING JOINT VENTURE, PURSUING
ITS OWN STRATEGY.   NONE OF THE PARENTS ACTIVITY
PURSUE THIS STRATEGY.

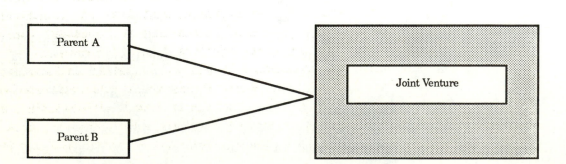

also be relatively straightforward, having to focus primarily on adjustments among the joint venture organization's members. The autonomy issue might be resolved by establishing standard responsibility control processes, authority limits, etc.

Finally it is up to the parents to equip the joint venture with a certain degree of redundancy, so that it will have the necessary capacity to be flexible. Not surprisingly, a number of successful joint ventures fall into this category.

Chart 2 shows a self-organizing system, consisting of parent A together with a joint venture that must adapt to be consistent with parent A's future strategic interests. Since parent B is no longer actively interested in the strategy, it is not part of the self-organizing system, but rather plays the role as a more passive investor.

To make this type of joint venture work in a self-organizing mode will typically be considerably more difficult than was the case in Chart 1. Maintaining a realistic level of complexity will be complicated by splitting the value-creating functions between parent A and the emerging joint venture organization. Often it may be hard to establish a sufficiently simple division of labor. The self-referencing issue may also become particularly difficult. As the joint venture adapts, and needs to redefine how it should execute its strategies (i.e. boundary adjustments), accepting changes in roles between parent A and the joint venture organization may become sensitive. Typical reactions in parent A's organization may be that the joint venture organization is too aggressive, trying to carve out its own "kingdom" in an unreasonable way. Within the joint venture organization similar negative reac-

Chart 2
A JOINT VENTURE THAT IS PURSUING A STRATEGY
WHICH ALSO IS BEING PURSUED BY PARENT A, BUT IS
NO LONGER BEING ACTIVELY PURSUED BY PARENT B.

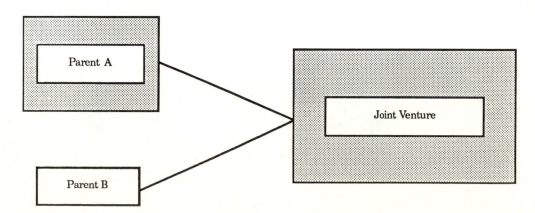

tions may exist, now based on frustrations from perceptions that the parent A organization is holding back too much.

The autonomy issue may be relatively easy to resolve provided that the self-referencing of boundary changes is working well. However, without agreements on such resulting shifts in tasks over time it will also be difficult to redistribute the balances of autonomy. Finally, the redundancy issue should be relatively easy to handle, assuming that the resource scarcity is not so high that a certain degree of redundancy cannot be established as was true in one case. Specialized technical management capacity was lacking, and could not be supplied by any means in the short run. There are examples of both successes and failures among joint ventures that fall into the Chart 2 category.

In Chart 3, *each* of the parents are continuing to have an active interest in the same type of business that the joint venture is set up to serve. Thus *two* interrelated self-organizing systems are to be considered. One consists of parent A together with the joint venture. This should facilitate adaptation challenges consistent with the strategic interests of parent A. A second self-organizing system will consist of parent B together with the joint venture, set up so as to facilitate parent B's adaptation consistent with *its* future strategic interests. Making this type of joint venture work may be quite demanding.

A careful delineation of potentially conflicting interests between the two partially overlapping self-organizing systems must be worked out. It is useful to

Chart 3
A JOINT VENTURE THAT IS PURSUING A
STRATEGY WHICH IS ALSO BEING ACTIVELY PURSUED
(AT LEAST IN PART) BY EACH PARENT.

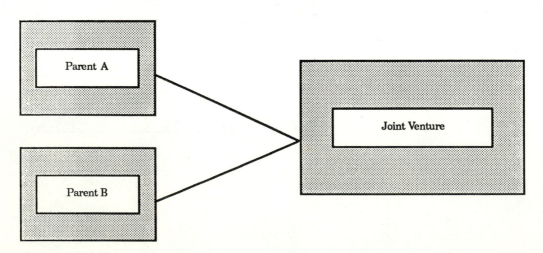

delineate such potential conflicts as they might occur along the four self-organizing principles that were proposed. First, in terms of complexity, the value-creating process will now involve both parents as well as the joint venture organization. Given potentially diverging perspectives among the partners regarding how the value-creating process is to be carried out might lead to excessively complex solutions, the result being compromises where both parties get their way without resolving their differences of opinions. Self-referencing boundary changes and resulting task reassignments may also be hard as was already discussed for Chart 2. In this case, it will be even more difficult, given that the joint venture organization must clarify its revised roles as part of *two* self-referencing processes. The autonomy issue, closely related to the self-referencing issue as it is, might also create conflicts. This may be particularly hard to resolve if one parent attempts to shift more autonomy over to the joint venture organization at a faster rate, while the other attempts to hold back.

Finally, a useful level of redundancy may be viewed differently by each parent, depending on their own resource bases as well as on what parts of the value-creating process they are responsible for and consequently how much flexibility they feel they need. Thus a Chart 3 type of joint venture is a demanding one and the risk of failure is quite high; however, there are still examples of success in this category.

An examination of these types of joint ventures reveals the importance of understanding what type of situation is at hand. The type of self-organizing system that should be considered in a given joint venture context should be clear. However, the joint venture itself, in its legalistic form, does not necessarily have to be a self-organizing system. Only in archetype 1 is this the case. Often this difference between legal boundaries and *de facto* boundaries confuses the various management teams involved. This confusion can create dysfunctional designs and management processes.

Further Structuring of the Joint Venture _____

We have seen that the task for establishing self-organization will differ from one archetype to another. To be clear and realistic about what these differences entail might in itself foster better self-organization. In addition, there are ways to further structure a joint venture to achieve even better self-organizing properties. Three such tasks for structuring the self-organizing features of joint ventures are discussed. Again, how these tasks might differ for the three archetypes will be explored. The three structuring tasks are: How to organize the joint venture; how to develop a set of unique know-how or "protected black-box features," allowing the parents and/or the joint venture to possess unique organizational capabilities on their own without having to fear that these will be "given away" to their "partners"; and how to appropriately tailor management processes to the given joint venture situation.

How to Organize a Joint Venture

The organizational delineation of the joint venture under archetype 1 would be a fairly complete, more or less free-standing organization. This complete organization should have the necessary requisite variety and redundancy, but should also be kept as simple as possible. The key here, in terms of summarizing the organizing task, is for the partners "not to be too skimpy" when they set up the joint venture, realizing that incurring realistic organizing expenses is critical.

Under archetype 2 the organizational design will typically be one of delineating a joint venture which would be reconcilable with parent A's organization. This joint venture organization will typically be small at the outset and be exemplified by the type of organizational form found in project-based strategic programs. It should be delineated very explicitly, and should enter a simple inter-relationship with the parent. Lack of respect for how much complexity can be handled may be a problem, and considerable emphasis on finding the right management team, and the joint venture head *cum* project manager is critical. Broad-based experience from previous project management tasks may be particularly valuable.

In archetype 3, the same considerations apply as before. The joint venture organization itself can be expected to be relatively small, drawing extensively on both parents A and B, at least at the out-set.

Thus, it is important that the joint venture is set up to ensure that both parents working independently of each other but together with the joint venture, have the autonomy to adapt and evolve. Similarly, it is important that the joint venture is created so that each of the parents have sufficient redundancy to cope with an unexpected event. If any or both of the parents give away critical functions, without allowing for sufficient redundancy, the self organizing capabilities of the parents, working with the joint venture, might be limited.

Unique Know-How and Black Box Protected Features

The creation of a "black box" in the self-organizing context refers to a partner's exercise of discretionary control over several types of strategic resources. Examples of strategic resources are: financial resources; discretionary technological know-how; unique marketing access and know-how; exclusive distribution channels; political contacts and clout; managerial resources and so on (cf. Lorange 1985). Unreflective creation of "black boxes" can represent a strain on the self-organizing properties of a joint venture. For archetype 1 this is not an issue in that unique competences and skills will have been vested in the joint venture organization itself, having the autonomy to control its own "black box," i.e. possess its own patents, know-hows and technology base.

For archetype 2 it is critical that a common "black box" gets developed between parent A and the joint venture. A problem might develop if partner A fails to provide the joint venture with access to its entire know-how base, but is "holding back." Loss of autonomy and redundancy may result. Due to the nature of this joint venture, parent B will probably not want to gain control over this "black box," but be satisfied with the financial returns it should receive as a "sleeping partner."

In archetype 3, it will be natural that both parents wish to maintain a certain control over their own black boxes, so that a full exposure of each of the parents' strategic positions to the other partner will not take place, at least not initially. Such "black boxes" can often be quite rigid *and* complex, making it difficult for the joint venture organization to be self-organizing. While such limiting effects on joint venture's self-organizing properties can not be ameliorated entirely, sensitivity to this potential problem should result in understanding and moderation on the part of each parent. The "black boxes" for each parent must provide *some* minimal protection while still leaving the joint venture flexibility to carry out its strategies. Similarly there must be enough redundancy, in terms of some degree of duplication of technology and other know-how.

Choice of Management Processes: Strategic Planning

A management process that is critical to strengthening self-organization is strategic planning. Strategic planning differs for each of the three joint venture archetypes. For archetype 1, the strategic planning process is contained within the joint venture organization, i.e. it delineates its own objectives and creates strategic programs for implementing them. The planning process should be simple and focused on the autonomous joint venture organization. The process should place sufficient emphasis on taking past experiences into account, so that the plans can reflect an accumulation of learning and on-going improvement and strengthening of the strategies. Facilitating effective self-referencing among the members of the organization and necessary emphasis on redundancy in developing plans is also key.

For archetype 2 the planning process will have to be worked out in parallel between parent A and the joint venture as well as between parent B and the joint venture. The critical importance the planning process can have for improving the self-referencing process is to be stressed. Establishing a basis for common understanding about the effects of boundary adjustments, such as task-redefinitions is critical. Here the strategic planning process is important.

For archetype 3 the execution of a strategic planning process is even more complex. The planning process that parent A together with the joint venture works out must be reconcilable with the one that parent B follows in consonance with the joint venture. A key challenge in carrying out these parallel planning processes is not to create too much complexity. Similarly the plans must be autonomous enough both from parent A's point of view and from parent B's point of view to allow for adaptability as well as for innovation. And finally these plans must allow for the accumulation of know-how in the form of self referential processes, seen both from parent A's and parent B's points of view. Needless to say, these types of planning settings are often very difficult to work out, due to the overlapping complex and potentially conflict-laden nature of these parallel processes. In total, the choice of planning process can be significantly different depending on the type of self-organizing setting. The appropriate choice of management processes for archetype 1 will be different from those appropriate for archetype 2 or archetype 3. Lack of sufficient attention to the tailor-made choice of management processes can lead to difficulties when it comes to effective self-organization, and thus hamper adaptation and innovation.

Conclusion

This paper has proposed that for joint ventures to be successful their self-organizing properties must be developed. By understanding and adapting the relationship of the joint venture to one or both of its parents, in light of these properties, more appropriate organizational forms and more effective management processes can be chosen, which lead to better performing joint ventures and improved long-term success.

References

Ben-Eli, M. and G. J. B. Probst. "The Way You Look Determines What You See—or Self-Organization in Management and Society," in R. Trappl, ed., *Cybernetics and Systems*, Reidel, Dordrecht, 1986, pp. 277-284.

Contractor, F. and Lorange, P. *Cooperative Strategies in International Companies*, D.C. Heath-Lexington Books: Lexington, MA 1987.

Fusfeld, H. J. and C. S. Haklisch. "Cooperative R&D for Competitors," *Harvard Business Review*, No. 11, 1985, pp. 60-76.

Foerster, H. V. "Principles of Self-Organization—In a Socio-Managerial Context," H. Ulrich and G. J. B. Probst, eds., *Self-Organization and Management of Social Systems*, Springer, Berlin, 1984, pp. 2-24.

Gomez, P. and G. J. B. Probst. "Organizational Closure in Management—A Complementary View to Contingency Approaches," *Cybernetic Newsletter*, Vienna, 1986.

Herbst, P. G. *Alternatives to Hierarchies*, Nijoff, Leiden, 1976.

Haag, I. and J. Johanson. *Firms in Networks: A New Perspective on Competitive Power*, Business and Social Research Institute: Uppsala, 1983.

Harrigan, K. R. *Strategies for Joint Ventures*, Lexington Books: New York, 1985.

Harrigan, K. R. *Managing for Joint Venture Success*, Lexington Books: New York, 1986.

Killing, P. *Strategies for Joint Venture Success*, London, Ontario, 1983.

Lorange, P. "Cooperative Strategies: Planning and Control Considerations," Wharton School Working Paper 5/1985, Philadelphia.

Lorange, P. "Human Resource Management in Multinational Cooperative Ventures," *Human Resource Management*, Spring 1986, Vol. 25, No. 1, pp. 133-148.

Lorange, P., Scott Morton, M. S. and S. Ghoshal. *Strategic Control*, West Publishing: St. Paul, 1986.

Morgan, G. *Images of Organization*, Sage, Beverly Hills, 1986.

Peters, T. J. and R. H. Waterman. *In Search of Excellence*, Harper & Row: New York, 1982.

Probst, G. J. B. "Some Cybernetic Principles for the Design, Control and Development of Social Systems," *Cybernetics and Systems*, Washington, 1985, pp. 171-180.

Probst, G. J. B. *Selbst-Organization*, Parey, Hamburg, 1987.

Riedl, R. Self-organization: Some Theoretical Cross-connections, H. Ulrich and G. J. B. Probst, eds. *Self-Organization and Management of Social Systems,* Springer: Berlin, 1984.

Susman, G. I. *Autonomy at Work*, Praeger: New York, 1987.

Trist, E. "The Evolution of Socio-Technical Systems," Occasional Paper No. 2, QWL Centre: Ontario, 1981.

Ulrich, H. and G. J. B. Probst, ed. *Self-Organization and Management of Social Systems*, Springer, Berlin, 1984.

Watson, T. J. *A Business and its Beliefs: The Ideals that Helped Build IBM*, McGraw-Hill: New York, 1963.

11. COMMON MISTAKES OF JOINT VENTURE EXPERIENCED FIRMS

MARJORIE A. LYLES

Marjorie A. Lyles is currently an Associate Professor of Strategic Management at the School of Business at Ball State University. Her research centers on strategic management and decision making. Of particular interest has been the descriptive rather than prescriptive models of strategic decision making and planning systems.

Four multinational firms with extensive experience in international joint ventures were surveyed to determine what mistakes they had made while joint venturing. They agree that mistakes often had little impact on the success or failure of the joint venture in meeting its objectives, but they do impact what the firms have learned from their joint venturing experiences. This paper reports on the nature of these mistakes, the apparent causes of these mistakes, and the learning that results.

Much of the current disenchantment with joint ventures stems from the frustration of having to deal with joint management. To help dispel some of this disenchantment, a variety of insights may be gained from firms with many and varied joint venture experiences in order to determine what has been learned. One method for determining the nature of organizational learning is to show imbalances or mistakes that serve as stimuli for learning.

This paper documents common mistakes which have occurred in four firms that have been successful at operating multiple international joint ventures over the last thirty years. The common causes of mistakes and the nature of these mistakes will be identified. The paper addresses what these firms have learned from their past mistakes. This discussion should be useful to all MNCs involved in or contemplating entering into joint ventures, who do not want to repeat others' mistakes.

Mistakes: Basic Character

Nothing would be more comforting than to suggest that the tendency toward making mistakes stems from poor management or ineffective organizations. If it

Reprinted from *The Columbia Journal of World Business,* Vol. XXII, No. 2, Summer 1987, pp. 79-85 by permission of the publisher.

were so, we would simply study only those firms which make no mistakes. Unfortunately the reality is that all firms, successful and unsuccessful, make mistakes.

One of the key distinctions of successful firms, however, involves learning from one's mistakes and taking corrective actions. The term "learning" refers to the development of insights, knowledge and associations between past actions, the effectiveness of those actions, and future actions.[1]

Organizational learning is not synonymous with change. Rather, it involves organizational adjustment triggered by an impetus or force for change or continuity. These forces for change are most frequently imbalances, difficulties, negative performance feedback, or in other words, mistakes. They generate stress that encourages the evaluation of traditional beliefs, strategies or norms.[2]

Part of learning is unlearning and reframing past behaviors that are no longer appropriate. To determine if unlearning occurs, one must look for environmental jolts, mistakes, failures, critical incidents, or changes in the standard methods for managing the operations of JVs.

Mistakes made by firms while joint venturing do not necessarily lead to the failure or to the termination of the joint venture. The joint venture may continue to operate and to accomplish its objectives. The mistake is usually recognized by the parent firm as it continues its involvement in the joint venture. It may not be recognized all at once, rather, recognition may evolve over time. These mistakes are frequently vocalized as "lessons" by the parent firm.

Mistakes and International Joint Ventures_____

Mistakes in joint venturing are all too familiar. Articles have frequently dealt with the failure or divorce rate of joint ventures. There is a tendency to assume that either these mistakes are country specific, that they are dependent on the stage of development of the MNC, that they are inevitable and therefore, cannot be resolved, or that they are joint venture specific. Unfortunately these approaches are not helpful for improving the effectiveness of joint venture management. What is required is a means of determining the cause of these mistakes and understanding how to link these mistakes to the organization's future actions or learning.

It is a mistake to understand or perceive something wrongly or to take a wrong action. Mistakes may result from the *lack of cognitive development* either because the situation is not understood or because it is rapidly changing or from *errors in the actions taken*. Most firms involved in international joint venturing are dealing with uncertain, changing environments and are frequently operating in unfamiliar political environments. Thus, mistakes in joint venturing are most frequently caused by poor judgments, actual human behavioral errors, or unanticipated events.

One reason that firms form joint ventures centers on reducing risks and minimizing the chance of making mistakes in uncertain environments. By sharing resources and information, firms attempt to eliminate the risk of making a mistake in achieving their strategic goals. However, forming a joint venture creates a risk in itself, namely, that of managing an entity jointly. Misunderstandings of the role of each partner and false concepts of the relatedness of the firms may exist. Difficulties arising from differences in size force partners to confront power issues. Unclear performance expectations create stress.

The critical strategic issues about which mistakes frequently occur are listed in Table 1. These are important issues that lend themselves to joint negotiations, inherent stakes, future uncertainties and evolution of expectations over time. They involve decisions about the division of labor, the division of authority, and who has power over what. Confounding this is the notion that these issues take on different dimensions at different points in time.[3]

The nature of mistakes in joint venturing has a certain context; namely, they may center on issues of technology or human resources, etc. Although most research on joint ventures has looked only at a particular point in time, analyzing mistakes involves looking backwards in time to determine why a certain action did not achieve the desired results. It involves an in-depth look at the joint venture to assess the motives, the frames of reference, the norms, and the expectations of the parents.

Research on Joint Venture Experienced Firms

By including an in-depth analysis of a few joint venture experienced firms and the various mistakes they have made, this paper gives a rare first hand look at the success of joint venture relationships and how to manage them. Four firms were selected based on their long histories with joint venturing and their current involvement in multiple JVs. Each has at least thirty years JV experience, at least twenty on going JVs, and experiences with a variety of JV configurations in numerous locations. Appendix I summarizes the business areas of each firm. Two were American and two were European, and each had sales of over $2 billion. All four firms have at least one joint venture that is fifteen years old.

Field interviews were conducted with the four firms, and some access was granted to interview partner firms and joint venture management. Corporate management, line and staff personnel involved in joint venture decisions were in-

Table 1
NATURE OF MISTAKES

1. Technology:
   - Licensing
   - Pricing
   - Transfer

2. Human Resources:
   - Career paths
   - Turnover

3. Negotiations:
   - Building in future conflicts
   - Ambiguous terminology

4. Partner Rapport:
   - Maintaining trust
   - Partner choice
   - Equity decisions

5. Goals/Objectives:
   - "Pinched shoe" effect
   - Acquisition of partner

cluded. These interviews covered the historical evolutions of the firm's JV decisions, the factors affecting future JV decisions, mistakes that were made, and what was learned from these mistakes. The field interviews were verified through archival data, other informants, and published accounts.

This methodology is appropriate because information about a firm's perceived mistakes and learning from these mistakes is not available outside that firm. It requires an in-depth analysis of a lagged phenomenon.

Common Categories of Mistakes _____

Table 2 summarizes the events mentioned by the respondents.[4] Two categories, future conflicts and partner rapport, were identified within three firms as influencing their learning. Both of these concern maintaining a good partner relationship.

Future Conflicts

Future conflicts acknowledges that at formation, there may be mixed motives and hidden agendas by both firms. For example, one firm formed a JV to have its products manufactured and marketed in a particular country. As time passed, the parent company acquired the skills necessary to market the product themselves and they thought their skills were better than the JV's. This created a conflict.

What the firms learned is to accept that one firm's reasons for participating in the JV may change, and to recognize that they want to acquire their partner's skills over a period of time. One person said, "The only general learning is that you have to be very, very careful that you think of all the potential conflicts of interest. It's more likely in your core business, core countries, than on the fringe." It appears that when the firms had less JV experience, they believed that a JV was forever and that there would be minimal conflict.

One firm openly admitted to having mixed motives at the time of formation that led to mistakes in managing its relationship with its partner firm. "We tried to be very open about our intent to learn the skills of our partner, but it still led to problems."

Partner Rapport

Mistakes relating to how to maintain partner rapport were frequently mentioned. These were verbalized in lessons such as "If you have 51%, you should not try to behave as if you have 100%. You should treat your partners with 49% as if they were yourself," and "Have the firm's president meet with top partners when he is traveling." These were seen as important as the firms learned to deal with the ambiguity of JVs' futures.

Table 2
UNLEARNING/MISTAKES

| Types | Firms | | | |
	C1	C2	C3	C4
Building in future conflicts	X		X	X
Partner rapport issues	X	X		X
Technology transfer issues		X	X	
Cultural issues				
Human resource			X	
Futuristic issues	X	X		
Equity issues				X
Partner choice				X

Several people remarked about the long-lived effect of a mistake on partner rapport. This is especially evident in joint ventures where the management is there to stay or where your partner is a family-owned firm. One manager said, "If you are dealing with an organization about a past mistake, the organization gets over it because the people change. If you are dealing with individuals, they don't forget—and maybe their children won't forget."

There are frequently mixed motives within the parent company about the JV. Some firms did not have agreement throughout their organizations about the goals and objectives of the JV which lead to mistakes in dealing with their partners. "The ventures have got to satisfy the real desires of both parties to be successful. That's sometimes not easy, and sometimes not perceived throughout your organization, because it means making trade-offs all the time." Several firms mentioned making mistakes by having the JV directly competing with the parent company in some markets and in producing the same products. This led to the staff of the parent company withholding information from or not cooperating with the JV.

Technology Transfer

All four of the firms frequently formed joint ventures that included technical cooperation agreements that specified the extent to which the technology and know-how would be transferred. It was also common for the partner firms to enter the JV for the primary purpose of acquiring the technology. The two American firms especially viewed Technology Transfer as an area in which they made mistakes. They said it takes experience to recognize that once you license your mature or stable technology, you sell your business and create a new competitor.

All of the firms have made a mistake in judgment about how to handle their technology at one time or another. In the core business area the possibility of conflict is higher than with a business on the fringe of the operations. One firm admitted that it had at least three joint ventures fail because it had licensed its technology in its core business areas and this led to major conflicts later. Another firm said that it was accused by its partner of taking the technology licensed to the joint venture and using the technology in its home office to compete with its partner.

Cultural Issues

Cultural differences have been discussed in the literature as a problem in JVs because of country differences and firm differences.[5] None of the firms in the present survey mention this as the nature of a major mistake or failure, although it was mentioned as important for getting along with your partner.

For example, one American firm mentioned a problem that they created by appointing two Australians to the board of a joint venture with the Japanese. The cultural differences between the Australians and the Japanese were an immediate issue for the American partner who corrected the situation within a short period of time.

Human Resources

One firm emphasized the learning that it had to make because of mistakes in the area of human resource management in joint ventures. It had to learn that their people should not be transferred every year or two. "You must guarantee a certain continuity of management." This same firm also emphasized that the type of people you need in managerial/operational positions in a JV need more diplomatic qualities than do the people you need in a wholly-owned subsidiary. "You can absolutely concentrate on 'Is he professionally capable?' for a technical manager in a wholly-owned subsidiary. If you put him in a JV relationship, you also have to look at whether he has enough sensitivity for the relationship."

One European firm identified a mistake of one of its American partners in assuming human resource management was the same in a local wholly-owned subsidiary as it was in a foreign joint relationship. One person said, "I remember people saying to me that those people coming from the States, they are used to making Americans work. They have a totally different style of factory management than you can do in Europe in a joint venture."

Futuristic Issues

The inability to predict the future has created problems for two of the firms. "You can't anticipate. What might have seemed a good mission—well designed—for you, fifteen years from now may look pretty constraining." For one firm, futuristic issues were closely tied to technology transfer: "There has been a tendency to license technology without real consideration of what the long-term implications might be. I think we are becoming more thoughtful." One firm openly stated that they priced their technology much too low initially and this led to problems later.

All firms have made mistakes in making judgment decisions about future legislation. It is impossible to predict ten years in advance what changes will occur. One firm formed a JV in Europe that became illegal when the EEC changed its laws. There were also mistakes in judgments about which ways the laws would go.

A mistake mentioned by one firm is that it used its own name in setting up a foreign JV. This proved to be a mistake for them because the local people perceived a large foreign firm taking profits out of the country. Also, problems emerged later when the JV was divested and its name had to be changed.

One European firm identified an important emerging issue for them. Despite the fact that they believed in decentralized management, they made the mistake of the parent firm's management becoming too closely involved in the day to day operations of the joint venture. This had emerged with the growing changes in communication technology. The joint venture management became more dependent on corporate headquarters, because of the ease with which they could call up on the telephone to say they had a problem.

Equity Issues

Issues regarding the amount of equity and who owned it became an area of concern for one firm. These mistakes took the form of changing the amount of equity in the future and also of changing the ownership of that equity over time. "We would try to avoid as much as possible having part of the company change into a public company where some of the shares were sold to the public on the stock exchange." This firm said that one of its biggest mistakes was allowing too much equity to become public because it forced the JV management to focus too closely on short term returns.

The firms mentioned that they had made mistakes by not having enough control over whom the partner firms might sell their equity to in the joint venture. In several examples, the partner firms sold their shares to firms that were direct competitors of the JV partner. Or, as in the case of one European firm, "We had to learn to live together with a partner which we had not selected . . . a partner which, moreover, had a similar relationship with our biggest competitor in the world."

Partner Choice

Partner choice was an area in which mistakes were made. "We prefer not to give the license to people who look upon it as sort of a lifebuoy, who say 'we are in trouble—maybe introducing your brand name may help us out.'"

A mistake identified by two firms was forming partnerships based solely on sound business reasons and ignoring their "gut" reactions. One person said, "You've got to have someone with whom you can work." Personalities are important. A number of the JVs had problems because the management of the partner firms or the JV president had a clash in styles.

Analyzing Mistakes: Three Basic Causes _____

One of the most frustrating parts of analyzing one's mistakes is the lack of a framework for organizing one's thinking about these problems. There are few (if any) models for sorting out key relationships related to making mistakes. As a result, few managers are able to anticipate a mistake and treat it before it occurs. They generally focus on the symptom rather than the cause of the mistake. This makes learning from the mistake even harder.

It was necessary to step back and analyze why these mistakes in joint venturing were made. Three basic models for managing the mistakes in joint venturing emerged. Each model links a cause, its effects, and its symptoms.

Chart 1: Poor Judgment

Poor judgment appears to be the cause of many mistakes that occurred in joint venturing. It is the result of a decision making process in which there is a lack of understanding or poor cognitive development about the current situation. It affects four primary mistake areas: technology transfer, human resources, future conflicts, and partner rapport. Some of the symptoms of poor judgment are listed in Chart 1. The mistakes caused by poor judgment are often not recognized immediately, but are recognized as the situation evolves.

To overcome poor judgments, the firms found several techniques useful. Developing reward systems that linked the manager's evaluation to future performance helped to overcome poor judgments that resulted from too little time being spent researching an issue. One of the most reliable methods for overcoming poor judgments was to involve different people with different joint venture experiences in the decision making process. Frequently, the process of gaining experience in forming and managing joint ventures helped to improve the judgment calls in decisions.

Poor judgment appears to be a cause of mistakes that can be handled and solved through an improved managerial process. The joint venture experienced firms found that as time passed, their knowledge of whom to involve in the process and the information they had available helped to minimize the possibility of judgment mistakes.

Chart 2: Human Behavioral Errors

Human behavioral errors are difficult to tackle since they involve mistakes that individuals have made. These are actions that have caused problems later. They may have to be corrected in a sensitive manner because it may involve admitting that senior management has made a mistake. Some of the symptoms of a human

Chart 1
EFFECTS AND SYMPTOMS OF POOR JUDGMENT

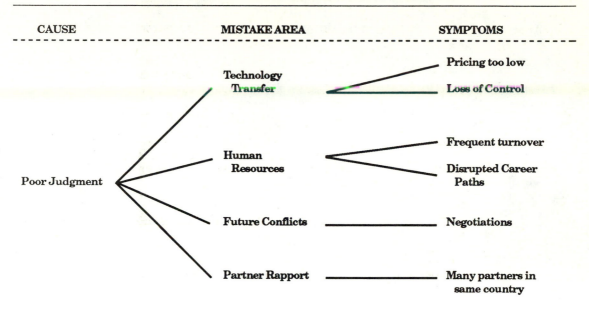

error are unclear terms in the negotiations, mistrust between the partners, or poorly matched expectations. Frequently human errors are immediately apparent and may be closely tied to poor judgment decisions.

The firms mentioned human errors as the least frequent cause of mistakes in joint ventures. It may be possible that the firms have difficulty acknowledging that an error was made that could have been prevented. In any case, human error caused the most difficulty for the firms when asked what they learned from these mistakes. The firms did suggest that one lesson that can be learned from human error is to look for similarities in the joint venture situations so that the same mistake is not made again. A typical method of handling this cause is to remove the person who made the human error. One firm conveyed how the manager of the JV made some mistakes in a contract that was signed. The partner firm who had chosen the manager asked him to turn in his resignation immediately. The removal of people who make human errors may, in fact, be unfortunate since they are the ones who may be able to best convey what should be learned from the mistake.

Chart 2
EFFECTS AND SYMPTOMS OF HUMAN BEHAVIORAL ERRORS

CAUSE   MISTAKE AREA   SYMPTOMS

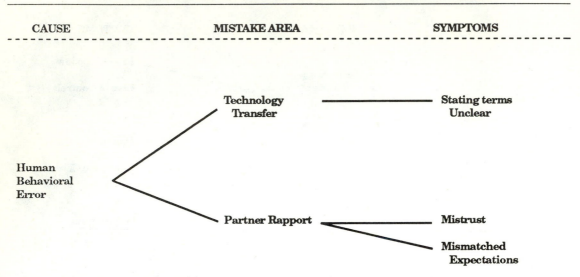

Chart 3: Unanticipated Events

Unanticipated events cause mistakes to be made by the very nature of uncertain futures and risks that are taken. It frequently influences mistakes and affects three primary mistake areas: futuristic issues, technology transfer, and partner rapport. It takes time to recognize these mistakes and frequently no responsibility for them is established.

To overcome mistakes caused by unanticipated events, the firms suggested that they had learned a couple of things. First, they utilized their contract negotiations to stipulate all possible future events. As it turned out, this was both good and bad. At times it was helpful to do this but at other times, the firms found that they were bound by contracts that were outdated or focused on the wrong sets of issues. Some partner firms view it as a sign of mistrust to have to specify everything.

Second, the lesson that the firms learned was to find people or firms with experience that can help to lessen the uncertainty of the future. The firms in the survey find themselves frequently being asked by less experienced firms for advice, and they also turn to others with experience for advice. With the growth of their experience base, the firms have begun to identify certain events that may occur during a JV's life. This helps them to better anticipate major issues and to prevent common mistakes.

Chart 3
EFFECTS AND SYMPTOMS OF UNANTICIPATED EVENTS

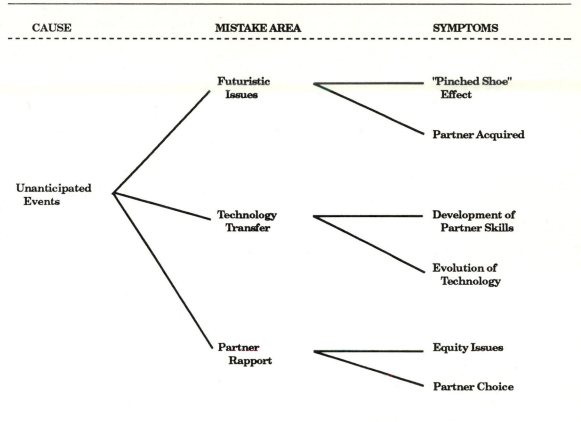

Conclusions _____

This paper has addressed the common mistakes that firms experienced in joint ventures have made. The nature of these mistakes and the common causes were addressed. The firms did not relate JV success to the making of mistakes. In fact, many times the JV may be viewed as a success because the effects of the mistake were overcome. The definition of joint venture success varied among profitability, operating ease, managerial control, JV stability, and/or overall performance.

The three basic causes seemed to account for most of the mistakes encountered by the joint venture experienced firms. By using the models presented, it should be possible for managers to more accurately diagnose the mistake areas and to take corrective actions. Managing mistakes in the context of joint ventures is never easy, and some may require long periods to overcome them. However, it is possible to learn from the mistakes of other firms and in the long run, to more effectively manage joint ventures.

Appendix I
DESCRIPTION OF FIRMS

Company	Gross Sales	Major Lines of Business
C1	$ 7.1 billion	Chemical products, coatings, pharmaceuticals, consumer products, misc. products.
C2	$ 6.3 billion	Air conditioning, chemical and plastics, industrial products, financial services, protective services, transportation equipment.
C3	$ 3.5 billion	Industrial chemicals, petroleum equipment, defense equipment, performance chemicals, specialized machinery.
C4	$ 2.0 billion	Brewing, soft drinks, wine.

Notes

1. Marlene Fiol and Marjorie A. Lyles. "Organizational Learning." *Academy of Management Review,* 10 (4), 803-813.
2. Robert H. Miles. *Coffin Nails and Corporate Strategies.* Englewood Cliffs, N.J.: Prentice Hall, 1982.
3. John I. Reynolds. "The 'Pinched Shoe' Effect of International Joint Ventures." *Columbia Journal of World Business,* 19 (2), 23-29.
4. Marjorie A. Lyles. "Learning Among Joint Venture Sophisticated Firms." Presented at Colloquium on Cooperative Strategies in International Business. Sponsored by the Wharton School and Rutgers Graduate School of Management, October, 1986.
5. Kathryn Rudie Harrigan. *Strategies for Joint Ventures.* Lexington, Mass.: Lexington Books, 1985.

ANNOTATED BIBLIOGRAPHY

ANNOTATED BIBLIOGRAPHY

Adler, Nancy J. "Pacific Basin Managers: A Gaijin, Not a Woman." *Human Resource Management* 26, no. 2 (Summer 1987): 169–191.

This article explores the question, Can North American firms send female managers to Asia or must they limit international management positions to men? Fifty-two women who held management positions in Asia were interviewed and found to be very successful. The author argues that the growing global competition makes the option of just sending male managers overseas old fashioned. Recommendations for change are offered.

Agthe, K. E., and Pendorgast, K. J. "Bhumiputra: What Is It? And Why do I Need It: (Organization Structure of Multinational Corporations)." *Business Horizons* 26 (November-December 1983): 60–68.

Growing nationalism puts many pressures on how multinational companies operate. But there are clear guidelines for choosing the right structure to match the situation: partnership, franchise, or wholly owned subsidiary.

Alpanda, G. G. "A Comparative Study of the Motivational Environment Surrounding First-line Supervisors in the Countries. (Netherlands, France, U.S.)." *Columbia Journal of World Business* 19 (Fall 1984): 95–103.

This article reports the results and implications of an exploratory study comparing the patterns of motivational factors among first-line supervisors in manufacturing organizations in Holland, France, and the United States. It concludes that these patterns differ greatly, with each country having different degrees of correlation of motivational factors and with markedly different loci of correlation.

Avishai, Bernard: "Managing Against Apartheid." *Harvard Business Review* 6 (November-December 1987): 49–56.

This article contains an interview with Anthony H. Bloom, a liberal South African business leader. He tells us why it is right for South African companies to struggle against apartheid and wrong for U.S. companies to pull out.

Badr. H. A., and others. "Personal Values and Managerial Decision Making: Evidence From Two Cultures." *Management International Review* 22 no. 3 (1982): 65–73.

This article describes an empirical study of the relationship between personal values and managerial decision making in a cross-cultural context—specifically, the United States and Egypt. The results indicate that while the personal value structures of the two groups studied were different, the managerial decisions of each group were basically consistent with their respective value structures.

Baliga, B. R., and Taeger A. M. "Multinational Corporation: Control System and Delegation Issues." *Journal of International Business Studies* 15 (Fall 1984): 25–40.

This paper has two major objectives: (1) to identify control and delegation issues confronting multinational corporation managers and (2) to develop a conceptual model to assist multinational corporation managers in selecting appropriate control systems and in determining the extent of delegation to be provided to subsidiary managers.

Barry, B. "Human and Organizational Problems Affecting Growth in the Smaller Enterprise." *Management International Review* (Britain) 20, no. 1 (1980): 39–49.

Although small firms are currently attracting considerable interest, until recently research in the field of management and organization has tended to concentrate on larger, more formal concerns, and its relevance to the small and medium-sized business enterprise may be questioned. This paper describes some of the problems in human and organizational difficulties faced by smaller enterprises. It also offers suggestions on how the problems may be solved.

Bartlett, Christopher A., and Ghoshal, Sumantra. "Organizing for Worldwide Effectiveness: The Transnational Solution." *California Management Review* 31, no. 1 (Fall 1988): 54–74.

Traditional organizational forms no longer seem to be competitively effective in the international environment. Companies with worldwide operations need to have global coordination and national flexibility simultaneously. The traditional structure usually provides one attribute but not the other. The authors show their point using two major competitors: Philips and Matsushita. They also discuss a new organizational model—the transnational organization, which is based on an integrated network of worldwide operations.

———. "Tap Your Subsidiaries for Global Reach." *Harvard Business Review* no. 6 (November-December 1986): 87–94.

Successful MNCs, like Procter & Gamble, Philips N.V., and NEC, are re-examining the usual top-down way of running national subsidiaries. They are encouraging initiative and enterprise and are seeing it pay off.

Beaty, David T., and Harari, Oren. "South Africa: White Managers, Black Voices." *Harvard Business Review* no. 4 (July-August 1987): 98–105.

This article examines the problem of productivity among South African black workers. The author found out after speaking with black workers that productivity is inseparable from politics. Blacks see the workplace as merely an extension of apartheid.

Beeman, D. R., and others. "Management Policies/Managerial Attitudes and Task Environmental Agents: A Cross-Cultural Empirical Examination." *Management International Review* 21, no. 2 (1981): 67–77.

This research was designed to develop and apply an instrument for measuring management policy such that the results were (1) reproducible and (2) effective in differentiating between the policies of management and the attitudes of managers in different organizations and different cultures.

Becker, Helmut, and Fritzsche, David J. "A Comparison of the Ethical Behavior of American, French and German Managers." *The Columbia Journal of World Business* 22, no. 4 (Winter 1987): 87–96.

A cross-cultural study testing the ethical behaviors of managers was done to see if behavior changes as a result of ethical setting. The following types of ethical problems were presented: (1) coercion and control, (2) conflict of interest, (3) the physical environment, (4) paternalism, and (5) personal integrity.

Black, Stewart J. "Work Role Transitions: A Study of American Expatriate Managers in Japan." *Journal of International Business Studies* 19, no. 2 (Summer 1988): 277–294.

Some individuals within the course of their careers may have the opportunity to accept an overseas transfer. This article looks at the relationship between some variables and the change in the work role if Japan was the overseas assignment. In this study, role ambiguity and role discretion had an effect on work adjustment, while predeparture knowledge, knowing local nationals, and family acceptance affected general adjustments.

Boseman, G., and Phatak, A. "Management Policy, Decentralization and Effectiveness of Firms Operating in Mexico." *Management International Review* 24, no. 3 (1984): 53–61.

This empirical study investigates the relationships that exist between management policy, decentralization, and effectiveness using a matched sample of ten Mexican firms and ten Mexican subsidiaries of U.S. firms.

Bourgeois, L. J., and Boltcinik, M. "OD in Cross-Cultural Settings: Latin America." *California Management Review* 23 (Spring 1981): 75–81.

Using the United States and Latin America as examples, the authors describe the obstacles and cultural differences, as well as the similarities and facilitating factors, that must be taken into account when a cross-cultural application of organizational development is contemplated.

Boyer, E. "Japan Manages Declining Industries." *Fortune* 107 (January 10, 1983): 58–63.

What makes Japan different from other industrial countries is that it has a comprehensive policy for helping those declining industries. Government, business, and labor have worked together to shift resources out of the ailing sectors of the economy into the healthy ones with relatively little pain.

Carney, Larry S., and O'Kelly, Charlotte, G. "Barriers and Constraints to the Recruitment and Mobility of Female Managers in the Japanese Labor Force." *Human Resource Management* 26, no. 2 (Summer 1987): 193–216.

Using information from interviewing 118 female Japanese workers, this article describes the organizational and attitudinal barriers Japanese women are confronted with in respect to recruitment and career mobility in Japanese corporations. It also examines the career implications of their roles as wives and mothers. Forces for change in the position of white-collar and managerial women are discussed with extra attention on the internationalization of the Japanese economy and society.

Davidson, Marilyn J., and Cooper, Cary L. "Female Managers in Britain—A Comparative Perspective." *Human Resource Management* 26, no. 2 (Summer 1987): 217–242.

This article presents the current position of female managers in Britain and explores the similarities and differences in areas such as: position, demographic profiles, career development, managerial styles, prejudicial attitudes, and occupational stress. Even though the major sex differences are not related to leadership, qualifications, mobility, efficiency, or performance factors, they are hurting career prospects of women in management. Recommendations for changes in corporate and legislative policies are proposed.

Davidson, William H. "Creating and Managing Joint Ventures in China." *California Management Review* 29, no. 4 (Summer 1987): 77–94.

Joint ventures are important vehicles of commercial interaction between the People's Republic of China and the rest of the world. However, joint ventures can cause problems in other settings. This article looks at the experience of 30 U.S.-P.R.C. joint ventures and how these firms have successfully met their challenges. Their experience provides useful information for firms thinking of participating in joint venture activities in China.

Dyment, John J. "Strategies and Management Controls for Global Corporations." *The Journal of Business Strategy* 7, no. 4 (Spring 1987): 20–27.

A global corporation will have to be managed differently than either a domestic or multinational company. The management control system must be constructed to fit the global strategy.

Doktor, R. "Some Tentative Comments on Japanese and American Decision Making." *Decision Science* 14, (Fall 1983): 607–612.

Ample literature attests to the existence of differential views of causation held by Japanese as compared to Americans. Some new evidence links these differing causation maps to physiological brain structure. Review of this new evidence somewhat clarifies the nature of the differences in views of causation and preliminary points toward the developmental phenomena underlying these differences.

Everett, J. E., et al. "Some Evidence for an International Managerial Culture. (Cross-Cultural Studies of Management)." *Journal of Management Studies* 19, (April 1982): 153–162.

An analysis is reported of the relations between the semantic responses obtained from managers of four nationalities. The results support the hypothesis that, for the groups considered, a shared international culture exists in the managerial context.

Earley, Christopher P. "Intercultural Training for Managers: A Comparison of Documentary and Interpersonal Methods." *Academy of Management Journal* 30, no. 4 (December 1987): 685–698.

This article reports on a study that explored documentary and interpersonal training methods of preparing managers to go overseas for their companies. The impact of the two training methods on managerial performance, perceived intensity of adjustments to a new culture, and international perspective were compared in an experiment with a two-factor, cross-factorial design. The results showed that the two training techniques have additive benefits in making managers ready for intercultural work assignments.

Fleet, D. Van, and Tukaih, S. Al. "Cross-Cultural Analysis of Perceived Leader Behavior. *Management International Review* 19, no. 4 (1979): 81–87.

This paper reports results of a study to determine if more agreement exists among subjects from differing cultures as to what is perceived as descriptive of actual leader behavior as compared to the subjects' normative perceptions of what leaders should do.

Garvin, David A. "Quality Problems, Policies, and Attitudes in the United States and Japan: An Exploratory Study." *Academy of Management Journal* 29, no. 4 (December 1986): 653–673.

This research was derived from surveys of first-line supervisors in a single, broadly representative industry to compare practices and attitudes toward quality in the United States and Japan. Two issues were stressed: (1) the changing kinds of problems with quality as quality performance improves, and (2) the relationships between management and work force commitment to quality, pressure to produce goods of high quality, and quality performance.

Gerlach, Michael. "Business Alliances and the Strategy of the Japanese Firm." *California Management Review* 30, no. 1 (Fall 1987): 126–142.

With the change of global capital markets, it has become necessary for American managers to think about capital market relationships as a part of their overall corporate strategies. This article examines these strategies from Japan's point of view, who is the leading industrial competitor.

Ghoshal, Sumantra. "Global Strategy: An Organizing Framework." *Strategic Management Journal* 8, no. 5 (September-October 1987): 425–440.

This article presents a conceptual framework dealing with a number of is-sues related to global strategies. The framework gives a basis for organizing infor-mation on the subject and for making a map of the field. The article also provides a foundation for relating and synthesizing the various views and solutions that are available for global strategic management.

Gillingham, D. W. "Future Environment of Canadian Business." *Management International Review* 19, no. 3 (1979): 5–16.

The dynamic social and economic environment of Canada will alter com-petitive conditions and marketing strategies of the future for local, international, and multinational corporations. This paper describes the results of a survey of 74 senior executives of Canada's leading corporations.

Gorovitz, E. S. "Adapting Japanese Management to American Organizations." *Training & Development Journal* 36 (September 1982): 9–10.

The article addresses the issue: Can the Japanese style of management be exported? The article suggests that it seems likely that American companies need to be highly selective in adapting Japanese concepts to their own needs. The danger lies in adopting programs too rapidly without integrating them into the corporate culture.

Grimald, Antonio. "Interpreting Popular Culture: The Missing Link Between Local Labor and International Management." *The Columbia Journal of World Business* 21, no. 4 (Winter 1986): 67–72.

Recent studies agree that conflicts between international managers and local cultures are unavoidable. This article states that if managers study cultural manifestations instead of just observing them, it will enable the managers to un-derstand some of the assumptions and motivational determinants that underlie a local worker's behavior. In this article, the Latin American Carnival is analyzed to demonstrate how values and sources of behavior can be identified to be used for managerial benefits.

Grinyer, P. H., et al. "Strategy, Structure, the Environment and Financial Perfor-mance in 48 United Kingdom Companies (with Discussion)." *Academy of Management Journal* 23 (June 1980): 193–220.

Among other results, the strategy/structure linkage is shown to be very stable, and the fit between strategy and structures was found to be negatively cor-

related with perceived environmental hostility but unrelated to financial performance.

Harrigan, Kathryn Rudie. "Joint Ventures and Competitive Strategy." *Strategic Management Journal* 9, no. 2 (March-April 1988): 141–158.

This article examines a framework for using joint ventures within different competitive environments, and hypotheses are made dealing with the impact of certain industry traits on firm's options in pursuing them. Examples of industry show the framework's hypotheses. In this framework, demand traits define what kinds of cooperative strategies are necessary. Competitor traits suggest how firms will react to these needs for cooperation.

Harris, D. G. "How National Cultures Shape Management Styles." *Management Review* 71 (July 1982): 58–61.

International trade expansion is sending more and more managers to overseas branches of MNCs. Language barriers and government regulations aside, they must cope with subtle differences in culturally influenced management styles.

Hatvany, N., and Pucik, V. "Integrated Management System: Lessons From the Japanese Experience." *Academic Management Review* 6 (July 1981): 469–480.

Japanese management is characterized by a focus on the maximum utilization of human resources. This philosophy of management is realized through three general strategies: (1) development of an internal labor market, (2) articulation of a unique company philosophy, and (3) intensive socialization of employees.

Hedlund, G. "Organization In-Between: The Evolution of the Mother-Daughter Structure of Managing Foreign Subsidiaries in Swedish MNCs." *Journal of International Business Studies* 15 (Fall 1984): 109–123.

In-depth case studies of four firms and a questionnaire survey of 52 companies show that the mother-daughter structure prevalent in Swedish MNCs is changing. The control style is changing in the direction of slightly more formal performance evaluation.

Hendryx, Steven R. "Implementation of a Technology Transfer Joint Venture in the People's Republic of China: A Management Perspective." *The Columbia Journal of World Business* 21, no. 1 (Spring 1986): 57–66.

This article uses the Tianjin-Otis Joint Venture to show the process and problems associated with getting a joint venture to operate. It discusses the "technical" tasks as well as the management tasks in personnel, finance, and marketing of transferring product and production technology. The authors concluded that fundamental management reform and commitment from the managers was pertinent.

————. "The China Trade: Making the Deal Work." *Harvard Business Review* no. 4 (July-August 1986): 75–84.

Confused loyalties, state interference, and poor coordination can cause problems that haunt foreign managers of joint ventures in China. By asserting their usual managerial prerogatives, they can make a Chinese company into a more autonomous and profit-minded enterprise.

Hennart, Jean-Francoise. "A Transaction Cross Theory of Equity Joint Ventures." *Strategic Management Journal* 9, no. 4 (July-August 1988): 361–374.

This paper contains information about transaction costs theory of equity joint ventures. It differentiates between two types of joint ventures: (1) scale joint ventures are parents who look to internalize a failing market, but indivisibilities due to scale or scope economies make full ownership of the relevant assets inefficient and (2) link joint ventures are those who come about from the simultaneous failing of the markets for the services of two or more assets whenever these assets are firm-specific public goods and acquiring the firm possessing them would result in high management cases.

Hildebrandt, Herbert W., and Liu Jinyun. "Chinese Women Managers: A Comparison With Their U.S. and Asian Counterparts." *Human Resource Management* 27, no. 3 (Fall 1988): 291–314.

Women holding managerial positions in China are held back by factors such as: traditional views, education, and government influences. One hundred fifty women managers from the People's Republic of China were interviewed, and the information gathered was used to compare the women to their counterparts in the United States and Southeast Asia.

Hofstede, G. "Motivation, Leadership, and Organization: Do American Theories Apply Abroad?" *Organizations Dynamic* 9 (Summer 1980): 42–63.

Many of the differences in employee motivation, management styles, and organizational structures of companies throughout the world can be traced to differences in the collective mental programming of people in different national cultures.

Hofstede, Geert, and Bond, Michael Harris. "The Confucius Connection: From Cultural Roots to Economic Growth." *Organizational Dynamics* 16 (Spring 1988): 4–21.

Managers in Japan and other Asian countries may have a competitive advantage over U.S. and European managers because Eastern ideals stress the art of synthesis and are not preoccupied with analysis, as are Western ideals.

Jaeger, A. M. "The Transfer of Organizational Culture Overseas: An Approach to Control in the Multinational Corporation." *Journal of International Business Studies* 14 (Fall 1983): 91–94.

This paper describes an alternative organizational ideal type that relies on an organizational culture for control. In this type of system, behavior is specified by the organizational culture, and performance is maintained via mechanisms of social pressure.

Johnson, Chalmers. "Japanese-Style Management in America." *California Management Review* 30, no. 4 (Summer 1988): 34–45.

This article looks at what Japanese-style management means and to what extent it is used in Japanese-owned and operated factories in the United States. It takes a closer look at the Japanese "lifetime employment" and whether Japanese-style management reflects their culture.

Johnson, Gerry, and Thomas, Howard. "The Industry Context of Strategy, Structure and Performance: The U.K. Brewing Industry." *Strategic Management Journal* 8, no. 4 (July-August 1987): 343–361.

This article examines the influences on the competitive performance of companies involved in the U.K. brewing industry. It tries to point out critical strategic characteristics, relate these to company performance, and explain the influences that come forth as influencing competitive standing. It supports the view that diversification strategies must be studied as an aspect of industry structure and illustrates that more focused, limited diversification and regional brewing strategies may be preferable in the U.K. brewing industry. These findings are contrary to previous studies that researched the diversification strategies of large firms from across-industry samples (e.g., Fortune 500 firms) and that identified higher performance for related diversification strategies. Therefore, the study backs up the hypothesis that there is an optimum level of diversification within an industry that balances economies of scope and diseconomies of scale.

Kakabadse A. "Politics of Planned Change." *Industrial Management Data System* (Britain) (September-October 1983): 10–14.

Change often seems fearsome and anxiety provoking, yet in today's fast-moving business world, both individual and organization must learn to cope with change. The purpose of this article is to identify the necessary steps to stimulate changes in organizations. It also explores what is required in terms of effort and action at each particular step.

Kelly, Lane; Whatly, Arthur, and Worthley, Reginald. "Assessing the Effects of Culture on Managerial Attitudes: A Three Culture Test." *Journal of International Business Studies* 19, no. 2 (Summer 1987): 17–32.

Many times in cross-cultural research, environmental influences are mistaken for cultural influences. This article reports on a study that uses a new research design that tries to isolate the influence of culture. Japanese, Chinese, Mexican, and their ethnic-American counterparts, and Anglo-American managers are used to test the model.

Kim, L., and Utterback, J. M. "The Evolution of Organizational Structure and Technology in a Developing Country: Korea." *Management Science* 29 (October 1983): 1185–1197.

This article examines an evolutionary pattern of relationship among technology, structure, environment, and other contextual variables in 31 manufacturing organizations in a developing country. The results of the study suggest ways in which international operations should be designed to correspond to their local environments.

Kim, Chan W., and Mauborgne, R. A. "Cross-Cultural Strategies." *The Journal of Business Strategy* 7, no. 4 (Spring 1987): 28–36.

The challenge for executives is to surpass the blinders imposed by their home cultures if operations in foreign cultures are to flourish.

Knon, T. "Japanese Management Philosophy: Can It Be Exported?" *Long Range Planning* 15 (June 1982): 90–102.

This paper analyzes the overall characteristics of Japanese management, with emphasis on strategic level of management practices.

Kriger, Mark P. "The Increasing Role of Subsidiary Boards in MNCs: An Empirical Study." *Strategic Management Journal* 9, no. 4 (July-August 1988): 347–360.

Subsidiary boards (SBs) are developing increasing importance in MNCs. In a two-phase survey research design involving 90 subsidiaries in 36 MNCs based in Japan, Europe, and North America, it was found that SBs are in a period of transition, going from lesser to greater productivity. It was also discovered that MNCs with parent headquarters in Japan, Europe, and North America perceive the usefulness of SBs in different ways. The results of the survey support an increasingly active role of SBs in selective advisory and strategic positions.

Lansing, Paul, and Ready, Kathryn. "Hiring Women Managers in Japan: An Alternative for Foreign Employees." *California Management Review* 30, no. 3 (Spring 1988): 112–127.

Women management students are growing in numbers in Japanese universities. However, these graduates find it hard to get jobs because of the traditional attitudes toward women in Japan. The authors examine the opportunity for foreign firms in Japan to hire females in managerial positions.

Laurita, Tom, and McGloin, Michael. "U.S.-Soviet Joint Ventures: Current Status and Prospects." *The Columbia Journal of World Business* 23, no. 2 (Summer 1988): 43–52.

This article assesses the political, economic, and human problems associated with U.S.-Soviet joint ventures. It reports on the status of overcoming such problems in the point of view of U.S. and Soviet organizations. It discusses ways in which to deal with obstacles encountered based on strategic commercial and economic interests of both sides. The chances for overall success are also addressed.

Lincoln, J. R., et al. "Cultural Orientations and Individual Reactions to Organizations: A Study of Employees of Japanese-Owned Firms." *Administrative Science Quarterly* 26 (March 1981): 93–115.

This study concerns cultural differences in the reactions of persons to work organizations. The data pertains to 522 employees of 28 Japanese-owned firms in the United States. The results were interpreted from a theoretical perspective that stresses the matching of organizational forms to cultural contexts.

Lovelace, D. J. "Universal Systems Model for Organizational Design." *Journal of System Management* 32 (August 1981): 27–31.

This article shows how to design a flexible organization. It provides a detailed explanation on the Universal Systems Model. The model offers a new approach to an old problem: designing a flexible and responsible organization that will meet present and future needs.

Marengo, F. D. "Learning from the Japanese." *Management International Review* 19, no. 4 (1979): 39–46.

This paper examines current Western interpretations of Japanese "groupism," consensual decision making, and reliance on growth rather than profit and shows that they are generally biased by Western perspectives.

Marsland, S., and Beer, M. "The Evolution of Japanese Management: Lessons for U.S. Managers." *Organization Dynamics* 11 (Winter 1983): 49–67.

The authors suggest taking a cue from Japan, where superior performance evolved from a match between new management concepts and some of Japan's traditional societal norms. Thus, U.S. managers seeking to increase productivity should reassess the match between U.S. societal norms and management practices.

Mendenhall, Mark E., et al. "Expatriate Selection, Training and Career-Pathing: A Review and Critique." *Human Resource Management* 26, no. 3 (Fall 1987): 331–345.

The authors explore the problems of failure and quick return of expatriates of U.S. MNCs. They also offer recommendations for improving human resource practices, including those for cross-cultural training programs and career pathing.

Misawa, Mitsuru. "New Japanese-Style Management In a Changing Era." *The Columbia Journal of World Business* 22, no. 4 (Winter 1987): 9–18.

As the Japanese economy and international business environment is changing, it is requiring the Japanese-style of management to adjust accordingly. This article probes the causes and direction of these changes.

Montebello, M., and Buigues, P. "How French Industry Plans." *Long Range Planning* 15 (June 1982): 116–121.

This paper presents briefly the results of an empirical study on long-range forecasting conducted in large French corporations. It demonstrates that forecasting differs quite widely according to its technical, economic, or social nature.

Nonaka, Ikujiro. "Self-Renewal of the Japanese Firm and the Human Resource Strategy." *Human Resource Management* 27, no. 1 (Spring 1988): 45–62.

The author describes a new style of human resource management, creative HRM, to begin the self-renewal of Japanese firms whose production-oriented paradigms and traditional human resource strategies are inefficient with the growing competitive global market. Three ideas support creative HRM:(1) the creation of the strategic vision through commitment of the employees, (2) emphasis of the middle managers, and (3) multi-dimensional personnel management.

Norburn, David. "Corporate Leaders in Britain and America: A Cross-National Analysis." *Journal of International Business Studies* 18, no. 3 (Fall 1987): 15–32.

This article discusses results and implications of a study testing for similarities between 1,798 American senior vice presidents and 418 British counterparts. The managers were selected from the largest national companies controlling domestic economics. The study concludes that there is a significant amount of differences between American and British managers in areas such as corporate grooming, educational and domestic experiences, and self-concept.

O'Connor, W. F. "New Globalism: A Game Every Multinational Will Have to Play." *Management Review* 72 (May 1983): 29.

The chief premise of the New Globalism is that many of the world's basic needs cannot be met by existing organizational structure. The article suggests that a truly global economy will not come easily. Cooperation and innovation will be the hallmarks of the New Globalism.

Ohmae, Kenichi. "The Triad World View." *The Journal of Business Strategy* 7, no. 4 (Spring 1987): 8–19.

Because Japanese consumers have achieved considerable purchasing power, multinational companies have to picture a triad market made up of Western Europe, North America, and Japan.

O'Reilly, Anthony J. F. "Establishing Successful Joint Ventures in Developing Nations." *The Columbia Journal of World Business* 23, no. 1 (Spring 1988): 65–72.

This is a case study of H. J. Heinz's company strategic action in developing countries. The article describes Heinz's joint ventures in Thailand, the People's Republic of China, and Zimbabwe.

Perlmutter, Howard V., and Heenan, David A. "Cooperate to Compete Globally." *Harvard Business Review* no. 2 (March-April 1986): 136–155.

Global strategic partnerships allow competitors to cooperate and utilize the strength of each to capture world markets. This article demonstrates how global partnerships work.

Peterson, Mark F. "PM Theory in Japan and China: What's In It For The United States." *Organizational Dynamics* 16 (Spring 1988): 22–39.

This article discusses how the Performance Maintenance Theory of Leadership used in Japan and China may seem like Western theories; however, it is different in some significant ways that can result in important benefits for managers in the United States.

Picard, J. "Organizational Structures and Integrative Devices in European Multinational Corporations." *The Columbia Journal of World Business* 15 (Spring 1980): 30–35.

This paper deals with U.S. subsidiaries of European enterprises located in the United States. Communications and coordination in marketing activities between subsidiaries and headquarters are the focus of this study.

Rehda, R. R. "What American and Japanese Managers are Learning From Each Other." *Business Horizon* 24 (March-April 1981): 63–70.

The author focuses on newly emerging nontraditional American and Japanese management and organization systems. The author identifies those management innovations from both countries that may hold promise as creative solutions to common problems in this healthy competitive race for world industrial supremacy.

Reich, Robert B., and Mankin, Eric D. "Joint Ventures with Japan Give Away Our Future." *Harvard Business Review* no. 2 (March-April 1986): 78–85.

U.S. companies are causing their own decline by letting the Japanese control the highest value-added segment of the production process. U.S. companies should rethink the structure of joint ventures, and the government should offer incentives for investments in workers' skills.

Shetty, Y. K. "Managing the Multinational Corporation: European and American Styles." *Management International Review* 19, no. 3 (1979): 39–48.

Both American and European multinational firms show a high degree of decentralization; however, in the case of European firms, the degree of decentralization is higher than in American multinational firms. Also, European-based multinationals deemphasize the dichotomy between international domestic business in their organizational setup compared to their American counterparts.

Sethi, S. P., et al. "The Decline of the Japanese System of Management." *California Management Review* 26 (Summer 1984): 35–45.

This article cautions American companies against attempting to imitate the Japanese system of management by demonstrating how many of the policies associated with Japanese management practices are in fact becoming less prevalent in Japan itself.

Sparrow, Paul R., and Pettigrew, Andrew M. "Britain's Training Problems: The Search for a Strategic Human Resources Management Approach." *Human Resource Managements* 26, no. 1 (Spring 1987): 109–127.

This article looks at the roots of Britain's training problem, linking it to the industrial decline and lack of competitiveness. A major research program in the U.K. is aimed at understanding and facilitating strategic change. HRM is described in detail.

Stephens, D. B. "Cultural Variation in Leadership Style: A Methodological Experiment in Comparing Managers in the U.S. and Peruvian Textile Industries." *Management International Review* 21, no. 3 (1981): 47–55.

This study is a cross-cultural comparison of various aspects related to leadership style of managers in the United States and Peru. Its purpose is to make such a transnational comparison while controlling for methodological and conceptual weaknesses common to earlier research efforts.

Sullivan, Jeremiah J., and Nonaka, Ikujiro. "The Application of Organizational Learning Theory to Japanese and American Management." *Journal of International Business Studies* 17, no. 3 (Fall 1986): 127–146.

Karl Weick, in The Social Psychology of Organizing, *theorized that organizational learning must be controlled by a theory of action. In a study of senior American and Japanese executives, the Japanese illustrated more commitment to the theory of action than the Americans did. The article discusses implications for strategy-setting behavior for both cultures.*

Tyebjee, Tyzoon. "A Typology of Joint Ventures: Japanese Strategies in the United States." *California Management Review* 31, no. 1 (Fall 1988): 75–86.

In the last decade, there has been an increase of Japanese foreign direct investment in the U.S. manufacturing industry in which a majority of them have been joint ventures with American partners. The author examines four types of joint ventures that the Japanese get involved in and how they differ in terms of the relative size of the partners, their relative power in the relationship, the strategic contributions each partner makes, and the territorial constraints put on the marketing activities. The information is from in-depth interviews with top managers in 21 joint ventures.

Von Glinow, Mary Ann, and Teagarden, Mary B. "The Transfer of Human Resources Management Technology in Sino-U.S. Cooperative Ventures: Problems and Solutions." *Human Resource Management* 27, no. 2 (Summer 1988): 201–229.

In order for Sino-U.S. cooperative ventures to succeed, Chinese HRM systems must change. This article probes assumptions underlying U.S. and Chinese HRM systems and offers suggestions on how modern HRM practices may be more effectively introduced in Sino-U.S. cooperative ventures.

Yoo, Sangjin, and Lee, Sang M. "The Management Style and Practice of Korean Chaebols." *California Management Review* 29, no. 4 (Summer 1987): 95–110.

Chaebols, groups of large business conglomerates, are the most important driving force behind Korea's economic success. The top five Chaebols' total sales make up more than 50 percent of Korea's GNP. They have enormous political and economic power. The author provides information about the unique characteristics, management style, and management practices of Korean Chaebols.

Thonet, P. J., and Poensgen, O. H. "Managerial Control and Economic Performance in West Germany." *Journal of Industrial Economics* 28 (September 1979): 23–37.

This is an empirical study on managerial control and economic performance in Germany. The results show that manager-controlled firms play a far less important role in Germany than in the United States.

Tsurumi, Y. "Two Models of Corporation and International Transfer of Technology." *Columbia Journal of World Business* 14 (Summer 1979): 43–50.

This article presents a useful paradigm of assessing American, Japanese, and other enterprises. The author's Model J and Model A types of corporations dispel the myth that there are uniquely Japanese or American corporate cultures. The author explores the impacts of different corporate cultures on the international transfer of technology.

Wortzel-Vernon, Heidi, and Wortzel, Lawrence H. "Globalizing Strategies for Multinationals from Developing Countries." *The Columbia Journal of World Business* 23, no. 1 (Spring 1988): 27–36.

In the 1980s, multinational enterprises from developing countries (MEDEC) have grown but haven't become dominant in their respective industries. This article analyzes the past and present competitive strategies of the MEDEC and then makes recommendations for necessary changes in order for the MEDECs to become strong multinational competitors.

Wright, P. "Organizational Behavior in Islamic Firms." *Management International Review* 21, no. 2 (1981): 86–94.

Managers of the subsidiaries of European and American multinational corporations operating in the Islamic markets face culturally bound difficulties that can be quite frustrating. Since few Western executives at the headquarters understand the Moslem mentality, they are at a loss when it comes to guiding their expatriate managers who are about to be assigned to organizations in the Islamic regions.

Yucelt, U. "Management Styles in the Middle East: A Case Example." *Management Decision* 22, no. 5 (1984): 24–35.

The purpose of this article is to point out management sectors of the Middle Eastern countries, particularly Turkey. To this end, applicability of different management systems is discussed and managerial implications are suggested for orderly decision-making purposes.

Zamet, Jonathan M., and Bovarnick, Murray E. "Employee Relations for Multi-national Companies in China." *The Columbia Journal of World Business* 21, no. 1 (Spring 1986): 13–20.

Human resource management in China is a great challenge. Managers must deal with issues not in the least familiar. They have to learn to handle the communist power structure that runs society, the extreme cultural differences, and the under-developed economy. How well managers can come to terms with the new issues affects the local work force and the expatriate personnel. Companies find that the basic principles are put to the test.